the illustrated directory of

healing crystals

a comprehensive guide to 150 crystals and gemstones

cassandra eason

the illustrated directory of
healing
crystals

a comprehensive guide to 150 crystals and gemstones

COLLINS & BROWN

First published in the United Kingdom in 2003
This paperback edition first published in the United Kingdom in 2008 by
Collins & Brown
10 Southcombe Street
London
W14 0RA

An imprint of Anova Books Company Ltd

Distributed in the United States and Canada by
Sterling Publishing Co, 387 Park Avenue South, New York, NY 10016, USA

Commissioning Editor: Miriam Hyslop
Design Manager: Gemma Wilson
Design: Justina Leitão and Sarah Rock
Senior Production Controller: Morna McPherson
Photography: Neil Sutherland

ISBN 978-1-84340-455-2

A CIP catalogue for this book is available from the British Library.

10 9 8 7 6 5 4 3 2 1

Reproduction by Rival Colour, UK
Printed and bound by SNP Leefung, China

This book can be ordered direct from the publisher.
Contact the marketing department, but try your bookshop first.

www.anovabooks.com

Acknowledgements

The publisher would like to thank Dolphin Minerals for supplying most of the beautiful crystals
shown in this book. They supply crystals and minerals by mail order and can be visited by special
appointment at the Old School Building, Wetherby Rd, Rufforth, York, YO23 3QB, tel 01904 738965.
Visit their website at www.dolphinminerals.com. Special thanks to Stephen Ash for his generous
assistance and to Mystic Dreams, East Street, Horsham, West Sussex.

CONTENTS

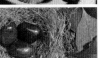
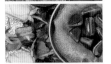

HEALING CRYSTALS

The Illustrated Directory of Healing Crystals is unique in that it offers detailed, accessibly presented information on more than 150 crystals. Beginning with their mythology and folklore, each entry explores how the crystals can be used for healing, magic, divination and for psychic development. The associated flowers, herbs, oils, incenses, planet, element, star sign, guardian angel and related chakra is presented in a box for each crystal, to allow quick and easy reference.

Crystals can help to bring harmony and joy to your life: each entry describes how to use each crystal for protection and to attract love, success, prosperity, self-confidence, health and happiness. The entries give examples of rituals, layouts and altars to further your spiritual and psychic development and explains which crystals are most suited to healing children and animals. Finally, the book describes, for beginners and crystal experts alike, methods of crystal healing, colour wisdom, ways of working with the chakras and aura, and the basics of crystal divination and magic.

Divided into sections by colour, the illustrations allow instant identification of individual crystals among the bewildering range available. This book is not only a comprehensive reference work, it is also an essential workbook, whether you use crystals to bring peace to your home or are a crystal healer looking for new ideas.

INTRODUCTION

According to the Ancient Greek philosopher Plato, crystals are formed from the stars and planets. The Australian Aboriginals and the Native North Americans consider crystals the bones of mother earth herself.

We know that the crystals we now enjoy and use were created in the womb of the earth over millions of years by the action of water, wind and volcanic fire. We know that they carry the life force and healing powers from earth and sky.

Their healing properties were recorded more than 3,500 years ago by the Ancient Egyptians, and by cultures in China and India. Indeed, crystals have always been part of the folk wisdom of ordinary men, women and children. Give any child a bag of crystals and he or she will instantly choose the correct crystal to relieve a headache or sore throat.

This book records the myths and the mystical and astrological associations of more than 150 crystals. Some of these stones have been used for thousands of years and enjoy a rich history and mythology. Others are more recent discoveries, cast up by the earth mother to heal modern ills and the pollution of earth, sea and sky caused by careless humankind.

Above all *The Illustrated Directory of Healing Crystals* forms a personal resource and workbook. It will be appropriate for both the complete beginner to crystal healing and for more experienced practitioners, who may welcome the new ideas and approaches they will discover here.

Ultimately, however, we are all crystal experts if we trust our intuitive powers: in our crystal work we can access a universal well of crystal wisdom, passed through our genetic heritage. By allowing each crystal to speak directly to our hearts and work, its healing energies will amplify our own innate healing powers to bring peace and spiritual harmony to people, animals and places.

ABOVE Crystals and gems were very important to the Ancient Egyptians as amulets. Lapis lazuli and red jasper were dedicated to the goddess Isis.

CHOOSING CRYSTALS

You will need two or three round or oval crystals the size of a large coin for healing and for spiritual development. If you already have personal crystals, you can use those, as they are endowed with your personal magic and energies. If you do not have any crystals, a small piece of tumbled or rough amethyst, citrine and clear quartz would make a good initial purchase.

ADDING TO YOUR COLLECTION

You can gradually build up your crystal collection, so that you have crystals in all the main colours for healing, divination and ritual. Some people prefer to have a separate set of healing crystals, but others feel, as I now do, that by using the same crystals for all their work, the crystals become very powerful and personalized. You may also decide to buy a crystal sphere (see p44) or geode and keep your special crystals and larger pieces in your magical crystal place (see p16).

CRYSTAL PENDULUM

A clear crystal pendulum is a very useful purchase. You can use it to cleanse and charge other crystals (see p19), make an instant intuitive decision (see p15), trace your inner bodily psychic energy pathways, and unblock stagnant chakras, the psychic energy centres within our body (see p9–10).

Your pendulum can also help you to find lost objects, to identify ley energies – the psychic power lines within the earth – and to pick up on ghostly presences. The spontaneous positive swing will affirm a yes response when questions are asked, indicate that energies are flowing freely within you and that you are on the right track if you are following a trail. The direction of this swing can be identified by thinking of a happy event in your life while holding the pendulum. It is often, but not always, a clockwise circling.

Think of a sad event to see the spontaneous negative response, usually an anticlockwise movement. It may indicate a blockage in the energy system or that you have moved away from the correct path physically.

You can deliberately circle your pendulum clockwise over your body to energize your system. If you circle it anticlockwise it will unblock a stagnant area in your body or remove pain or sickness.

An amethyst or rose quartz crystal will cleanse gentler crystals and both are good for clearing negative earth energies in the home.

THE CHAKRAS

Each of the 150 crystals in this directory is assigned to the chakra that it will most effectively cleanse and energize. Each chakra is associated with an area of the body and an emotional state. Chakras are swirling psychic energy centres within the body, inter-connecting points for thousands of tiny energy channels. Apply a crystal a few inches above a chakra point, rotating it anti-clockwise to unblock, cleanse and calm if the energies are too intense and then clockwise to energize. Let your hand and intuition guide your actions. You can also lie with the appropriate chakra crystal on each chakra point to rebalance the whole system.

THE ROOT OR BASE CHAKRA
COLOUR: Red.
LOCATION FOR HEALING: The base of the spine, the perineum or the soles of the feet (the feet chakras are ruled by the root chakra).
AREAS OF INFLUENCE: Legs, feet and skeleton (including the teeth), bowel and large intestine. The root chakra relates to material comfort and awareness of reality. It is the source of the kundalini (or serpent energy) that provides the driving power for the chakra system.
IMBALANCES: Pain and tension in the body parts it controls, constipation or an irritable bowel. A lack of energy and an inability to relax: the flight-or-fight mechanism in over-drive. Irritability, anger or paralyzing fear.

THE SACRAL CHAKRA
COLOUR: Orange.
LOCATION FOR HEALING: The centre of the sacrum/lower abdomen; around the reproductive system.
AREAS OF INFLUENCE: The blood, all bodily fluids, hormones, the reproductive system, kidneys, circulation and bladder. Sensuality, desires and cravings.
IMBALANCES: Fluid retention, menstrual or menopausal problems. Mood swings. Impotence in men and frigidity in women.

BELOW It is possible to balance the body's energy and circulate healing throughout the body by using the crystals associated with each of the chakras (psychic energy centres).

Emotional problems with food, alcohol, cigarettes or compulsive behaviour.

THE SOLAR PLEXUS CHAKRA
COLOUR: Yellow.
LOCATION FOR HEALING: Above the navel, around the central stomach area or, according to some chakra practitioners, further up towards the central cavity of the lungs.
AREAS OF INFLUENCE: Digestion, the liver, spleen, gall bladder, stomach, small intestine and the metabolism. The solar plexus chakra affects will-power, independence and the ability to learn from experience.
IMBALANCES: Digestive disorders, gallstones, sluggish metabolism. Food intolerances. Inflexible attitudes, hyperactivity and lack of self-confidence.

THE HEART CHAKRA
COLOUR: Green or pink.
LOCATION: The centre of the chest, level with the heart. There are minor chakras in the palm of each hand.
AREAS OF INFLUENCE: Heart, lungs, breasts and arms. The development of compassion and spiritual love. The awareness of past lives and ancient worlds. Healing powers, especially using herbs and crystals.

IMBALANCES: Constant coughs and colds, breathing difficulties, food intolerances and allergies, and heart palpitations. Psychosomatic illnesses and oversensitivity to the problems of others.

THE THROAT CHAKRA
COLOUR: Blue.
LOCATION: Close to the Adam's apple in the centre of the neck.
AREAS OF INFLUENCE: Throat and speech organs, mouth, the neck and shoulders and the passages that run up to the ears. The ability to communicate and creative powers. Healing with sound. Out-of-body experiences, divination, psychic dreams and clairaudience. Access to the cosmic memory bank.
IMBALANCES: Sore throats, swollen glands in the neck, mouth ulcers and ear problems. Inability to express feelings or translate thoughts and ideas into workable plans.

THE BROW OR THIRD EYE CHAKRA
COLOUR: Indigo/purple.
LOCATION: Just above the bridge of the nose, in the centre of the brow.
AREAS OF INFLUENCE: Eyes and ears, sinuses, the left and right hemispheres of the brain and the central cavity of the brain. Communication with angels and devas. Spiritual healing abilities, mediumship and prophetic powers. The brow chakra connects us to our guides and our own higher knowledge.
IMBALANCES: Unexplained blurred vision, headaches and migraines and blocked sinuses. Earache, insomnia and nightmares.

THE CROWN CHAKRA
COLOUR: White/violet.
LOCATION: The top of the head, where the skull bones meet. The crown chakra extends to about three finger breadths above the top of the head.
AREAS OF INFLUENCE: The brain and the whole body. The soul/psyche. Experience of archangels, ascended beings and the source of divinity through mystical experiences. Healing through prayer. Through the crown chakra we may momentarily glimpse divinity and feel at one with the universe.
IMBALANCES: Headaches and migraines. Inefficient functioning of the immune system. Forgetfulness and frequent minor accidents. A lack of meaning in life.

BELOW Amethyst opens the brow chakra, giving access to dreams, inner vision and intuitive powers.

CRYSTAL COLOURS

Each colour contains qualities and strengths that are amplified by the power of crystal. Colours are absorbed through the skin and the optic nerves. Psychically they are assimilated into the human energy field or aura and from there, via the seven chakras, they go to wherever specific colour strengths are needed in the body or mind.

THE AURA

The aura is a constantly flowing coloured rainbow. It extends about an arm span all around the body and head in an ellipse. Because it filters pollution and negative emotions, the aura becomes discoloured or dull and needs regular cleansing and energizing at least once a week.

SEEING YOUR AURA

If you want to check the health of an aura, stand in front of a mirror, or set your subject framed with light, and focus on the area around the head, where the aura is most visible. Stare hard, close your eyes, open them, blink and look again and you will see, either in your mind's vision or externally, the rainbow colours. With practice you will see areas of darkness or any missing colours from what should be a rainbow spectrum.

If in doubt as to which colour to use, either for the aura or for general empowerment, arrange a crystal of each colour (include grey, brown and pink as these often appear in auras as well) in a circle on a table. Pass your pendulum clockwise a couple of inches above each crystal slowly; your pendulum will vibrate and pull down over one or more colours, showing you what you need.

LEFT Clear quartz is especially powerful for cleansing the auric field. It fills the entire system with joy, light and a sense of optimism.

AURA COLOUR CLEANSING

Find the edge of the aura by holding both palms over the head a few inches away and continuing to move your hands outwards till you encounter resistance: this is the extent of the auric field. Spiral the chosen crystals in turn (or one in each hand simultaneously if you have two) over your head or that of your patient, first anticlockwise to cleanse and then clockwise to energize the aura.

ABSORBING CRYSTAL COLOURS

❖ Carry a crystal in a pouch or wear it as jewellery to infuse yourself slowly and continuously with the chosen colour quality.
❖ Sleep with a stone under your pillow.
❖ Soak a crystal in a cup of still mineral water for eight hours and drink the water, splash it on your pulse points or add it to your water when you bathe.
❖ Add coloured crystals to your bathwater.
❖ Hold the chosen coloured crystal in cupped hands and gently breathe in its light through your nose. Exhale visualized dark light as a sigh through your mouth.
❖ Once a week, by candlelight or in natural sun- or moonlight, sit inside a circle of crystals, one of each colour. Visualize the colours entering your aura. You will absorb the colours in which you are deficient.

LEFT Chrysoprase brings freshness and vitality to counteract the stresses and pollution of urban life.

THE MEANING OF COLOUR IN MAGIC AND HEALING

WHITE: White increases the flow of the life force. It is good for new beginnings, enthusiasm, clarity of purpose, spiritual insights or inspiration.

The colour white heals the body, mind and spirit at all levels. It effectively relieves pain, depression and inertia. White helps bone and tooth maintenance and promotes the flow of breast milk in nursing mothers.

RED: The colour red increases power, determination, physical energy and health. It denotes courage, sexual passion and potency and positive change.

Red instantly boosts energy levels and it will kick-start a sluggish immune system. It is good for the reproductive organs in both men and women. It increases fertility and helps menstrual problems, sexual dysfunction, blood and the circulation.

ORANGE: Vibrant orange increases self-esteem and confidence and strengthens a sense of identity. Orange is a joy bringer and promotes peace and harmony.

Orange is good for the pulse rate, and the gall bladder. It relieves bladder and kidney problems, food allergies and eating disorders. It aids rheumatism, arthritis and exhaustion.

YELLOW: The colour yellow is associated with the mind and aids logic, memory, concentration, will-power and communication. It helps skills to do with technology. It is good for job changes and local house moves and short-term or time travel. Use yellow for overcoming money troubles.

Yellow stimulates the nervous system, calms the digestive system, aids eczema and skin problems and increases metabolic rate.

GREEN: Green increases love, empathy and compassion. It is good for working with nature and the environment. It brings a gradual increase of prosperity and good fortune.

Green strengthens the heart, lungs and respiratory system and helps fight infections and viruses. Green is useful to counter panic attacks and addictions.

BLUE: Blue increases existing opportunities in career, business or finances and improves leadership qualities. Blue aids long-distance travel and house moves and promotes success in both legal and official matters.

The colour of healers, blue is a natural antiseptic. It also relieves headaches and migraines, fevers, high blood pressure, eye strain, earache and sore throats.

PURPLE: Purple relates to the inner self, unconscious wisdom, increasing psychic powers, meaningful dreams, accurate divination, meditation, past-life work and psychic protection.

An all-healer, purple relieves allergies, asthma, sleep disorders, eye, ear, nose and skin problems and migraines. The colour purple is a natural sedative.

PINK: Pink represents kindness, reconciliation, families, friends and children. Pink also symbolizes the development of new love and trust after a betrayal or abuse.

This gentle healer relieves ear and gland problems, headaches and psychosomatic illnesses. It is helpful for disorders relating to babies, children, adolescent girls and pregnant and menopausal women.

BROWN: The colour brown is associated with the element of earth and offers physical and psychic protection. It relates to the home, property matters, day-to-day finances and learning new skills, especially later in life.

Brown absorbs pain and sorrow and increases long-term stamina. It relieves disorders of the feet, legs, hands and bowels. It is useful in animal healing.

GREY: This useful colour lowers your profile in dangerous or confrontational situations. It neutralizes negative energies or feelings, aids compromise and adaptability and helps you to keep secrets.

Grey heals the immune system, reduces stress and fear and dulls chronic pain.

BLACK: The colour of regeneration, black represents beginnings after natural endings in life. Black banishes negativity, helps to heal old sorrows and allows you to move on from redundant or destructive relationships.

Black slows down an overactive, stressed system. It heals the skeletal system, especially the spine, removes blockages in the lower body, and overcomes trauma and shock. It is useful in debilitating illnesses.

CRYSTALS AND HEALING

Crystals act as a transmitter and amplifier of healing energy whether the patient is present or absent and whether healing power is directed through the hands, the voice or the mind – or all of these simultaneously. Almost every healer asks for help in healing from a higher source, whether from God, the Goddess, a healing deity, an angel, a spirit guide or the wise light of the universe.

At the beginning and end of a healing session, hold your crystal in your hands, raise it to your heart and ask in your own words that your healing may be for the highest good and in the form that is right for the patient. Also request protection and blessings for yourself and the patient in the name of your chosen higher power. Afterwards thank the source of your healing power.

CONTACT CRYSTAL HEALING

Contact healing means the patient is present at the healing session. Some healers and patients prefer no physical skin contact except between relations and close friends.

HOW TO HEAL

Use your intuition and your heart as a guide and allow the crystal to find its own movements and pathways, one or two inches away from the body. Sometimes you may want to hold the crystal over a part of the body that is seemingly unrelated to the symptoms described – listen to the crystal.

You may move the crystal constantly or feel it suddenly pull down over a particular spot, perhaps drawing out a tangled knot of energy that rises as a strand of pale grey mist skywards, to be transformed into a sunbeam or starlight. There are several effective methods from which to choose.

CRYSTAL PAIRS

Use a pair of crystals, one to draw out pain or remove blockages and one to infuse the system with healing light. You can use crystal palms (round flat stones you hold in your hand) or ordinary round tumbled stones. The following pairs are good combinations:

CLEAR CRYSTAL QUARTZ AND AMETHYST: These are good for all-purpose healing and routine cleansing and energizing.

TURQUOISE AND ROSE QUARTZ: These help an overloaded system or a person who is constantly under pressure.

Amber and blue coral or blue chalcedony: These are good for deep healing and for restoring natural immunity.

PURPLE FLUORITE AND NEPHRITE OR JADEITE: This is a good combination for healing over a long period, for chronic conditions or those that are difficult to diagnose and treat.

RED JASPER AND CELESTINE OR ANGELITE: These are useful for balancing, strengthening and harmonizing body and mind.

TIGER'S EYE AND BANDED AGATE: Use to soothe and empower very nervous or emotional patients or those in crisis situations.

BLUE LACE AGATE AND PINK MANGANOCALCITE: This combination is good for healing the very young, the very old or people who are extremely ill or in intense pain.

HEALING WITH CRYSTAL PAIRS

❖ Hold the more active vibrant crystal (the first in the list above) in your power hand (the one you write with) and the other in your receptive hand. Establishing a rhythm, simultaneously move your power crystal clockwise and the receptive crystal anti-clockwise over any pain or discomfort. Do this two inches away from the body.

❖ Next, slowly spiral up and down the body, still moving the crystals harmoniously.

BELOW Rose quartz can be used to send gentle healing to people, animals and places that are far away.

You want to develop a mesmeric rhythm if possible. You may find that healing words emerge spontaneously.

❖ You may find the crystals stop over a chakra energy centre and move much faster as they balance or unblock it.

❖ Flow with the movement: when you find yourself slowing, the healing is complete.

CREATING A HEALING CIRCUIT WITH PAIRED CRYSTALS

Try this with a pointed crystal quartz and a pointed amethyst.

❖ If healing yourself, sit on the floor and hold the receptive crystal to the sole of the foot on the power side of your body (the same one as the hand you write with) and the power crystal point touching the other sole.

❖ Visualize warm, glowing, healing liquid light passing upwards through the power crystal and spiralling round your body, finding the natural psychic pathways and swirling round the chakras.

❖ You need do nothing, but if you wish close your eyes and you will be rewarded by visions of the glowing channels within.

❖ See the power leaving via the receptive crystals and re-entering the body, transformed, as it passes through the power crystal. When the energies slow, healing is complete.

You can create a healing circuit for other people by holding the crystals in your hands against the soles of their feet or, if they prefer, the centres of the palms of their hands.

ABSENT HEALING

Use a large crystal as a focus, a crystal or amethyst sphere, a geode or unpolished rose quartz or calcite in any shade.

❖ Work if possible by candlelight.

❖ You can send healing crystal light to people who are not present, to animals, war- or famine-torn places, the seas, the skies, the melting ice caps or to the whole planet.

❖ Work either alone, holding the crystal in your hands, or with a group of healers or friends who can pass the large crystal round a circle as each empowers it with special prayers or wishes.

❖ Name the person or place and say a prayer or a healing mantra (a continuous rhythmic chant) for healing into the crystal. Breathe in the light of the crystal, exhaling darkness.

❖ When you are filled with light, send the light as continuous out breaths to the subject.

Meanwhile, keep repeating your chosen healing prayer or mantra in your mind.

❖ Leave the candle to burn through and restore energy to the crystal.

❖ You may wish to have a healing book in your special crystal place, to record names of anyone who is sick. You can then send them light through the crystal every week.

DIVINATION

Named after the practice of consulting the divus or diva, a god or goddess, divination helps to determine the right course of action in a particular situation, or what the outcome of an event will be. It involves selecting, apparently at random, symbols such as tarot cards, Viking or Anglo Saxon rune staves or crystals, through which the divus or diva would make their will known. In modern divination we consult the god or goddess within, the wise part of ourselves that is not bound by the limitations of time. This part of ourselves can reach the universal store of knowledge, so that we are not bound by the facts as known to our conscious mind.

RIGHT For thousands of years, clear quartz crystal spheres have been used to reach the unconscious depths of personal and cosmic wisdom.

The selection of particular crystals or other symbols occurs through the process of psychokinesis, the ability of the mind to move matter, in this case our hand, to select one crystal rather than another so that it answers our question. Crystals are a very powerful form of divination, because not only do the colours and the individual crystal type have certain core meanings, but also when we hold the crystal we have selected unconsciously, information from it floods our minds. This knowledge is transmitted through our finger-tips and in the form of words, sensations of heat or cold, feelings of reassurance or sudden doubt about a planned course of action as well as rich visual images in our mind.

CREATING A CRYSTAL DIVINATION SET
On page 159 there is a list of crystals that are suggested for divination. You can use as few as eleven crystals, one for each of the main colours: white, red, orange, yellow, green, blue, purple, pink, brown, grey and black.

❖ Choose crystals of similar size, shape and smoothness; round or oval tumbled stones about the size of a medium coin are ideal.

❖ You can add to the selection at any time and may aim initially to double your original set so you have a vibrant shade of each colour that would indicate a more immediate active response and a softer, more muted hue.

❖ You can use as many or few crystals as you wish, from eleven to two hundred or more, as the selection is made by your unconscious wisdom no matter how few stones you use. I have known people who needed a practical, down-to-earth approach to a problem pick only matt brown stones out of more than 150 crystals in my divinatory bag.

❖ Keep the crystals for divination in a drawstring bag (or place them in this bag prior to divination).

❖ You can read for yourself or others. Crystal divination is remarkably good for creating a psychic dialogue between questioner and reader, even if the questioner has never used crystals before.

❖ Ask a question or get your subject to do so. Place your power hand in the bag (or ask the questioner to make the selection) and choose three crystals, one at a time, that feel right. Do not look in the bag. Set them on the table.

❖ As you buy more crystals for divination, choose up to six for an important question.

❖ Hold each crystal in turn in the order that

ABOVE Choosing crystals from a bag is a way of allowing our unconscious mind to guide us.

feels right, in your cupped hands.

❖ Close your eyes and allow impressions to form. If you are reading for someone else, ask that person to pick up each crystal first and say what it makes them feel, before handing it to you for interpretation.

❖ Use this intuitive method first. The meanings of colour and kind are just guidelines and will help you to give structure to the message.

❖ If the answer is not clear, tell a story, using the images you have seen from each crystal.

❖ You can also select a single crystal each morning to alert you to the mood of the day ahead and offer you the strengths you will need. Carry it as a talisman in a tiny purse.

CRYSTAL PENDULUM DIVINATION
You can also use a crystal pendulum for decision-making at work or at home. Alternatively, choose a favourite birthstone pendant or a crystal point that you hold between the thumb and first finger of your power hand.

❖ On a piece of paper, draw a circle and divide it into four, six or eight segments, according to the number of options. Alternat-ively, draw a square and make a grid of boxes.

❖ In each segment write down the different options you have. The decision could be about your career, a relationship or foods you suspect may be causing an allergy.

It could even be possible holiday destinations or properties you have visited when seeking a new home. Shade in any left-over segments.

❖ Very slowly, move the pendulum over each option in turn, allowing images and words to form in your mind.

❖ Then pass the pendulum a second time over the options and this time it will pull down strongly over one of the options.

❖ If it does not respond to any option, leave the reading overnight and your dreams may suggest another avenue to add to your list.

RIGHT Crystal pendulums are a quick but accurate way of making intuitive decisions.

MAGIC AND PSYCHIC DEVELOPMENT

Crystals amplify and transmit our innate psychic energies. They offer doorways to other dimensions and within their depths our minds can travel beyond the immediate material world with its rigid restraints. We can also empower crystals to hold prosperity, love or success energies that can be released when we need them in our daily lives.

CREATING A CRYSTAL PLACE

Crystals are magical anywhere. However, if you create a special crystal place in your home for meditation, contemplation and healing

work, it will increasingly become an oasis of calm and healing power that can restore your inner harmony after the most fraught day.

❖ You will need a small table with a cloth to serve as an altar and comfortable seating, perhaps floor cushions if it is a low table.

❖ On the altar set white candles, an all-purpose incense such as sandalwood, lavender or rose, fresh seasonal flowers and a statue or picture of a favourite angel or deity.

❖ You can display large crystals, spheres, geodes, crystal point formations or clusters and wands and the unpolished pieces you keep for absent healing.

❖ Keep open your healing book (see p14); read a name every night as well as your weekly ritual. Send blessings through a crystal.

❖ In the centre, keep a dish of your favourite crystals, through which you can run your fingers or create patterns with the crystals on the altar, the floor or in a special sand box (use a large tray and children's sand).

❖ Make crystal grids, mandalas (regular circular patterns), labyrinths, medicine wheels or any formation that intuitively seems to bring power and healing. Touch each crystal in turn and send a blessing or healing to a person, animal or place.

❖ When you have the time, explore the energies of an individual crystal by setting the altar with its related incense, relevant candle colour, a dish of its herbs or oil and its flowers (see individual entries). Hold the crystal and allow impressions to come of its personal functions for you.

CRYSTAL MAGIC

Each crystal has its strengths, for example as a money or luck bringer, and simply by carrying the crystal you absorb these powers.

❖ You can empower a crystal even more intensely for any purpose by drawing over it in the air a word or symbol for what you need, while stating the purpose aloud as a soft continuous mantra.

❖ Sprinkle a few grains of sea salt over your chosen crystal for the power of the earth, spiral it with smoke from its associated incense for the power of air, pass the crystal through the flame of its own coloured candle for the power of fire and shower it with drops of still mineral water for the power of water, at each stage repeating the mantra. Say: 'So may it be, the power flies free as I count three. Three two one. Blessings come.'

MAKING A CHARM BAG

You can add the empowered crystal to a charm bag, a tiny purse or drawstring bag containing symbols related to the wish, for example the crystal's herbs, a gold coin for wealth, a tiny doll for fertility or a silver heart for love. Carry your charm bag until your desire is fulfilled.

PSYCHIC POWERS

If you were just to sit holding a crystal in candlelight, gazing into its depths, you would enter a light meditative state in which your innate psychic powers would spontaneously unfold. In the individual entries are listed the psychic properties each crystal best amplifies. The following are a few ways you could begin to use crystals if you are new to psychic work.

ABOVE Making crystalline formations, mandalas and medicine wheels captures the essence of ancient powers.

SCRYING WITH CRYSTALS

Scrying means perceiving images in a reflective surface, though in fact we often see them, at least initially, in our mind's vision. See page 44 for scrying with a crystal ball.

❖ Gaze into a large polished crystal, preferably one that has inclusions, with reflected candlelight shining into it.

❖ Ask a question and, through half-closed eyes, allow images to form as crystal and light combine into magical shadowy forms.

❖ If you find this difficult, fill a bowl with water and gently drop crystals into it one at a time to create ripples. Surround the bowl with a ring of candles or set it in shimmering sunlight or full moonlight.

EXPLORING CRYSTALLINE WORLDS

For past-life exploration, identify a doorway in a large cloudy crystal, in candlelight or intense sun- or moonlight.

❖ Breathe in the crystalline light all round you so that you are within the crystal and can walk through the doorway.

❖ You may find yourself in a wood, beside a river. Walk along the path, which is strewn with crystals. You may see scenes from the past and a person with whom you identify, that will answer some present question. You can return to the everyday world by counting slowly down from ten to nought.

❖ For an out-of-body experience (astral travel), surround a large crystal with candles and gradually blow them out one by one while picturing the crystal just as bright in your mind's vision, but getting larger and larger and steps of crystal rising up one side.

When it is physically dark and all the candles are extinguished, in your mind climb the crystal steps higher and higher and feel feather wings sprouting. At the top you can fly or float towards the stars, dive deep into the clear ocean below or follow another crystal staircase inside a huge tree to a mythical land with talking animals and wise guides.

Whichever route you choose, you can again return by counting slowly from ten to nought.

LEFT Scrying with crystals in water is one of the most ancient forms of divination.

CLEANSING AND EMPOWERING CRYSTALS

Cleansing and empowering are two aspects of the same process. As you work with your crystals, whether for healing, magical or protective functions, they do naturally become depleted of energy and absorb negativity as people talk of their sorrows or pain flows from the person into the crystal.

Though some recently discovered crystals do not seem to need cleansing or charging, the ritual is a good way of ensuring that any negativity that has penetrated our aura is dissipated (see p20–21 for more general crystal psychic protection).

WHEN TO CLEANSE AND CHARGE CRYSTALS

❖ Cleanse any crystal that is new to you, to remove the impressions of those who have mined, handled and sold it, even though these energies may not be negative. You can then endow the crystal with your personal power and that of the earth, seas and skies.

❖ If a crystal appears dull or feels heavy, it probably needs restoring and maybe resting for a while if you use it every day. Have two or three of your favourite kinds of crystal so that you do not exhaust them.

❖ Cleanse and recharge your healing and divinatory crystals once a week or after particularly intense or emotional work. Home and workplace crystals, especially ones that have to protect against technological pollution or that hold at bay negative earth energies, will also rapidly become depleted.

❖ You can cleanse more than one crystal by placing them in a circle and working over or round the crystal circle.

METHODS OF CLEANSING CRYSTALS

In each individual crystal entry is listed the specific ways that you can charge the crystal according to its unique qualities. However you can also use any of the following methods, unless for example, it is suggested you should not use sunlight for a specific crystal because it may crack or fade.

RIGHT Fragrant incense will restore the energies of a crystal that has been used for healing.

USING A CRYSTAL PENDULUM

❖ Hold a clear-crystal pendulum over the crystal (very delicate shades are best cleansed with an amethyst or rose-quartz pendulum).

❖ Pass the pendulum over the crystal nine times with slow anticlockwise circles to remove negativity.

❖ Dip the pendulum into a bowl of cold water nine times and shake it dry.

❖ Finally, move the pendulum nine times clockwise over the crystal to empower it.

CLEANSING AND EMPOWERING WITH SALT AND WATER

❖ Add three pinches of salt to a small bowl of still mineral water and stir clockwise with a clear, pointed crystal.

❖ Sprinkle three circles of the salt water round the crystal, moving outwards as you sprinkle. As you do so, ask the blessing of a deity, angel or the benign light of the universe to remove all darkness from the crystal and infuse it with healing light.

USING EARTH ENERGIES

❖ Visit a place where earth energies are strong: a standing stone, a stone circle, a long barrow, burial mound or fairy hill, an old stone medicine wheel or a sacred rock. If possible, go soon after dawn.

❖ Set your crystal or crystals on top of a flat stone or at its foot if it is too tall or pointed.

❖ Leave the crystals for at least thirty minutes so that the negative energies can flow into the earth and power can rise through the stones.

SMUDGING YOUR CRYSTALS

This is especially good for a circle of crystals.

❖ Use either a sage or cedar smudge stick (a tied bundle of dried herbs) or large, broad-based incense sticks in cedar, sage or pine.

❖ Light the smudge or incense and, before you begin, face the four directions, starting with the east, then point your smudge downwards to the earth and upwards to the sky. Ask at each direction that the guardian of the east, south, west and north will purify and empower your crystals. Then ask the same of the earth mother and finally the sky father.

❖ Spiral the smudge alternately upwards and downwards, combining anticlockwise and clockwise smoke rings. Repeat this mantra as you work: 'Above, around, to the ground, peace surround.'

❖ Alternatively, circle the crystal in the smoke.

CLEANSING WITH NATURE

❖ Leave the crystal in sunlight and moonlight for a twenty-four hour period or in a rainstorm for just two or three minutes. The day of the full moon is good because the moon rises around the time the sun sets and so you have a continuous flow of energies.

❖ Put the crystal in a pot of herbs associated with general healing, for example lavender, sage or rosemary. Leave it for a day and wash off any soil with running water.

❖ Leave the crystal in a stream for an hour.

Left Running water will empower a crystal by releasing its innate healing energy.

CLEANSING WITH CRYSTALS

❖ Wrap the crystal you have used for healing with a large unpolished piece of amethyst in dark silk. Leave the crystals in a closed drawer to rest and recharge.

USING A HERB INFUSION

❖ Use one teaspoon of whichever dried herb is appropriate for three cups of water.

❖ If you are using fresh herbs, use three teaspoons of the herb.

❖ Pour boiling water over the herbs in a pot and leave the infusion to cool.

❖ Strain the infusion into a ceramic or glass dish. Discard the herbs.

❖ Add your healing crystals to the infusion and leave them for twelve hours.

❖ Hold them under running water.

❖ For delicate crystals, substitute dried lavender heads, chamomile flowers or rose petals in the infusion and make a circle of the sprinkled infusion round the crystal/s, first in an anticlockwise direction and then clockwise.

CRYSTALS IN THE HOME AND WORKPLACE

Crystals have been used for thousands of years in every culture to bring power, harmony and protection to people and places. In the modern fast-moving world, our personal crystals create a small oasis of calm at home and work. They accumulate energies upon which we can draw when we are becoming overstressed or need to focus our attention on an urgent task and temporarily shut out distractions.

CHANGING THE ATMOSPHERE

Even a small dish of crystals will subtly improve the atmosphere in a room at home or in the workplace. It will maintain a stable, positive mood in spite of fluctuating emotions or sudden changes of focus.

❖ Have a dish of gentle-coloured crystals in places where there are frequent personality clashes, a mixture of strong egos or a frantic or pressurized atmosphere.

❖ Use more vibrant stones to enhance concentration and enthusiasm and to encourage positive communication and exchange of ideas.

❖ Have a small dish of your favourite crystals on your desk or workbench, so that when you are stressed or need a sudden infusion of energy you can close your eyes and intuitively pick one for the quality you most need.

❖ Keep money-attracting crystals, such as jade, peridot and tiger's eye, in your purse, with credit cards at home, or near your tools of trade or account books at work.

❖ Make restorative crystalline waters by soaking individual crystals for eight hours in small bottles or jars to keep in your fridge. You can take the bottle of needed crystalline strength to splash on your pulse points at work or use them to make drinks for family members or visitors.

Blue lace agate water softens a critical tongue, labradorite water will encourage compromise, while orange carnelian will fill you with confidence. Those seeking love can drink rose quartz water or add nine rose quartz crystals to a pre-date bath.

❖ Carry sparkling crystal quartz, carnelian or citrine when you want to be noticed, whether socially or in a work situation.

BELOW Crystalline pyramids create an area of stillness and calm. They also enhance self-healing abilities and awaken our psychic powers.

PROTECTIVE CRYSTALS

All crystals have protective properties but over the millennia, in cultures from Ancient Babylon to the Orient, the same crystals have assumed importance as guardians of people, homes and places of work. They include amber, amethyst, bloodstone, brown and red jasper, carnelian, dark banded agates, garnet, jade, jet, lapis lazuli, malachite, rose quartz, sodalite, tiger's eye, topaz and turquoise.

If you carry out psychic or healing work, you need ongoing extra crystalline protection. Set protective crystals at the four corners of your healing room or the table where you give readings. Place another crystal on either side of the entrance to your crystal place to filter out negativity from the everyday world. Make sure you cleanse them frequently.

CRYSTAL PROTECTION AT WORK AND HOME

Crystals can shield us from spite at work, and from difficult relations. They can also protect us from neighbours who drain our energies and from those who ill-wish us out of envy.

❖ Smoky quartz buried at the corners of your home (in plant pots if necessary) will keep all within and your possessions safe from harm.

❖ Place an amethyst or obsidian crystal point, sharp end outwards, in your workspace to deflect gossiping or an over-critical boss.

❖ Keep rose quartz or amethyst by the phone and computer at home and work to soften confrontational calls or emails.

❖ Green and black malachite will help to absorb the headache-inducing rays of computers and high-tech equipment.

PROTECTION WHILE TRAVELLING

Hide turquoise or a pink kunzite (a recently discovered protective stone) in the glove box of a car or in your luggage to guard you against attack, accident and road rage. Sodalite is a protective crystal for air travel. Carry a smoky quartz, misty obsidian or labradorite if you must travel alone late at night or are in a potentially dangerous crowded area. Breathe in the misty energy and exhale your fear as dull-red light to act as a shield and lower your profile so you will be less visible to hostility.

NEGATIVE EARTH ENERGIES

Sometimes our homes and workplaces are built on land where there are very strong earth energies that are not meant for dwellings and we can feel constantly exhausted or even become ill as the strong psychic currents permeate our aura. Negative energies can also be caused by major manmade constructions such as a main road. Electricity pylons, mobile-phone masts and mine workings may cause negative energies, as can unhappy or evil events, even if they occurred years ago.

Set dishes (or single, larger stones) of amber, amethyst, brown jasper and dark banded agate, obsidian and tiger's eye in the centre of any room that feels dark or unfriendly. These crystals will also help a room where quarrels and bickering seem to break out for no reason.

CHILDREN AND CRYSTALS

Children have an instinctive understanding of crystals and, because they are so spiritual and psychically open, are very receptive to crystal healing. Indeed a child will not only instinctively select the correct crystal for a particular ill, but will move the crystal quite naturally over the afflicted area, drawing out pain and infusing healing light in a way envied by the most experienced adult healer.

CRYSTALS FOR CHILDREN

It is never too early to introduce a child to crystals. Indeed, some women intuitively select a crystal for a child soon after conception. They place this crystal on the womb when communicating with the foetus, hold the crystal during labour and then hang it over the infant's crib for protection in the early hours and days of life. This birth crystal becomes the first of a child's personal crystal collection and can be added to by relations and friends at the naming ceremony, birthdays and other landmarks in the child's life. When the adult child leaves home, the crystals provide a link with the love of the family

However you can begin a child's crystal collection at any time in his or her life or start one for a relation's child or a grandchild. Buy a zodiacal birthstone as a very special gift.

BELOW Rose quartz is a perfect stone for children and animals because it gently brings calm and counteracts the frantic pace of the modern world.

❖ Earth stones, such as brown and banded agates, golden-brown rutilated quartz and brown jasper, will infuse animals with gentle, healing earth energies. They are useful for chronically ill or very old animals or those who are recovering from an operation or intensive treatment.

❖ Cat's eye is good for all cat healing, and dalmatian jasper is excellent for dogs. Hawk's eye (blue tiger's eye) benefits birds, while aquamarine or blue coral aids fish. Tiger's eye or leopardskin jasper assists exotic pets and both are good for sending healing to wild creatures that are under threat of extinction.

❖ For thousands of years, turquoise has offered animals protection against being stolen, straying or being hurt in accidents or by animal haters. It can be attached to a horse's mane or bridle, an animal collar, the mirror in a birdcage or the back of a small animal hutch.

It can be worn or carried by the child on significant occasions. Often the crystal selected before birth reflects the child's inner nature and potential while the official birthstone represents their persona to the world. As soon as a child is old enough not to swallow or chew crystals, they can keep them in a drawstring bag and will often spontaneously begin healing teddy bears, dolls and willing adults.

HEALING CHILDREN WITH CRYSTALS

Amethyst, coral, blue lace agate, jade and rose quartz are excellent all-purpose healers for children. Amethyst and rose quartz relieve nightmares and head pains, while rose quartz aids earache, colic and stomach pains. Coral is beneficial for teething pains and protects against falls. Jade is useful for all fevers, growing pains and fears of all kinds. Blue lace agate soothes restless children and is useful when a child is learning to walk.

CRYSTALS FOR HEALING THE ENVIRONMENT

Because crystals are formed in the earth, moulded from volcanic fire and affected by wind and water, even the smallest crystal has the power to heal the environment. When we hold any crystals and speak a prayer or empowerment, we release healing medicine from the earth mother herself. We can direct this energy to heal polluted land, the seas or atmosphere or to assist any of the species endangered by human carelessness.

Green and brown crystals are good for the land and the forests and their creatures. Blue and turquoise crystals support the air and seas,

HEALING ANIMALS

Animals are also very responsive to crystal healing. Owners often have great success healing their pets with crystals because of the strong bond of love and trust between them, which amplifies the crystal's healing powers.

❖ A healthy animal can benefit from drinking water in which jade has been soaked every day; this will maintain vitality, especially in an older animal. Amethyst water deters fleas and other parasites.

❖ Moss agate or brown-banded agate placed under a pet bed will calm hyperactive, aggressive or very nervous animals. It is especially useful for pets from a rescue centre.

birds and sea creatures of all kinds. Have a small dish of these environmental crystals on your altar and, once a week, hold one crystal. Focus on a particular place under threat that you have seen on the news or a local issue that needs extra input. Speak to the earth mother or your special angel and ask that the forces within the crystal and of the earth will restore the balance.

To assist damaged land, place a healing crystal at each of the corners of a photograph of the polluted place, of belching smoky chimneys or of waste-filled seas. Surround the picture with a circle of small candles of the same colour as the crystals and, as you light each one, speak a blessing or wish for healing. Leave the candlelight to shine on the crystals and picture until the candles are burned through (do not leave candles unattended).

To heal wasteland, especially urban waste, bury moss agate and jade crystals in the earth, asking that life may return and healing follow. Bury tree agate close to saplings in any areas where there is reforestation or where forests have been ripped down to make way for roads. Encircle a photograph of a rainforest with tree agates and waft the smoke of cedar or pine smudge or incense over the image to regenerate the lungs of the earth.

To help protect the oceans, on the night of the full moon drop three orbicular jasper, aquamarine or blue coral crystals, one after the other, into a bowl of salt water. As you do so, make a wish for each crystal to cleanse the seas and protect seals, dolphins, whales and other endangered species. Or, cast three blue-glass nuggets one after the other into the sea at high tide, calling your wishes to the waves.

ABOVE Crystal spheres are traditionally used to direct healing sunlight, to take away pain and enhance the body's innate healing ability.

THE DIRECTORY

Each of the crystals in the directory is identified by its main colour and is cross referenced to other crystals of the same kind that share characteristics. For example, the balanced energies of all agates can be found under the main heading.

For each crystal, the associated herbs, flowers and so on are listed. These correspondences are drawn from a variety of traditions and the practice of modern healers, as well as from my personal research, healing and magical work.

Many of the zodiac references are based on ancient associations. These astrological strengths indicate not only that a crystal is especially powerful for a person born under that sign, but also that the crystals' powers are concentrated during that astrological period.

In some cases the references are straightforward and a crystal will be ruled by the traditional planet or element. More complex crystals may display more than one astrological energy line and another planet or even two planets may contribute to its healing qualities, while it may display properties of two elements.

As you work with the crystals you may find different herbs or oils amplify the healing powers of a crystal or that your own guardian angel is a better focus than the ones listed. Crystal work is personal, based on the interaction of the crystal, the user and the energies of the patient. So experiment and change anything that is not right for you.

CLEAR QUARTZ

See also rose (p100), smoky (p144), rutilated (p113) and blue quartz (p58)

Pure clear quartz is the most common mineral on earth. The word crystal comes from krystallos (clear ice in Ancient Greek) – celestial water from the heavens that the deities froze so it would never melt.

MYTHOLOGY AND HISTORY

According to legend, Hercules dropped the crystal of truth from Mount Olympus and it shattered into the millions of pieces that we find today as clear quartz crystal. That is the reason a person using a crystal for scrying can never lie (see spheres, p44).

Australian Aboriginals called quartz the living spirit and mekigars (magic men and women) had crystal quartz inserted into their skin by, it was said, Balame, the All Father, which gave them magical and healing powers. In the Orient, crystal quartz was regarded as the essence of the dragon; it was considered to be pure chi, or life force.

DIVINATORY SIGNIFICANCE

Quartz is the stone of the sun, of health, wealth and happiness. When crystal quartz appears in a reading you can be optimistic, especially about a planned new beginning.

HEALING PROPERTIES

Clear crystal quartz is probably the most versatile of all crystals and can be used for any healing, energizing or cleansing work. In its clear form, quartz is pure yang energy, associated with masculine properties, light, an active response and the power of the sun.

Quartz crystal absorbs energy from sunlight and the life force in flowers, trees and all plants and can draw down divine light. It will store and concentrate this energy, to be released in healing or magic or just as pure vitality. The white light radiates through the body as the seven chakra colours (see p9), each ray unblocking and energizing its own associated chakra. Crystal points are most frequently used for healing.

To restore and maintain health, for nine consecutive days drink water in which nine tiny quartz crystals have been boiled. This is an ancient Celtic practice.

BELOW A clear quartz cluster will promote a calm and harmonious atmosphere at home or in the workplace.

PROPERTIES

TYPE: Silicon dioxide, crystalline quartz. Six sided or faced in its natural formation

COLOUR: Clear, glassy, sparkles in the sun

SYMBOLIC ASSOCIATIONS

ZODIAC SIGN: Leo

PLANET: Sun

ELEMENT: Fire

CANDLE COLOUR: Gold

GUARDIAN ANGEL: Michael

CHAKRA: Crown

HERBS, INCENSES AND OILS: Bay, frankincense, orange, rosemary and St John's wort

FLOWERS: Golden chrysanthemum, marigold and sunflower

ASSOCIATED CRYSTALS: Diamond, white sapphire and white topaz

LEFT Clear quartz contains pure light and undiluted life force, bringing vitality, joy and health and driving away all fears.

USES AT WORK AND HOME

Crystal clusters in the centre of a room help people to live and work together harmoniously. They instil a sense of optimism and clear purpose and make others more receptive to innovation if they are by nature pessimistic and closed to new ideas.

A quartz cluster is an excellent antidote to harsh lighting at work and will enliven a home that is always dark, even in summer. Some people keep a special personal crystal quartz wrapped in silk or a tiny purse for their own private work.

CHILDREN

Give a newborn child his or her special quartz crystal in a purse that can be put in the nursery and kept throughout life. It will increase in power and serve as a personal guide, talisman and source of light and hope.

ANIMALS

Place quartz beneath an old animal's bed to make it more energetic, playful and healthier.

PROTECTIVE FUNCTIONS

Clear crystal quartz will absorb negativity from the atmosphere and transform it into rays of healing and positive feelings.

PSYCHIC PROPERTIES

Crystal quartz amplifies any innate psychic, magical or healing power and is traditionally used to increase the power of prayer, especially for healing. It will also act as a channel for angelic powers and spirit guides (see below). Hold a quartz crystal to send telepathic messages. A clear crystal pendulum will aid in making decisions and will also trace fluid, useful if looking for the source of an oil leak in your car or finding a blockage in a pipe. More esoterically, a crystal pendulum will identify energy pathways in the body and unblock and energize chakras.

ENVIRONMENTAL WORK

Even the tiniest piece of crystal quartz will send healing vibrations to the planet and help towards creating a world community based on tolerance and diversity. Bury tiny quartz crystals in soil to regenerate wasteland and help bring back wildlife.

RECHARGING ITS ENERGIES

Leave it in midday sunlight among greenery.

MILKY QUARTZ

PROPERTIES

TYPE: Silicon dioxide. The cloudiness is caused by tiny inclusions of fluids that are trapped in the crystal during formation. Quite greasy to touch

COLOUR: Clouded white

SYMBOLIC ASSOCIATIONS

ZODIAC SIGN: Cancer

PLANET: Moon

ELEMENT: Water

CANDLE COLOUR: Silver

GUARDIAN ANGEL: Muriel

CHAKRA: Sacral

HERBS, INCENSES AND OILS: Jasmine, lemon balm, peach, rose and vanilla

FLOWERS: Lily, narcissus and white lotus

ASSOCIATED CRYSTALS: Moonstone, pearl and water opal

MYTHOLOGY AND HISTORY

These cloudier crystals, like their opaque sisters (snow quartz, see p29), are female, yin stones associated with the moon, see-through clouds and the moon goddesses. More opalescent types can be called girosol quartz, though this is a name that is also given to a very rare clear quartz.

DIVINATORY SIGNIFICANCE

There are new beginnings and new opportunities coming into your life, but you will see the changes gradually over the coming weeks and months.

HEALING AND THE ENVIRONMENT

Cloudy quartz will relieve blurred vision, headaches or a loss of balance. It can be used to draw out pain or to unblock a chakra (clear quartz can then energize) and to slow down the body and mind when they are running on empty but rest will not come. Cloudy quartz also alleviates acute anxiety states, panic attacks and phobias.

USES AT WORK AND HOME

Every modern household should have a cloudy as well as a clear quartz to create a boundary between the world and the home and to encourage family members to spend time just being together rather than always indulging in frantic activity. If your workplace is always mayhem, with clamouring voices,

constantly ringing phones and clattering faxes, use cloudy quartz to blur the edges and muffle sounds.

CHILDREN AND ANIMALS

Give cloudy quartz to sensitive children who do not enjoy the rough and tumble of the playground or playgroup: it will help them to create a private space. Attach a tiny crystal to your dog lead if you have to walk your pet by busy roads.

PSYCHIC ASSOCIATIONS

Trace the labyrinthine pathways within the stone to mesmerize yourself and allow your mind to slip into gentle meditation.

RECHARGING ITS ENERGIES

Recharge milky quartz with gentle sunlight on a misty morning.

SNOW QUARTZ

MYTHOLOGY AND HISTORY

It is the stone of the snow moon, the moon that heralds the month known by Amerindians as Gnawing on Bones, the time of the deep snow. A yin stone, it is associated with winter.

DIVINATORY SIGNIFICANCE

Let unprofitable situations run their course and build up your strength for the future.

HEALING AND THE ENVIRONMENT

Snow quartz strengthens bones, bone marrow and teeth and aids calcium absorption. It improves lactation and helps a baby feed, whether or not the mother is breast feeding.

USES AT WORK AND HOME

Snow quartz gives you resourcefulness and stamina for tasks you may not relish. It favours ventures where you rely on yourself, whether in juggling finances, filling in your tax forms or finding a new source of income. It will help you to survive tricky patches in your life until luck smiles on you again.

CHILDREN AND ANIMALS

It soothes colicky, fretful or teething babies. It gives strength to the runt of any animal litter.

PSYCHIC ASSOCIATIONS

It can gradually change your fortunes. Use in ice magic: melt ice or snow to soften a cold relationship or release your frozen feelings.

RECHARGING ITS ENERGIES

Wash snow quartz in melted ice or ice cubes.

PROPERTIES	
TYPE: Silicon dioxide. The crystals can be quite chunky	
COLOUR: Polar white. Opaque	
SYMBOLIC ASSOCIATIONS	
ZODIAC SIGN: Capricorn	
PLANET: Moon	
ELEMENT: Water	
CANDLE COLOUR: White	
GUARDIAN ANGEL: Shalgiel	
CHAKRA: Crown	
HERBS, INCENSES AND OILS: Cypress, angelica, cedar, jasmine and mimosa	
FLOWERS: Glastonbury Thorn blossom, snowdrop and white crocus	
ASSOCIATED CRYSTALS: Sardonyx, snowflake obsidian and white opal	

FADEN QUARTZ

MYTHOLOGY AND HISTORY

It is a symbol of wounded heroes, or people who have overcome tragedy or disability.

DIVINATORY SIGNIFICANCE

Time is a healer; what you have lost recently is outweighed by new wisdom, with which you can help others avoid similar pitfalls.

HEALING AND THE ENVIRONMENT

The 'mender crystal' repairs bones, cartilages, torn muscles, broken blood vessels or a grieving heart. It generates self-healing abilities and the will to recover. Use it to heal the damage done to the earth by careless humans.

USES AT WORK AND HOME

Faden quartz helps you put things right, whether fixing your car or mending quarrels with family, reaching compromises at work or turning past mistakes into future triumphs.

CHILDREN AND ANIMALS

Faden quartz will teach children to make do and mend and sometimes accept less than designer chic. It relieves lameness in animals.

PSYCHIC ASSOCIATIONS

A crystal for working with the inner world and for exploring past lives to understand present dilemmas and fears. Potent for all ending rites, for example to mark a divorce.

RECHARGING ITS ENERGIES

Encircle with red and white flowers overnight.

PROPERTIES	
TYPE: Silicon dioxide; crystal quartz. Usually flat (tabular) crystals with straight or curving thread-like lines at the centre	
COLOUR: Clear with white line(s)	
SYMBOLIC ASSOCIATIONS	
ZODIAC SIGN: Aries	
PLANET: Mars	
ELEMENT: Fire	
CANDLE COLOUR: White	
GUARDIAN ANGEL: Charoum	
CHAKRA: All	
HERBS, INCENSES AND OILS: Almond, juniper, nutmeg, sweet tobacco and tangerine	
FLOWERS: Edelweiss, red and white carnations	
ASSOCIATED CRYSTALS: Rutilated quartz, tourmalated quartz and tree agate	

PHANTOM QUARTZ

MYTHOLOGY AND HISTORY

Phantom quartz is formed when the growth of quartz crystal is interrupted and a shadowy, smaller crystal, like a veil within the larger host, appears. Sometimes another coloured crystal can grow around it, for example rose quartz and green chlorite. Often the phantom quartz forms a pyramid shape. A wonder of nature, in myth phantom quartz crystals have been thought to house fairies, angels or earth spirits. They are also the traditional tool of ghost hunters.

DIVINATORY SIGNIFICANCE

Focus on your inner world and for the moment keep your own counsel about matters dear to your heart.

HEALING AND THE ENVIRONMENT

Phantom quartz will help a healer to see psychically the root of problems that may be very different from the symptoms. Use it to help conditions such as ME for which the cause is not understood by medical science and for psychosomatic conditions. It assists tissue and organs deep within the body. Phantom quartz can encourage people to talk about deeply buried sorrows and is helpful for unborn children.

FUNCTIONS AT WORK AND HOME

Keep phantom quartz in a room where you sense a paranormal presence, to help the ghost to move on peacefully. At work use it for projects or long-term ventures whose outcome is unclear and for taking over from a person who has done a job for years.

CHILDREN AND ANIMALS

A pregnant woman can place it on her womb to aid communication with the foetus. Children can talk to their guardian angel within. It will drive away fears of paranormal visitations (except from deceased kindly great-grandparents). This stone confuses animals.

PSYCHIC ASSOCIATIONS

Look through it to see benign ghosts at old houses or ancient sites. Good for connecting with your spirit guides and with earth and air nature essences.

RECHARGING ITS ENERGIES

Use steam from a hot drink, bath or kettle, being careful not to burn yourself.

RAINBOW QUARTZ

MYTHOLOGY AND HISTORY

Like rainbow opal, rainbow quartz is the stone of Iris, Greek goddess of the rainbow, and the Hindu goddess Maya Shakti, who created the wondrous colours of nature behind her seven rainbow veils. Rainbow quartz was a bead which fell from the necklace of the Great Mother as she laughed. It formed Bifrost, the rainbow bridge over which the Viking deities travelled to Asgard.

DIVINATORY SIGNIFICANCE

As the wish crystal, rainbow quartz promises that happiness and the restoration or increases of fortune in the way you most need are within your grasp.

HEALING AND THE ENVIRONMENT

Rainbow crystal healing in sunlight will cleanse, balance and energize all the chakras and fill the aura with light. It transforms areas of pain, darkness or blockage into free-flowing light energy, panic states into calm and depression into happiness. It helps the body perform its routine transformative processes more efficiently, especially regarding blood oxygenation and blood sugar levels, the regeneration of cells and tissue, especially the liver, pancreas, the stomach and intestines, bowel and bladder.

USES AT WORK AND HOME
Rainbow quartz will breathe new vitality into any situation where expectations were not met, whether the disappointment was in love or career or creative ventures that proved less fulfilling and rewarding than anticipated. Use it also to forgive the failings of others.

CHILDREN AND ANIMALS
Rainbow crystals comfort crying babies and disappointed children. Use one to uplift an animal who has lost its will to live.

PSYCHIC PROPERTIES
Rainbow quartz is the best of all wish crystals for focusing on dreams and desires. Use it in rituals for rekindling love or passion, and for prosperity or good fortune after loss. It is an excellent first choice for channelling wisdom from angels or bringers of light from higher dimensions. It is associated with the rainbow goddesses in various cultures.

RECHARGING ITS ENERGIES
Sprinkle it with water in shining sunlight.

PROPERTIES

TYPE: Silicon dioxide. Clear quartz with prismatic fractures in the crystal

COLOUR: When light catches the fracture(s) it forms rainbows

SYMBOLIC ASSOCIATIONS

ZODIAC SIGN: Cancer

PLANET: Moon

ELEMENT: Water/fire

CANDLE COLOUR: Silver or gold

GUARDIAN ANGEL: Matriel

CHAKRA: All

HERBS, INCENSES AND OILS: Lemon, frankincense, myrrh, orange and sandalwood

FLOWERS: Roses of different colours

ASSOCIATED CRYSTALS: Pearl, rainbow obsidian and any precious opal

---

TOURMALATED QUARTZ

MYTHOLOGY AND HISTORY
Like all crystals with inclusions, tourmalated quartz has always been an object of wonder. This black within white stone has come to represent both a doorway into hidden realms and the triumph of light over darkness, day over night, good over evil. In more modern Westernized thought, it is seen to represent the balancing of polarities, yin and yang, as it always has in Oriental philosophy.

DIVINATORY SIGNIFICANCE
Acknowledge and express what you really feel and not what you think is expected of you. The fears in your mind will then dissolve in the clear light of day.

HEALING AND THE ENVIRONMENT
Tourmalated quartz restores balance to the body, mind and spirit, unclogs arteries and heals scars and lesions both in the body and on the skin. It relieves sinus-related headaches. It helps people suffering from Aspergers Syndrome and other personality problems that make social interaction difficult. It aids recovery after road accidents.

USES AT WORK AND HOME
A good crystal for clearing away cobwebs left from the past at home and for neutralizing unfriendly ghostly or poltergeist activity. At work use it to dispense with pettiness among colleagues and to clear the air about

long-standing minor resentments. It also offers great resources of inner strength when you are tired but cannot rest.

CHILDREN AND ANIMALS
It helps over-sensitive children and animals to tolerate noise or sudden movements.

PSYCHIC ASSOCIATIONS
Focus on tourmalated quartz in candlelight to aid astral projection or hold when reading the I Ching. Use in knot rituals when you are binding others from harming the vulnerable.

RECHARGING ITS ENERGIES
Set between a dark and a light candle and allow them to burn through.

PROPERTIES

TYPE: Ring silicate in quartz. Needles or rutiles of black tourmaline in clear quartz. Occasionally green or even pink tourmaline inclusions

COLOUR: Clear transparent with sparkling black tourmaline

SYMBOLIC ASSOCIATIONS

ZODIAC SIGN: Scorpio

PLANET: Pluto

ELEMENT: Water/air

CANDLE COLOUR: White

GUARDIAN ANGEL: Sataral

CHAKRA: Crown/brow

HERBS, INCENSES AND OILS: Cypress, juniper, mugwort, rosewood and wintergreen

FLOWERS: Hyacinth, sea lavender and thistle

ASSOCIATED CRYSTALS: Rutilated quartz, snowflake obsidian and tree agate

MOONSTONE

See also rainbow moonstone (p34)

Because from early times the moon was associated with female reproductive cycles and the moon goddesses were associated with love and fertility, the moonstone is the most powerful of all fertility crystals.

PROPERTIES
TYPE: Feldspar
COLOUR: Translucent white, cream, peach, pink, grey and less commonly blue, all with an iridescent shimmer
SYMBOLIC ASSOCIATIONS
ZODIAC SIGN: Cancer
PLANET: Moon
ELEMENT: Water
CANDLE COLOUR: Silver
GUARDIAN ANGEL: Gabriel
CHAKRA: Sacral and brow
HERBS, INCENSES AND OILS: Jasmine, lemon, mimosa, myrrh and wintergreen
FLOWERS: Lotus, poppy and lily
ASSOCIATED CRYSTALS: Opal, pearl and selenite

HISTORY AND MYTHOLOGY

The Romans thought moonstone was formed out of pure moonlight because of its silvery gleaming hue. It is the stone of moon goddesses everywhere, especially the Greek moon and love goddess, Aphrodite, and Selene, the Greco-Roman full moon goddess. According to legend, blue moonstones, the most rare and precious moonstones, are washed up on shore only on the night of the blue moon, the second full moon to fall in the same month.

Throughout the Orient and in Europe the moonstone is associated with love and was worn to attract a lover. In India lovers spoke their vows over matching moonstones

RIGHT Moonstone is a magical crystal that increases in power and translucence as the moon waxes. It is the stone of dreams and inner visions.

empowered by the light of the full moon to ensure continuing love and fidelity so long as the moon is in the sky.

DIVINATORY SIGNIFICANCE

Trust your intuition rather than external appearances when making a decision. Listen especially to your dreams. Others may take a less than open approach. Beware of taking the path of least resistance or the easiest route.

HEALING PROPERTIES

Moonstone is especially healing for women, though it helps with hormonal and thyroid problems with both sexes. For women it eases troubles with fluid retention, PMT, menstruation, pregnancy, childbirth, the menopause and fertility. Moonstone helps to lessen mood swings and prevents overreacting to situations and the pressures of others. It relieves insomnia, nightmares and hormonal and stress-related headaches.

USES AT WORK AND HOME

A dish of moonstones in the main sitting area at home helps to ease the tensions of the day and to mark the transition between the world of work and home. A friend to shift workers and those whose jobs involve constant travelling and irregular hours, moonstone helps the body clock to adjust.

CHILDREN

Moonstone is a favourite with children. It prevents night terrors and helps wakeful children establish a regular sleep pattern. Moonstone will promote calm in hyperactive children by helping them to get in touch with natural rhythms.

ANIMALS

Moonstones are beloved of cats and sometimes those with 'eye' markings are called cat's eyes (see also p144). A moonstone near the cat bed will prevent the cat from straying too far at night.

PROTECTIVE FUNCTIONS

Moonstones protect travellers, especially those who travel at night and on the sea. Frequent travellers should keep one in the glove box of a car for safe night driving and as a protection against road rage. Other travellers can keep a moonstone in their luggage or in a small charm bag.

PSYCHIC PROPERTIES

As one of the most magical stones, the moonstone plays a central part in allowing positive energies to flow in rituals, especially moon magic, and for developing psychic abilities in a safe, gradual way. During the full and waning moon, and for all readings at night, moonstone is a powerful trigger for divination and prophecy.

For personal divination, ask a question and drop five moonstones into a crystal bowl of water lit by the moon or by silver candles. The ripples as each falls into the water will suggest an image in your mind's eye and the five images will answer your question. Alternatively, place a moonstone on your brow before sleep while you ask your question. The answer will appear in a dream.

You can substitute a moonstone for rose quartz in the fertility ritual on page 102.

THE ENVIRONMENT

Moonstone is associated with the growth of plants. Bury one in the soil when planting herbs in the three days before the full moon, the traditional time for peak growth.

SPECIAL PROPERTIES

Moonstone is believed to absorb the powers of the moon, becoming deeper in colour, more translucent and more powerful for healing as the moon waxes until it reaches full moon. As the moon wanes, the moonstone becomes paler and releases gentler energy, encouraging rest and withdrawal from frantic activity.

RECHARGING ITS ENERGIES

On the night of the full moon, leave your crystals in a dish from moonrise to moon set.

RAINBOW MOONSTONE

MYTHOLOGY AND HISTORY
Believed in Classical times by such writers as the Roman Pliny to absorb moon- and starlight, rainbow moonstone is the original mood stone, increasing in translucence or becoming dull in response to the underlying mood of the person carrying or wearing it. (This happens to some extent with all moonstones.)

The iridescence is caused by what may appear to be insect-like inclusions: these are in fact tiny prismatic fractures that reflect rainbows. Moonstones, especially rainbow ones, are given on the thirteenth wedding anniversary to counter fears of bad luck.

DIVINATORY SIGNIFICANCE
You may want to try new methods of psychic work or divination. If in doubt, begin with dream interpretation.

HEALING AND THE ENVIRONMENT
Rainbow moonstone is gentler than rainbow quartz and so is helpful in cases where a person has low resistance or their immune system is not working properly. It alleviates post-operative stress for women who have had surgery relating to their breasts, ovaries or womb and helps with any scarring. It is excellent for people who harm themselves or consider doing so as a cry for help.

Rainbow moonstone will aid all places torn apart by war or internal abuses of power.

USES AT WORK AND HOME
Rainbow moonstone is protective for all who live in rural or remote areas. It helps both men and women who work irregular hours to adjust their body clocks. It relieves jet lag when flying overnight.

CHILDREN AND ANIMALS
Rainbow moonstone improves speech problems and learning difficulties in children. It also helps the conservation of butterflies, moths and dragonflies.

PSYCHIC PROPERTIES
Moonstone is a wish stone for long-term projects. Use it also in love rituals, in ceremonies to increase inner radiance and for all full-moon magic.

RECHARGING ITS ENERGIES
Leave it under the light of the full moon, or as near to the full moon as you can.

PROPERTIES
TYPE: Particularly opalescent feldspar. Lustrous

COLOUR: Often white, cream or with a blue tinge. It shimmers with rainbow brilliance in light

SYMBOLIC ASSOCIATIONS
ZODIAC SIGN: Cancer

PLANET: Moon

ELEMENT: Water

CANDLE COLOUR: Silver

GUARDIAN ANGEL: Gabriel

CHAKRA: Sacral

HERBS, INCENSES AND OILS: Lemon balm, coconut, lotus, mimosa and papyrus

FLOWERS: Jasmine, magnolia and white water lilies

ASSOCIATED CRYSTALS: Rainbow quartz, pearl and precious opals

APOPHYLLITE

MYTHOLOGY AND HISTORY

Apophyllite was discovered at the beginning of the nineteenth century. According to the Gaia hypothesis, mother earth revealed this crystal so that its energies might counter the more materialistic attitudes arising out of the Victorian Industrial Revolution and colonization, while at the same time encouraging the spirit of discovery.

DIVINATORY SIGNIFICANCE

Now is the time to formulate long-term plans about your future and make commitments. Do not be distracted by the lure of short-term gains or instant fulfilment.

HEALING AND THE ENVIRONMENT

Apophyllite is a regulator crystal, helping the heart to beat strongly and regularly and encouraging the body to function like a well-tuned engine. It also brings mental clarity, improved memory and concentration and increased optimism.

USES AT WORK AND HOME

Apophyllite is good for efficient organization at home and work and so is helpful for planning any major life changes that will have long-term repercussions, whether buying a house, becoming pregnant, undertaking a major training course or entering a structured career path. It will help you to prioritize your responsibilities and to fine-tune the details so that you are confident of success. It is an excellent crystal for those who job share, for people returning to work after an absence, for inventors, accountants and bookkeepers, long-distance athletes and those making long-term investments.

CHILDREN AND ANIMALS

Apophyllite helps older children to plan examination courses and to save money. It is helpful for working or show horses.

PSYCHIC ASSOCIATIONS

Use the crystal for deep meditation, astral projection, for improving clairvoyance through scrying, for past-life recall, especially of old talents and languages, and for remembering your dreams. Use it also for invoking pyramid-healing energies (some crystals can be found as pyramids) and for work with angels, spirit guides and with power animals.

RECHARGING ITS ENERGIES

Use sunlight to recharge apophyllite.

PROPERTIES

TYPE: Sheet silicate, striated, cube-like and glassy. Before separation crystals can look flower- or plant-like. Can be sparkling. Broken surfaces shimmer like mother-of-pearl

COLOUR: Colourless / white but can take on the colour of other minerals, pale pink, pale green, blue-green, yellowish and transparent

SYMBOLIC ASSOCIATIONS

ZODIAC SIGN: Gemini

PLANET: Mercury

ELEMENT: Air

CANDLE COLOUR: Lemon yellow

GUARDIAN ANGEL: Akriel or Livet

CHAKRA: Crown

HERBS, INCENSES AND OILS: Lemon, bergamot, lemongrass, lime and rosemary

FLOWERS: Lavender, lily of the valley and flowering mint

ASSOCIATED CRYSTALS: Danburite, faden quartz and prehnite

CLEAR FLUORITE

See also green (p76) and purple (p49) fluorite

PROPERTIES

TYPE: Halide/fluorspar

COLOUR: Its purest form is colourless. Often twin crystals

SYMBOLIC ASSOCIATIONS

ZODIAC SIGN: Pisces

PLANET: Neptune

ELEMENT: Water

CANDLE COLOUR: White

GUARDIAN ANGEL: Vocatiel

CHAKRA: Brow

HERBS, INCENSES AND OILS: Lily of the valley, chamomile, lemon verbena and yarrow

FLOWERS: Bluebell, harebell and wild daffodil

ASSOCIATED CRYSTALS: Apophyllite, milky quartz and water opal

MYTHOLOGY AND HISTORY

Though often used as a diamond simulant, white fluorite has none of the greed associated with diamonds that has led to diamonds being stolen or people being killed for their possession. Although fluorite has been around for some time, it is nevertheless one of mother Gaia's gifts to the New Age as a spiritual substitute for the diamond.

DIVINATORY SIGNIFICANCE

Matters are becoming much clearer and you will soon have no doubts about which option or person to choose to make you happy.

HEALING AND THE ENVIRONMENT

Clear fluorite increases the flow of the life force through all creation. This gentle but powerful healer strengthens teeth and bones, improves eyesight and relieves problems with the sinuses, spleen, skin and bones. It encourages the growth of healthy cells and all connective tissue, fights colds and eases arthritis. It increases the production of breast milk and aids a new mother's recovery after a more complex birth, such as a Caesarean.

USES AT WORK AND HOME

A stone of cooperation, clear fluorite nevertheless cuts through woolly thinking and vague plans or promises so that necessary tasks and projects are set in motion with a definite time scale for completion.

CHILDREN AND ANIMALS

Clear fluorite can heal young children and animals that might find the more intense clear white stones a shock to the system.

PSYCHIC ASSOCIATIONS

If you have not prayed or explored your psychic nature since childhood, use clear fluorite as a channelling stone for prayer or spiritual disciplines. It is good for increasing the telepathic links between mothers and children of all ages.

RECHARGING ITS ENERGIES

Use running water, best of all by moonlight.

DIAMOND

MYTHOLOGY AND HISTORY

According to Aristotle, Alexander the Great first discovered diamonds in a valley guarded by snakes. He ordered his men to polish their shields so that the snakes saw their own reflections and, thinking they were enemies, stung themselves to death. Another Greek myth relates that diamonds were fragments of stars. Cupid's arrows were reputedly tipped with diamonds, leading to its association with love. Diamonds are associated with the sixtieth wedding anniversary.

DIVINATORY SIGNIFICANCE

Diamond is not used in divination.

HEALING AND THE ENVIRONMENT

Diamond purifies the body and detoxifies the whole system, dispersing any negativity and integrating mind, body and spirit. It increases the healthy functioning of the brain, affecting both the skull bones and brain cells, and balance the hemispheres, clearing anxiety, neuroses and depression. Diamond also increases female fertility.

USES AT HOME AND WORK

At work, diamond increases the ability to learn new skills and information quickly and to think objectively.

Diamonds may seem cloudy if you become overheated emotionally or if mental and physical functions go into overload. This can be a good signal that you need to slow down in life and take things more easily.

CHILDREN AND ANIMALS

It is not suitable for children or animals.

PSYCHIC ASSOCIATIONS

Use diamond for contacting angels and devas and for increasing the power of prayer. Magically, diamond enhances clairvoyance. You can use diamond for scrying, both by candlelight and in sunlight.

Use diamond in love, fidelity and prosperity rituals and to discover the truth about a matter. If you wish to achieve fame, wearing diamonds will enhance your aura of success and make others notice you. To bring

faithful love, surround a diamond with white roses. Light a gold candle and recite nine times: 'Rose of white, diamond bright, bring to me fidelity'. Burn the candle through and wear the diamond close to your heart.

RECHARGING ITS ENERGIES

Cleanse diamond often as it absorbs negativity. Polish with a soft cloth and smudge it.

PROPERTIES
TYPE: Carbon. It is 150 times harder than any other mineral
COLOUR: Usually clear
SYMBOLIC ASSOCIATIONS
ZODIAC SIGN: Aries
PLANET: Sun
ELEMENT: Fire
CANDLE COLOUR: Gold
GUARDIAN ANGEL: Asmodiel
CHAKRA: Crown
HERBS, INCENSES AND OILS: Bay, frankincense, lime, neroli and ylang ylang
FLOWERS: Sunflower, white roses and white lotus
ASSOCIATED CRYSTALS: Crystal quartz, Herkimer diamond and zircon

HERKIMER DIAMOND

MYTHOLOGY AND HISTORY

Although they are in fact double-terminated quartz crystals, Herkimer diamonds resemble diamonds in both their shape and their brilliance. Named after the place they are mined, Herkimer County, New York, Herkimer diamonds are valued as a New Age stone because their unrestricted growth in soft mud makes them one of the prime liberators of the human spirit. Therefore Herkimer diamonds are considered to give access to the user's own unlimited potential for growth.

DIVINATORY SIGNIFICANCE

It is not used in divination.

HEALING AND THE ENVIRONMENT

Herkimer diamond affects the body on the deepest level, bringing the deeper brain wave patterns that enable the mind to influence body health positively and opening the aura and chakras to spiritual healing from divine sources. It will stop physical burnout and activate the body to fight not only disease but also potential illnesses that are building up.

USES AT WORK AND HOME

Herkimer diamond enables you to function effectively in the world, but also to see a much wider picture of your own life. It is excellent for making interconnections with other people on a spiritual level. If circumstances or other people have been forcing you and a lover or

PROPERTIES
TYPE: Silicon dioxide. Double-terminated quartz crystals with triangular-shaped faces
COLOUR: Clear, but may contain rainbow inclusions, water and air bubbles
SYMBOLIC ASSOCIATIONS
ZODIAC SIGN: Aries
PLANET: Sun
ELEMENT: Fire/water
CANDLE COLOUR: Gold
GUARDIAN ANGEL: Sandalaphon
CHAKRA: Crown/brow
HERBS, INCENSES AND OILS: Neroli, avocado, lemon, lime and olive
FLOWERS: Cyclamen, dahlia and tiger lily
ASSOCIATED CRYSTALS: Clear fluorite, diamond and faden quartz

permanent partner apart, Herkimer diamond will unite you on a very deep creative level, helping you to face together any situation that arises. It is very useful for anyone who comes into contact with illusions, lies and trickery as it helps you to see through deception and hear the truth of what people are actually saying to you, despite their words.

CHILDREN AND ANIMALS
Herkimer diamonds make children, teenagers and animals too spaced out to make them useful for anything more than occasional use.

PSYCHIC ASSOCIATIONS
Herkimer diamond is the stone of beautiful spiritual dreams and accurate dream recall. It will enable you to have out-of-body experiences/astral travel if you have previously had a problem letting go psychically. Herkimer diamond is also useful for visualization, though you may find that your deeper self alters what you thought you were going to visualize into what you really need spiritually.

RECHARGING ITS ENERGIES
Use sunlight in an unglazed pottery dish.

SELENITE

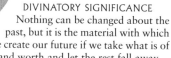

MYTHOLOGY AND HISTORY
Selenite can grow naturally as wands, which are sometimes twinned. Selenite is named after Selene, the Greek goddess of the full moon. Selene was a prolific mother, producing Pandia, goddess of brightness, Ersa, goddess of the dew and Nemea, the mountain goddess. By her mortal lover Endymion she had fifty daughters. A goddess of marriage, married women and mothers, she is mistress of enchantment and ritual.

DIVINATORY SIGNIFICANCE
Nothing can be changed about the past, but it is the material with which we create our future if we take what is of beauty and worth and let the rest fall away.

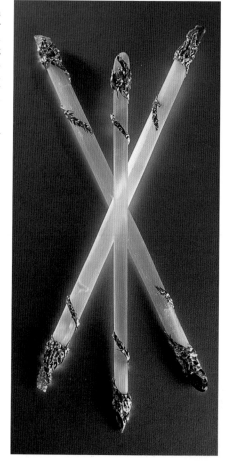

RIGHT AND ABOVE Selenite wands tipped with calcite, quartz or other crystals (right), or a selenite crystal circle (above), can direct light towards a person, animal or place in healing or for protection.

HEALING AND THE ENVIRONMENT
Selenite heals the cells of the body and ensures the fluid system flows harmoniously, including the spinal fluid. It improves skin tone and increases the body's capacity to absorb calcium. A stone of fertility, pregnancy and motherhood, Selenite protects the health of the pregnant woman and the unborn child. It also increases libido.

USES AT WORK AND IN THE HOME
Selenite is the crystal of partnerships, both in love and relationships, and creates a firm foundation for long-lasting commitment. Selenite gently encourages all forms of communication and enables you to see through lies or deception.

CHILDREN AND ANIMALS

Young children love selenite magic wands that they can wave to dispel their fears. Selenite enhances telepathy with all creatures.

PSYCHIC ASSOCIATIONS

Selenite is a powerful crystal of psychic communication. It aids interaction with the wise ancestors, angels and spirit guides, and loved ones telepathically and, through divination, with the cosmic records of wisdom. It is therefore a stone that should be used by mediums and clairvoyants. It also promotes the recollection of dreams and past lives. Keep one in a love charm bag to ensure fidelity until the seas run dry.

RECHARGING ITS ENERGIES

Use still mineral water in which full moonlight has shone to revitalize selenite.

PROPERTIES	
TYPE: Gypsum, hydrous calcium sulphate	
COLOUR: White, transparent or semi-transparent, sometimes striated, translucent and white. As Satin Spar it has bands of moving white light that resemble satin	
SYMBOLIC ASSOCIATIONS	
ZODIAC SIGN: Cancer	
PLANET: Moon	
ELEMENT: Water	
CANDLE COLOUR: Silver	
GUARDIAN ANGEL: Ergediel	
CHAKRA: Brow / sacral	
HERBS, INCENSES AND OILS: Jasmine, lemon balm, peach, rose, vanilla and myrrh	
FLOWERS: Chamomile, gardenia, grape hyacinth and poppy	
ASSOCIATED CRYSTALS: Milky quartz, moonstone and pearl	

WHITE OPAL

MYTHOLOGY AND HISTORY

There are two kinds of opals, common and precious. Milk opals or plain common opals do not have flashes of colour or what is called play of colour. With a precious opal the flashes of colour can be seen from different angles when the opal is held in the light.

According to Hindu legend, the first opal was created when the Mother Goddess changed the young virgin Goddess of the Rainbow into an opal, because the gods Brahma, Shiva and Vishnu were relentlessly pursuing her.

DIVINATORY SIGNIFICANCE

White opal is not used in divination.

HEALING AND THE ENVIRONMENT

The properties for common and precious opals are the same but iridescent white opals have more intense, faster-acting powers.

White opal regularizes the biorhythms of the user, avoiding discordant energies that can lead to uncontrolled behaviour between frantic activity or total inertia. It harmonizes sexual desire so that sexuality becomes true lovemaking rather than pure appetite or a power trip. It also restores pleasure to eating and so alleviates food-related disorders.

AT WORK AND IN THE HOME

White opal increases our pleasure in life. It inspires creativity, especially for writing poetry, drama and children's literature. It aids expression through dance, yoga and tai chi.

CHILDREN AND ANIMALS

A white opal, especially a common one, will help children to express their feelings if they bottle them up. Opal is not an animal stone.

PSYCHIC PROPERTIES

Opals can increase the power of Tantric sex or sex magic, resulting in joint astral travel at the point of sexual union. They are also a focus for rituals to enhance beauty and to call a twin soul psychically.

RECHARGING ITS ENERGIES

Opals are delicate and should not be exposed to sunlight. Wipe with virgin oil or water often but sparingly, as they absorb emotions.

PROPERTIES	
TYPE: Silicon dioxide with water trapped inside	
COLOUR: Pale precious opals are called white, but the term popularly refers to white opals with or without iridescent fire	
SYMBOLIC ASSOCIATIONS	
ZODIAC SIGN: Cancer	
PLANET: Moon	
ELEMENT: Water	
CANDLE COLOUR: Silver	
GUARDIAN ANGEL: Gabriel	
CHAKRA: Brow / sacral	
HERBS, INCENSES AND OILS: Myrrh, eucalyptus, jasmine, peach and sandalwood	
FLOWERS: Night stock, orchid and white water lily	
ASSOCIATED CRYSTALS: Milky quartz, selenite and white pearl	

WATER OR JELLY OPAL

MYTHOLOGY AND HISTORY

The word opal probably comes from the Sanskrit world upala, which means precious stone. Opals, especially colourless ones, were believed to render the wearer unseen and in medieval times opal was called the friend of thieves and wrongdoers. However, water opal can help you lower your profile for more positive reasons.

DIVINATORY SIGNIFICANCE

Water opal is not used in divination.

HEALING AND THE ENVIRONMENT

Clear opal is good for the eyesight, for hair and skin. It gently alleviates exhaustion and is

useful in all illnesses where the person lacks energy or strength. It will ease hormonal imbalances and breast tenderness, especially in younger women, and will aid people of both sexes when they are exploring their sexuality, banishing guilt, fears or pressures to have sex before they are ready.

AT WORK AND IN THE HOME

Water opal will absorb powerful feelings, softening harsh or thoughtless responses and bringing a more caring attitude even to a fiercely competitive workplace.

CHILDREN AND ANIMALS

Water opal is useful for pubescent boys and girls; it will overcome their fears and any sense of shame at their body changes. It is good for calming adolescent animals and those on heat.

PSYCHIC ASSOCIATIONS

Water opal will increase your understanding if you are studying different religious faiths and forms of spirituality. It enhances prophecy through automatic writing (when you allow your pen to write without consciously formulating the words).

RECHARGING ITS ENERGIES

Water opal is especially delicate. Regularly hydrate it gently with a little water while reciting a favourite prayer or mantra.

PEARL

See also black pearl (p152) and mother-of-pearl (p41)

MYTHOLOGY AND HISTORY

According to many legends, pearls are tears that fell into the ocean into open oyster shells; one myth states that they are the tears of the angels for the sins of humankind. More cheerfully, it is told in India that the god Vishnu chose the most beautiful pearls as a wedding gift for his daughter Pandaia. In European custom pearls are the stone given on the thirtieth wedding anniversary. Like opal and jet, pearl best belongs to one person.

DIVINATORY SIGNIFICANCE

Pearl is not used in divination.

HEALING AND THE ENVIRONMENT

Pearl harmonizes bodily rhythms with those of the natural cycles of the moon and the seasons. This enables hormonal cycles and biorhythms to find their natural level, making it a particularly useful stone for women. It also eases mental overload.

AT WORK AND IN THE HOME

Pearl increases spiritual as well as romantic love. It develops nurturing qualities in both men and women. This can foster a caring and harmonious atmosphere in the workplace, which is usually more productive as well.

CHILDREN AND ANIMALS

Give a girl a pearl each year for a necklace to be strung on her eighteenth birthday. Collect them for a belt for a boy or, if he prefers, to save for his future love partner. Pearl is not a suitable stone for animals.

PSYCHIC ASSOCIATIONS

Pearls are a powerful focus for prosperity magic and for breaking the psychic or psychological hold of a destructive or over-dominant person in your life.

RECHARGING ITS ENERGIES

Recharge in waxing moonlight at least once a month. If used for healing or in divination, cleanse at any time with a silver candle.

PROPERTIES	
TYPE: Organic. Formed when an oyster coats an irritant with layers of calcium carbonate (nacre). May be salt or freshwater	
COLOUR: White or pale cream, pink/peach. Iridescent	
SYMBOLIC ASSOCIATIONS	
ZODIAC SIGN: Pisces	
PLANET: Moon	
ELEMENT: Water	
CANDLE COLOUR: Silver or turquoise	
GUARDIAN ANGEL: Rahab	
CHAKRA: Crown/sacral	
HERBS, INCENSES AND OILS: Elder, ambergris (synthetic), gardenia, rose and sandalwood	
FLOWERS: Lotus, sea holly and sea lavender	
ASSOCIATED CRYSTALS: Aquamarine, blue coral and mother of pearl	

MOTHER-OF-PEARL

MYTHOLOGY AND HISTORY

In many cultures, mother-of-pearl is associated with the sea mothers. In Peru pearl is sacred to Mother Sea, the whale goddess. First worshipped by the Incas, she has been revered through the ages by the peoples living along the South American Pacific Coast.

DIVINATORY SIGNIFICANCE

This is a time to keep your counsel and any secrets you have heard from a third party, as they may not be correct.

HEALING AND THE ENVIRONMENT

Mother-of-pearl is very soothing for any skin complaints, allergies or rashes. It is a stone of preconception, pregnancy, birth and

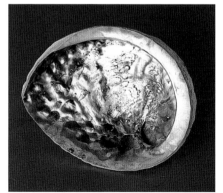

motherhood. It is also helpful for a gentle weight-loss programme for both men and women at any time of life. Mother-of-pearl relieves fluid retention.

AT WORK AND IN THE HOME

Keep either money or gold jewellery in a mother-of-pearl shell to attract prosperity to your home or workplace. Mother-of-pearl helps to ease mothers back into the workplace, no matter how long the break from paid employment has been.

CHILDREN AND ANIMALS

Traditionally mother-of-pearl was placed on a newborn infant's stomach for a few seconds to endow him or her with the protection of the mother even when the mother leaves the child with another carer. Mother-of-pearl comforts an animal whose young have been given away after weaning.

PSYCHIC ASSOCIATIONS

Mother-of-pearl is excellent for sea magic. Find two halves of an oyster shell and insert a small coin or gold earring in the shell. Carefully bind it together with seaweed and cast it on the seventh wave, asking the sea mother to grant your wish.

RECHARGING ITS ENERGIES

Use sea water or add a pinch of sea salt to water to revitalize mother-of-pearl.

PROPERTIES	
TYPE: Organic, the lining mainly of pearl oysters shells, formed from the nacre or calcium carbonate that forms the shell lining. You may find it naturally after the sea creature has died. Iridescent	
COLOUR: White, cream or brown	
SYMBOLIC ASSOCIATIONS	
ZODIAC SIGN: Cancer	
PLANET: Neptune	
ELEMENT: Water	
CANDLE COLOUR: Aquamarine	
GUARDIAN ANGEL: Tamiel	
CHAKRA: Brow/sacral	
HERBS, INCENSES AND OILS: Kelp, lemon verbena, musk (synthetic), tea tree and willowherb	
FLOWERS: Madonna lily, passionflower and peach blossom	
ASSOCIATED CRYSTALS: Amber, pearl and water opal	

WHITE HOWLITE/MAGNESITE

See also blue howlite (p56)

See also blue howlite (p56)

PROPERTIES

TYPE: Calcium Boro-silicate hydroxide. Smooth stones. Opaque. Also found in a form that looks like a cauliflower floret or chewing gum, called magnesite

COLOUR: White or white with grey or black web-like streaks. The magnesite formation is sometimes pale or lime green

SYMBOLIC ASSOCIATIONS

ZODIAC SIGN: Virgo

PLANET: Earth

ELEMENT: Earth

CANDLE COLOUR: Grey

GUARDIAN ANGEL: Hamaliel

CHAKRA: Root

HERBS, INCENSES AND OILS: Caraway, clary sage, lemongrass, honeysuckle and patchouli

FLOWERS: Heather, mosses and wallflowers

ASSOCIATED CRYSTALS: Blue chalcedony, snow quartz and sodalite

MYTHOLOGY AND HISTORY

Howlite is named after Henry How, a geologist who discovered it in Nova Scotia. It is called the home-blessing stone. It is traditionally buried around the boundaries (or in indoor plant pots) at the four main compass directions and a small piece is placed over the front and back doors.

DIVINATORY SIGNIFICANCE

You may need to touch home base for a while. Spend time in familiar places with friendly faces and draw on their loyalty and reassuring strength.

HEALING AND THE ENVIRONMENT

White howlite relates to the skeleton, bones, teeth and to the absorption of necessary minerals. It strengthens the effects of basic health-care and fitness programmes. It is primarily a stone of preventative care and protects against the user or healer neglecting their own health: it is an important component of any charm bag for health.

AT WORK AND IN THE HOME

Howlite encourages high standards of integrity and open, non-confrontational communication. Therefore it is valuable at extended family gatherings and is useful in a workplace where there are factions. It is also conducive to brainstorming sessions.

CHILDREN AND ANIMALS

White howlite reassures children who are afraid to sleep in the dark and encourages a peaceful night's sleep. It persuades nomadic cats to stay near the fireside.

PSYCHIC ASSOCIATIONS

White howlite is effective in visualization, perhaps because it provides both the openness necessary to visualize needs and the earthing to make them manifest in the daily world. It protects against unfriendly phantoms.

RECHARGING ITS ENERGIES

Set it in a white ceramic bowl and leave it in the centre of your home at a happy gathering.

WHITE SAPPHIRE

See also sapphire (p63) and ruby (p132)

See also sapphire (p63) and ruby (p132)

HISTORY AND MYTHOLOGY

The stone of purity, white sapphire was worn as an amulet against infidelity. In medieval times it was exchanged as a peace token. It marks the forty-fifth wedding anniversary.

DIVINATORY SIGNIFICANCE

White sapphire is not used in divination.

HEALING AND THE ENVIRONMENT

White sapphire is a purifier of the blood and will relieve problems with blood cells or bone marrow, the brain and the nervous system. It

works on the whole system like a shimmering shower of rain, cleansing impurities from the chakras and aura and awakening the core of healing and of divinity within us all. Use white sapphire for world peace and wise leadership by elected leaders.

AT WORK AND IN THE HOME

A stone of purity of purpose that sometimes seems at odds with modern consumerism and the need to succeed at all costs. But some of the most successful business people use white sapphire and so benefit from a high reputation in their particular field for honest dealings and customer/staff care. It is also an important stone of internal monitoring, to help set personal standards that do not waver even when the wearer is alone.

CHILDREN AND ANIMALS
White sapphire will help older children and teenagers to create personal rules for living rather than rely on externally imposed ones. It is a good crystal for guide dogs.

PSYCHIC ASSOCIATIONS
A token of first love or one endowed with love and trust in a more mature relationship to remove jealousy or doubts about fidelity. Use it for justice without revenge.

RECHARGING ITS ENERGIES
Wipe gently with a silk cloth and surround it with pink or white petals whenever it feels as though its light is fading.

PROPERTIES
TYPE: Corundum

COLOUR: White, the purest form of sapphire, often substituted for diamonds. Sometimes dyed blue or red by heating

SYMBOLIC ASSOCIATIONS
ZODIAC SIGN: Gemini

PLANET: Mercury/sun

ELEMENT: Air/fire

CANDLE COLOUR: White

GUARDIAN ANGEL: Raphael

CHAKRA: Crown

HERBS, INCENSES AND OILS: Fennel, ferns, lavender, lilac and sweetgrass

FLOWERS: White carnation, hyacinth and rose

ASSOCIATED CRYSTALS: Herkimer diamond, diamond and white topaz

WHITE TOPAZ
See also blue topaz (p71) and golden topaz (p118)

MYTHOLOGY AND HISTORY
The Ancient Greeks prized clear or white topaz because they believed it prevented the owner being enchanted and made the wearer invisible in times of danger. Of all the topaz shades, white is most connected with the moon cycles and is said to increase in lustre and power as the moon waxed, becoming at its most brilliant and powerful on the night of the full moon (see rainbow moonstone, p34).

DIVINATORY SIGNIFICANCE
White topaz is not used in divination.

HEALING AND THE ENVIRONMENT
White topaz is like an internal valve, regulating the amount of energy needed in the

system at any time. It controls the endocrine system and relieves conditions such as asthma and allergies, where external factors attack the body. It also builds up resistance to pollution and harmful rays from the environment. White topaz relieves insomnia caused by system overload and helps the body find its natural weight and level of fitness.

AT WORK AND IN THE HOME
A crystal of truth, it filters information coming from different sources and activates your automatic radar that will guide you if you trust it. It will lower your psychological profile if you don't want to be noticed.

CHILDREN AND ANIMALS
White topaz reduces the power of advertising jargon on impressionable young minds. It is not an animal stone.

PSYCHIC ASSOCIATIONS
Wearing topaz jewellery, especially as earrings, increases your clairaudient and clairvoyant powers. A white topaz ring (the stone need only be tiny) will help you to channel psychic power through the minor chakras on the palms of your hand for effective psychometry.

RECHARGING ITS ENERGIES
Recharge under the full moon, beginning as the sun is setting for solar and lunar powers.

PROPERTIES
TYPE: Hydrous aluminium silicate

COLOUR: The purest form of topaz, clear and sparkling. Also called silver topaz. Translucent. Sometimes irradiated to produce blue topaz

SYMBOLIC ASSOCIATIONS
ZODIAC SIGN: Leo

PLANET: Sun/moon

ELEMENT: Fire/water

CANDLE COLOUR: Gold

GUARDIAN ANGEL: Verchiel

CHAKRA: Crown

HERBS, INCENSES AND OILS: Bay, basil, frankincense, lime, tangerine and rosemary

FLOWERS: Calendula, daffodil and yellow lily

ASSOCIATED CRYSTALS: Clear quartz, diamond and moonstone

CRYSTAL SPHERES

Crystal spheres are characterized by their shape. Those with inclusions are generally easier to read psychically (and are cheaper). Some have double refraction, where light waves bend and double.

PROPERTIES
TYPE: Various
COLOUR: Various
SYMBOLIC ASSOCIATIONS
These will be the same as the kind of crystal from which the ball is formed. All crystal balls operate through the crown chakra

MYTHOLOGY AND HISTORY

Crystal ball divination became popular in Europe in the fifteenth century when it was believed that spirits or angels would appear in the glass. One of the most famous scryers was Sir John Dee (1527–1608), astrologer to Queen Elizabeth I. On 21 November 1582, he bought an obsidian crystal ball. It is said that this crystal provided forewarning of the arrival of the Spanish Armada.

DIVINATORY SIGNIFICANCE

Crystal-ball reading is a multi-sensory experience. Hold the ball and allow feelings and impressions, words as well as images, to enter your mind spontaneously. Images usually appear within your mind initially, but with practice you can project them into the ball by visualizing them on the surface and then picturing them entering the crystal until this happens spontaneously. The images may make a story that answers the question.

HEALING AND THE ENVIRONMENT

Crystal spheres are wonderful transmitters of healing energy. Use a cloudy ball if the healing is to be gradual, or a clear ball when you need a fast infusion of energy. You and the person being healed should hold the ball at the same time: you can send rays of love, which will be amplified through the ball. Traditionally, clear spheres are used to reflect the rays of the sun on to a painful or injured part. Be careful the ball does not get too hot.

AT WORK AND IN THE HOME

Crystal spheres will absorb negativity and transform it into light. Place your hands round it to centre yourself and fill yourself with its light. Use a clear ball for energizing and a soft cloudy one such as amethyst for its calming effect.

CHILDREN AND ANIMALS

Children will see angels and other lands even in the clearest sphere. A crystal sphere will make animals grow quiet and still – who knows what they see?

PSYCHIC ASSOCIATIONS

You can work with really small spheres. If possible have three to consult: first, an amethyst, calcite or rose quartz sphere, then clear quartz or citrine and finally a smoky quartz or blue beryl. In the first gentle ball you can see unknown aspects of the past of yourself or the other person or glimpses of past lives. Cup the sphere between your hands and start talking (record on tape if you wish). The clear or sparkling ball will clarify aspects of the present that may be linked to the past. Finally, the smoky quartz or beryl ball will allow you to look through the cracks of time to future potential/opportunity.

RECHARGING ITS ENERGIES

Use sunlight for a clear or sparkling ball and full moonlight for a cloudier one.

RIGHT A Schalenblende sphere. FAR RIGHT Crystal spheres have from earliest times been regarded as tools of personal wisdom. Holding one to reflect sun, moon or a candle awakens our innate clairvoyant powers and enables us to access the cosmic pool of knowledge of all times and all places. Clockwise from top: rose quartz, serpentine, red jasper, lapis lazula and jet, with a fluorite sphere in the centre.

AMETHYST

Amethyst is particularly effective in meditation and psychic work to develop clairvoyance and clairaudience. It also brings memories of past worlds and past lives if placed in the centre of the brow.

MYTHOLOGY AND HISTORY

Amethyst is considered to be the stone of St Valentine and of faithful lovers. Indeed St Valentine reputedly wore an amethyst ring engraved with an image of Cupid. The Greeks believed it to be particularly effective against drunkenness – hence the name amethustos, which means not to be drunk. Wealthier Greeks, and later the Romans, would make wine goblets out of amethyst to guard against the excessive effects of wine. Legend tells that Amethysta, a beautiful maiden, attracted the unwelcome attention of Bacchus, the god of wine. Diana, the virgin goddess of the hunt, saved Amethysta by turning her into the gleaming gem, saying henceforward all would behave in a restrained manner in her presence.

Amethyst is also the stone of integrity and was worn by Egyptian soldiers in battle so they would not lose their courage in dangerous situations. In the Christian Church, amethyst was the gem of purity and is associated with bishops, who traditionally wear an amethyst ring, especially in the Roman Catholic Church.

Amethyst is the stone of the Buddha and is popular for Buddhist prayer beads, especially in Tibet. In Northern Africa it is a rain-making stone, and is dropped into water by medicine men and women.

DIVINATORY SIGNIFICANCE

Amethyst indicates that you may be feeling stressed or exhausted or have experienced difficulties recently and need to give gentle love to yourself until energy flows again.

HEALING PROPERTIES

Often called the all-healer, amethyst is one of the most effective crystals for any kind of healing work. It is effective for people, animals and plants and can even recharge other crystals with healing powers. It is potent for ailments of both mind and body, especially emotional problems.

It is particularly helpful for addictions, including those to alcohol and food. Placed on the stomach or liver, amethyst helps to soothe problems in these areas.

If worn when sleeping, or kept under the pillow, amethyst prevents insomnia and nightmares. It soothes headaches if placed on temples or the point of pain, relieves eyestrain and helps to maintain the blood-sugar balance. It is excellent for absent healing.

AT WORK AND IN THE HOME

Amethyst soothes anger and impatience and so is good to have in the workplace or at home in a room where you may have to deal with awkward or truculent visitors. Place amethyst geodes, spheres or amethyst pyramids around your home and workspace and focus on one if you become anxious about potential conflict or feel overwhelmed by the tasks you have to finish.

CHILDREN

Children who suffer from nightmares can use an amethyst geode or sphere as a talisman. They should be encouraged to look at the crystal while breathing slowly and imagining that they are breathing in purple light and

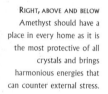

RIGHT, ABOVE AND BELOW Amethyst should have a place in every home as it is the most protective of all crystals and brings harmonious energies that can counter external stress.

PROPERTIES

TYPE: Quartz with very large crystals. Translucent, semi-transparent and transparent

COLOUR: From pale lilac to deep purple; also white

SYMBOLIC ASSOCIATIONS

ZODIAC SIGN: Aquarius

PLANET: Jupiter

ELEMENT: Air

CANDLE COLOUR: Dark blue/purple

GUARDIAN ANGEL: Cambiel

CHAKRA: Brow

HERBS, INCENSES AND OILS: Dusky rose petals, patchouli, lavender, chamomile and sweetgrass (smudge)

FLOWERS: Lavender, violet and lilac

ASSOCIATED CRYSTALS: Rose quartz, moonstone and jade

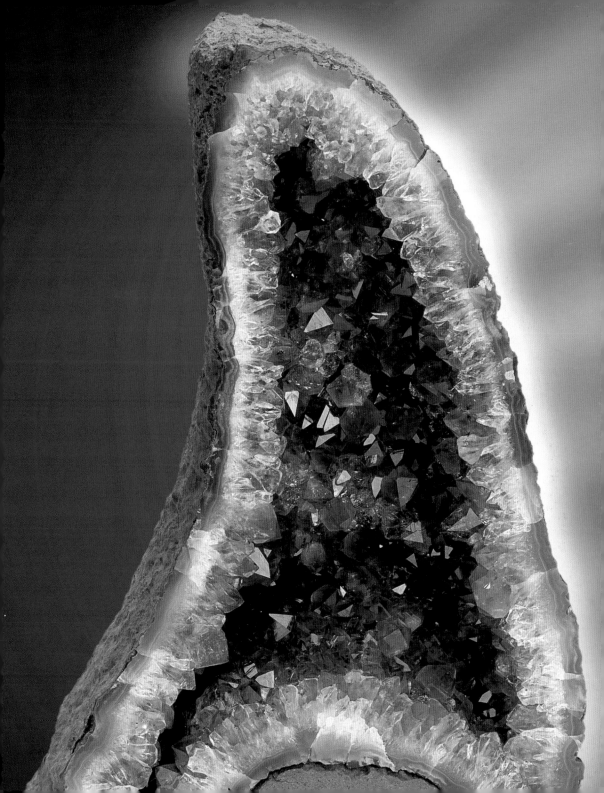

exhaling darkness. Finally, they should visualize themselves as safe and secure in a crystalline castle for the night.

To bring peaceful sleep, soak an amethyst in still mineral water for eight hours and serve as a bedtime drink. Amethyst water is also good in the daytime if a child finds it hard to relax and settle to activities.

ANIMALS

Ill pets can drink amethyst water to energize them and to calm hyperactivity. This helps to stop excessive barking in a dog or feather ripping in a bird. Amethyst also deters fleas.

PROTECTIVE FUNCTIONS

If your home or workplace feels unfriendly or always seems cold and dark even in summer, you may be suffering from streams of dark psychic energy beneath the building. Place amethyst inclusions over any spot that feels hostile and near doors and windows. You can also put tiny amethysts under the carpet to absorb negative earth powers.

Amethysts are naturally protective against technological pollutants, such as a constantly ringing telephone or jangling fax. They are especially good placed on a computer table to avoid excessive strain on eyes and mind.

PSYCHIC ASSOCIATIONS

A powerful psychic enhancer, an amethyst under your pillow will bring peaceful but psychic dreams. An amethyst pendulum aids personal decision making, using a yes/no response. Alternatively, hold it or a pointed amethyst crystal over a series of written options and see over which of the choices the pendulum or crystal pulls down.

ENVIRONMENTAL WORK

An amethyst in the soil of a plant in the workplace will restore energies depleted by noise and over-bright artificial lighting. You can set several tiny amethysts in a polluted place or around the edges of a photograph of a despoiled or war-torn land. Light a purple candle and leave it to burn through.

SPECIAL PROPERTIES

A large unpolished piece of amethyst will cleanse and restore energies to any other crystal you have used for healing, divination or protection. Carefully wrap the crystal with the amethyst in dark silk.

RECHARGING ITS ENERGIES

Recharge amethyst under the light of the moon rather than in sunlight.

PURPLE FLUORITE
See also green fluorite (p76) and clear fluorite (p36)

MYTHOLOGY AND HISTORY
The most spiritual colour of this New Age stone, purple and lavender fluorite have come to represent mystical powers associated with higher planes. They are amplifiers, especially in their naturally occurring pyramid forms, and contain healing light and channelled wisdom from evolved teachers of humanity who live in higher realms.

DIVINATORY SIGNIFICANCE
Your healing gifts may be manifest in the way others seek you out for wise counsel, but you may wish to develop them more formally.

HEALING AND THE ENVIRONMENT
Purple fluorite clears tension headaches and eases problems associated with the ears, sinuses, throat and tonsils. It calms buzzing thoughts that stop you relaxing and sleeping. Purple fluorite also builds up resistance, especially against colds, flu and childhood illnesses that are far more serious in adulthood. Use it as a focus for world peace.

AT WORK AND IN THE HOME
Lavender fluorite will lower levels of tension at home and work and absorb negative or panic vibes. Purple fluorite will make writing course materials, presentations and learning

material for examinations or interviews much easier. Take a piece with you to any meetings when you will be on trial.

CHILDREN AND ANIMALS
Purple fluorite works well with hyperactive children. It helps dogs behave well in public.

PSYCHIC ASSOCIATIONS
It is one of the best stones for meditation, for channelling from higher beings of light and for archangel work. It is good for pyramid work.

RECHARGING ITS ENERGY
Use running water to recharge fluorite.

PROPERTIES
TYPE: Halide / fluorspar
COLOUR: Purple and blue. Transparent or semi-transparent
SYMBOLIC ASSOCIATIONS
ZODIAC SIGN: Pisces
PLANET: Neptune
ELEMENT: Water
CANDLE COLOUR: Lilac
GUARDIAN ANGEL: Raziel
CHAKRA: Crown / brow
HERBS, INCENSES AND OILS: Clary sage, chamomile, star anise, rosewood and sweet pea
FLOWERS: Hebe, lavender and lilac
ASSOCIATED CRYSTALS: Amethyst, blue calcite and watermelon tourmaline

SUGILITE

PROPERTIES

TYPE: Ring silicate

COLOUR: Lilac to violet, dense and opaque with black, white, orange or brown or less commonly blue. A rare dark purple kind is translucent

SYMBOLIC ASSOCIATIONS

ZODIAC SIGN: Aquarius

PLANET: Jupiter

ELEMENT: Air

CANDLE COLOUR: Dark blue

GUARDIAN ANGEL: Ausiel

CHAKRA: Brow

HERBS, INCENSES AND OILS: Acacia, benzoin, lavender, mace and star anise

FLOWERS: Cyclamen, fuchsia and violet

ASSOCIATED CRYSTALS: Amethyst, kunzite and lapis lazuli

MYTHOLOGY AND HISTORY

A relatively recent discovery, sugilite, like kunzite, is said to have been offered up by mother earth to meet the needs and problems of the modern world. Sugilite has become associated with the Age of Aquarius and with a new, more compassionate world view.

DIVINATORY SIGNIFICANCE

Sugilite indicates that your healing powers are developing, whether you are training formally in healing or not. You may find that other people are increasingly seeking your help and advice and that you intuitively know what is wrong with them.

HEALING AND THE ENVIRONMENT

Sugilite directs energy to wherever it is needed in your system and removes energy blockages.

It is especially effective if you continually feel slightly unwell or stressed, as sugilite will realign your body and help to balance the all-important pineal, pituitary and adrenal glands. Some cancer sufferers have found sugilite to be helpful.

Use sugilite in rituals to heal the planet and to restore ecological balance.

USES AT WORK AND HOME

Sugilite will preserve your integrity and self-esteem in a workplace where profit is considered more important than people and where you feel you are just a cog in a machine. You can also use it to bring spiritual values into the home if outside influences are working against you.

CHILDREN AND ANIMALS

Sugilite helps children and teenagers to resist peer pressure and advertising that stresses the importance of designer goods as the route to happiness. It also encourages ecological awareness from a young age.

Sugilite is particularly loved by cats because it is the colour of their aura.

PSYCHIC ASSOCIATIONS

Sugilite makes meditation and channelling easier and creates a space between the psychic world and the everyday world. Use it to contact spirit guides and light beings and for an awareness of other dimensions.

RECHARGING ITS ENERGIES

Sugilite is surprisingly delicate: recharge it by placing it next to an unpolished chunk of amethyst covered by a dark silk scarf for twenty-four hours.

LEPIDOLITE

MYTHOLOGY AND HISTORY

Each lepidolite crystal is believed to have a keeper, either a guardian spirit or angel that is said to choose you. You may find your lepidolite crystal when you least expect it or may be given one: the keeper of the crystal will guide you in your sleep and, if you wish, to other lands in dreams.

DIVINATORY SIGNIFICANCE

Lepidolite indicates the strong positive influence of a woman (it could be you), who will make sure your opinions are heard in a current issue that may affect your community or livelihood. Don't be swayed by other people's moods and dramas: they are often attention-seeking, not a real cry for help.

PROPERTIES

TYPE: Hydrous potassium lithium aluminium silicate

COLOUR: Violet to lavender to pink. Transparent or translucent and shiny. Lithium gives the crystal its colour. If you scratch the surface with your fingernail, it may flake

SYMBOLIC ASSOCIATIONS

ZODIAC SIGN: Capricorn

PLANET: Saturn

ELEMENT: Earth

CANDLE COLOUR: Deep purple

GUARDIAN ANGEL: Aftiel

CHAKRA: Crown / brow

HERBS, INCENSES AND OILS: Cedar, comfrey, patchouli, vetivert and wintergreen

FLOWERS: Dark tulip, foxglove and verbena

ASSOCIATED CRYSTALS: Charoite, diopside and kunzite

HEALING AND THE ENVIRONMENT

Lepidolite is a powerful pain remover. It can also reduce the ill-effects of anaesthetic and dependency on medicines (especially anti-depressants and tranquillizers), alcohol, tobacco or food. It provides a useful shield against the effects of modern pollution. Some people have reported finding it helpful for relations who suffer from mental illnesses, dementia, Alzheimer's disease and other degenerative conditions.

USES AT WORK AND HOME

Lepidolite will clear out all the redundant messages and voices from the past that hold us back from happiness or success. It will attract supportive friends and colleagues and bring opportunities to succeed. It will help anyone living an unavoidably stressful existence, especially city dwellers, to maintain a still, calm centre.

CHILDREN AND ANIMALS

Lepidolite will cleanse the atmosphere after quarrels between siblings or toddler or teenage tantrums. It effectively restores peace and harmony to the household.

Lepidolite is also excellent for dogs that have behavioural problems.

PSYCHIC ASSOCIATIONS

Lepidolite is a reassuring stone for people new to psychic work or those who have had a bad psychic experience or dabbled with ouija boards or held séances when younger. It screens out negativity.

RECHARGING ITS ENERGIES

Use a pendulum (amethyst is preferred) or a watermelon tourmaline wand.

SUPER SEVEN

See also amethyst (p46), clear quartz (p26), rutilated (p113) and smoky quartz (p144)

MYTHOLOGY AND HISTORY

Also called the Sacred Seven, this crystal is a fusion of seven other minerals: amethyst, cacoxenite (which assists the flow of energy through the body), goethite (good for blood and survival instincts), lepidocrocite (a fire stone similar to hematite), clear quartz, rutile and smoky quartz. It is the crystal of Sirius A, the brightest star in the sky. Sirius is famed in Egypt for its reappearance for ten days around mid-July, which heralded the annual flood and so ensured the fertility of the land. Sirius and super seven are associated with Isis.

DIVINATORY SIGNIFICANCE

This is a special time spiritually. If you have been struggling to reconcile your spiritual and everyday worlds, you will feel them merge.

HEALING AND THE ENVIRONMENT

An all-healer, super seven operates on spiritual levels. It affects your whole body – you start to feel at home in your skin physically and emotionally. It relieves conditions caused by allergies and eases the management of hereditary or congenital conditions. Use it to promote universal peace and love.

RIGHT A simple altar representing the four elements, with feathers representing air in the east, a candle for fire in the south, a bowl of water in the west and a stone to symbolize earth in the north. Super seven, in the centre, represents Akasha, all the elements.

AT WORK AND IN THE HOME
It increases understanding of yourself and your life path so that you act rather than react and can be yourself in any situation.

CHILDREN AND ANIMALS
Ask young children how to use super seven. Use at the beginning and end of a pet's life.

PSYCHIC ASSOCIATIONS
Super seven increases your awareness of all your innate psychic powers. It helps you link with the magic of Ancient Egypt.

RECHARGING ITS ENERGIES
Super seven does not need cleansing.

CHAROITE

MYTHOLOGY AND HISTORY
Charoite is sometimes called the stone of courage in exile, because it is found only near the Chara River area of Siberia, where political dissidents were once sent.

DIVINATORY SIGNIFICANCE
It is definitely a time for giving rather than receiving. Your generosity, whether with your time, emotional support or practical help, will make a real difference to the recipient and so is worthwhile.

HEALING AND THE ENVIRONMENT
Charoite relieves difficulties with blood pressure, eye and liver problems and migraines or headaches with severe visual disturbance. It will prevent insomnia and sleep disturbances including sleepwalking or talking. It alleviates fears of illness, pain, the unknown and mortality.

AT WORK AND IN THE HOME
Charoite is a crystal for all who live away from friends and family or who work away for long periods. It will give stamina for long periods of intense work or caring for sick or elderly relations and prevents people from repeating past mistakes.

CHILDREN AND ANIMALS
Charoite is helpful for children with autistic tendencies or any with social and behavioural difficulties. It soothes homesickness in children who are at boarding schools or who are in residential care. Charoite prevents animals from being too territorial.

PSYCHIC ASSOCIATIONS
Charoite is excellent for facilitating past-life recall. It is also very useful for overcoming fears of ghosts and for dealing with unwanted spontaneous psychic experiences. Charoite will connect you telepathically with absent friends. Hold it for a minute at the same time each evening to exchange loving thoughts.

RECHARGING ITS ENERGIES
Set charoite within the sound of natural running water for an hour or so to recharge.

PROPERTIES
TYPE: Silicate. Marble-like and translucent
COLOUR: Swirling purple, violet, lilac and/or lavender, black and white
SYMBOLIC ASSOCIATIONS
ZODIAC SIGN: Pisces
PLANET: Neptune
ELEMENT: Water
CANDLE COLOUR: Any shade of purple
GUARDIAN ANGEL: Cassiel
CHAKRA: Brow/heart
HERBS, INCENSES AND OILS: Blessed thistle, gardenia, lemon, nutmeg and sandalwood
FLOWERS: Michelmas daisy, plantain and thistle
ASSOCIATED CRYSTALS: Lapis lazuli, lepidolite and lavender fluorite

TURQUOISE

Associated with the throat chakra, turquoise will help you communicate more effectively. Known for its strength, it is associated with qualities of leadership and makes the wearer less sensitive to negative influences.

ABOVE AND FAR RIGHT
Turquoise is traditionally considered the stone of travellers. It offers worldly success and authority and the power to soar spiritually.

PROPERTIES

TYPE: Phosphate of aluminium with copper and traces of iron. Opaque

COLOUR: Light blue/blue-green

SYMBOLIC ASSOCIATIONS

ZODIAC SIGN: Sagittarius

PLANET: Venus/Neptune

ELEMENT: Fire/air

CANDLE COLOUR: Bright blue

GUARDIAN ANGEL: Zadkiel

CHAKRA: Throat

HERBS, INCENSES AND OILS: Cedar, hyssop, sage, mistletoe and sandalwood

FLOWERS: Honeysuckle, carnation, chrysanthemum

ASSOCIATED CRYSTALS: Azurite, lapis lazuli and blue howlite/howzite

---

MYTHOLOGY AND HISTORY

The name turquoise comes from Turkey, where the Crusaders discovered it, although it was in use thousands of years before. It is a stone associated with the gods and goddesses in cultures as far apart as Ancient Egypt and China and the Americas.

One of the most prized stones in Ancient Egypt, its name means delight. Hathor, the goddess of love, marriage dance, music, joy and women, was called the Lady of Turquoise, giving the stone a feminine association (in a number of other cultures it was a male power stone). In Ancient Egypt turquoise was also linked to the sun gods and the sun at dawn and so, like lapis lazuli, it is a symbol of rebirth. The hair of the Sun God Ra was said to have been made of turquoise. It was mined in Sinai.

Known as a male stone of power in the Americas, only warriors could wear it; in some parts it was only used as an adornment for the statues of male deities. It was regarded as a sky stone, a sacred manifestation of the source of creation.

Turquoise is sacred to many American Indian tribes, including the Pueblo Indians. Indeed, in the Chaco Canon groups of ruins in Mexico, nine thousand turquoise beads and pendants were discovered in the grave of a single warrior chief. Some were carved in the shape of animals or birds to attract favourable spirits to enter the crystals.

Among the Apaches, turquoise was a powerful talisman and healer and was an important tool of the medicine man or woman. After a storm it was believed turquoise would be found in the damp earth at the point where the rainbow ended; these were especially prized and fixed to the end of a bow or gun to ensure an accurate aim.

The Navajo placed tiny pieces of turquoise on their magical sand paintings as a way of ending drought and, like the Pueblo Indians, they set pieces of turquoise under their dwellings to protect their homes and their families against evil spirits.

As late as CE 1400 the Aztecs offered Queztalcoatl, plumed serpent god of the sun, a death skull inlaid with hundreds of small turquoise crystals.

DIVINATORY SIGNIFICANCE

You may be called upon to arbitrate in a quarrel, perhaps at work, or to speak out if you feel strongly about a matter. You may also need to take the lead to bring a matter or project to fruition.

HEALING PROPERTIES

Turquoise detoxifies the system of pollutants, and relieves migraines, sore throats, rheumatism, arthritis, bone disorders, lung and chest infections, and asthma and other allergies. It is excellent for inner ear and eye problems. It also eases cramps and over-acidity and gives resistance to fight viruses.

USES AT WORK AND HOME

Keep turquoise near stairs to prevent falls, especially if there are children, elderly people or the infirm in the house. Hide turquoise in outhouses or near entrances to your home to repel intruders.

Turquoise will also attract prosperity and success; place it in your workspace or where you keep your financial papers.

CHILDREN AND ANIMALS

Turquoise is a good stone for a child to carry to protect against bullying and to help a timid child to take the initiative and to answer questions in class. Children could also drink water in which the crystal has been soaked for eight hours.

Fix turquoise to pets' collars and to the mirror of caged birds to prevent theft or the creature getting lost or straying.

PSYCHIC ASSOCIATIONS

Absorbing all negative forces, turquoise endows wisdom on those who wear it and increases prophetic powers. Turquoise is said to give access to the collective wisdom of humankind. Hold your turquoise in cupped palms and name your intentions seven times.

PROTECTIVE FUNCTIONS

Turquoise is traditionally plaited into the mane of a horse or attached to the bridle to prevent it stumbling; a similar sized turquoise should be held or carried by the rider. Famed as a protection against poison, turquoise is reputed to change colour if poison or other dangers are near.

ENVIRONMENTAL WORK

Because of its strength and association with leadership it is sometimes called the campaigner's stone, favouring those who initiate or play active roles in peaceful movements for the protection of the environment and for human rights.

SPECIAL PROPERTIES

Turquoise has the dual function both of energizing and balancing mood swings or extremes of emotions, making the wearer strong within but less sensitive to negative outer influences. Turquoise should be given as a gift, not bought.

RECHARGING ITS ENERGIES

Turquoise fades in sunlight and from exposure to oils. Recharge it with an Amerindian smudge – cedar, sagebrush or sweetgrass.

BLUE HOWLITE

PROPERTIES

TYPE: Calcium boro-silicate hydroxide

COLOUR: Bright sky-blue. Opaque

SYMBOLIC ASSOCIATIONS

ZODIAC SIGN: Sagittarius

PLANET: Jupiter

ELEMENT: Air

CANDLE COLOUR: Bright blue

GUARDIAN ANGEL: Gediel

CHAKRA: Throat

HERBS, INCENSES AND OILS: Anise, bergamot, cinquefoil, lemongrass and lemon verbena

FLOWERS: Blue poppy, iris and cornflower

ASSOCIATED CRYSTALS: Chrysocolla, lapis lazuli and turquoise

MYTHOLOGY AND HISTORY

Howlite, sometimes called the bones of the earth, is white or grey. It is frequently dyed vivid blue and acts as a cheaper form of turquoise. What is remarkable is that in this blue form, it adds to the gentle stone a powerful sky deity influence that gives it an enduring strength to meet any challenge.

DIVINATORY SIGNIFICANCE

Your talents and strengths are greater than you realize, so take new opportunities even if you do not feel you are qualified or sufficiently experienced.

HEALING AND THE ENVIRONMENT

Blue howlite will flood the system with strength and stamina long after the treatment has ceased. It is excellent for bones and teeth and the upper part of the spine and neck, as well as easing recurring throat or tonsil

infections. It will energize a new mother who has twins, triplets or a premature infant who needs constant care.

USES AT WORK AND HOME
Blue howlite will bring many blessings to your home. It helps you to upgrade your property and get the best deals in selling or buying. At work it wil hasten long-term success and give you the stamina to survive if there is in-fighting or a whispering campaign. It is an empowering and protective stone for young people during their gap years or for anyone who wants to leave the rat race.

CHILDREN AND ANIMALS
Blue howlite encourages children and animals to exercise and to be more adventurous. Blue howlite protects both a physically weak child or the runt of an animal litter.

PSYCHIC ASSOCIATIONS
Blue howlite is a dream stone: it will bring healing in dreams and will also assist astral travel during sleep.

RECHARGING ITS ENERGIES
Place blue howlite with watermelon tourmaline or amethyst to rest it.

VIOLAN

MYTHOLOGY AND HISTORY
Violan is a relatively recent discovery that is already gaining a reputation for channelling angels and star beings. Some people believe it is a caretaker stone brought by travellers from Sirius B that resonates with the songs of the dolphins and radiates blue healing rays of Sirian energies.

DIVINATORY SIGNIFICANCE
Make space for your spiritual development, if only a few minutes stargazing, even if you are pressed for time.

HEALING AND THE ENVIRONMENT
Violan is a spiritual healer that works by drawing down from angelic and stellar powers energy that will relieve whatever part of your body, mind or soul is suffering dis-ease. It is especially good at enabling you to talk about your feelings if you feel restricted, either physically or emotionally.

USES AT WORK AND HOME
Place a piece of violan in the heart of your home, the central place where you and anyone who lives with you gathers regularly to relax. This will make your home a spiritual place and a sanctuary from the world. Use violan at work if you are part of a firm where the profit motive dominates everything.

CHILDREN AND ANIMALS
Violan is wonderful for sending healing to children who are suffering abuse or poverty, or living in famine-stricken areas or in

war-torn lands. It is especially healing for dolphins, whales and all sea creatures. However, violan will help any animal that is being cruelly treated or imprisoned in a small cage or pen.

PSYCHIC ASSOCIATIONS
Violan is in tune with the higher energies: hold this crystal to channel wisdom from star guardians and beings of light as well as from angels. A palm stone (shaped to be comfortable in the palm of your hand) is excellent for banishing worry. You can also add a piece of violan to your bath water to harmonize your spirit with the positive healing forces of the universe.

RECHARGING ITS ENERGIES
Use starlight or a very soft pearl-grey dawn light to re-energize violan.

PROPERTIES
TYPE: Silicate. Rare form of diopside found in Italy
COLOUR: Soft light-blue, streaked with white and silver rutiles, also lavender to pink-purple

SYMBOLIC ASSOCIATIONS
ZODIAC SIGN: Libra
PLANET: Uranus
ELEMENT: Air / pure spirit
CANDLE COLOUR: Light blue
GUARDIAN ANGEL: Raphael / all star beings
CHAKRA: Crown
HERBS, INCENSES AND OILS: Star anise, magnolia, marjoram, mugwort and vanilla
FLOWERS: Apple blossom, orchid and sweet pea
ASSOCIATED CRYSTALS: Blue lace agate, lapis lazuli and sapphire

BLUE LACE AGATE

PROPERTIES

TYPE: Agate

COLOUR: Pale, powdery blue, sometimes brighter periwinkle blue, with white lace threads

SYMBOLIC ASSOCIATIONS

ZODIAC SIGN: Aquarius

PLANET: Neptune

ELEMENT: Water / air

CANDLE COLOUR: Pale blue

GUARDIAN ANGEL: Cambiel

CHAKRA: Throat

HERBS, INCENSES AND OILS: Fern, star anise, vervain, vetivert and yarrow

FLOWERS: Bluebell, forget-me-not and periwinkle

ASSOCIATED CRYSTALS: Aquamarine, blue calcite and celestite

MYTHOLOGY AND HISTORY

Blue lace agate is sometimes associated with the Virgin Mary and so is an icon of motherhood. In Scandinavia blue lace agate is sacred to Nerthus, the earth mother.

DIVINATORY SIGNIFICANCE

Speak the truth and express your inner feelings and you will receive a favourable response.

HEALING AND THE ENVIRONMENT

Blue lace agate relieves sore throats, thyroid problems, headaches and painful or swollen glands in the neck. Soak one in water for eight hours and gargle with the water. Blue lace

agate calms stress and stress-related conditions, quietens high blood pressure and soothes skin allergies and problems with bones. Healers should carry blue lace agate to increase their own healing energies and stop them becoming exhausted.

Blue lace agate can send peaceful energies to war-torn places. It should be placed on pictures of world leaders when they attend conferences to encourage moderation.

USES AT WORK AND HOME

The stone of the peacemaker, use blue lace agate water in drinks to make words kind and to avoid confrontations at family gatherings. At work use it when addressing a meeting or for public speaking. It helps you be coherent if you are thinking on your feet and facilitates communication, especially on the telephone. It protects against outbursts of anger by others.

CHILDREN AND ANIMALS

Use it when an infant is learning to talk and to soothe a restless child. It reduces barking in a dog, screeching in birds and yowling in cats.

PSYCHIC ASSOCIATIONS

Blue lace agate develops clairaudience and will make even the most difficult divinatory reading you give others positive and uplifting.

RECHARGING ITS ENERGIES

Use moonlight as the moon begins to wax.

BLUE QUARTZ

See also aqua aura (p66)

MYTHOLOGY AND HISTORY

Since natural blue quartz is not often of gem quality, clear quartz is dyed or grown in the laboratory with added cobalt impurities to produce more perfect specimens. You may prefer nature's untouched offerings (except for a polish) or feel that the qualities are enhanced by the beautification. Hold both kinds before choosing which is for you.

DIVINATORY SIGNIFICANCE

You may be aware of your growing spiritual powers. Explore your special psychic ability.

HEALING AND THE ENVIRONMENT

Blue quartz will strengthen the immune system and the thyroid and aid the absorption of the B vitamins, zinc, iron and iodine. It clears sinuses, reduces fevers and soothes heat stroke and sunburn. It also cleanses the aura, lowers anxiety levels and improves eyesight.

USES AT WORK AND HOME

Blue quartz will raise your consciousness, so the goals you used to have may no longer be sufficiently challenging spiritually. It will encourage singing and musical abilities.

CHILDREN AND ANIMALS
Children are entranced by even the roughest piece of blue quartz, perhaps because it is a reminder of the spiritual knowledge with

which they were born. Blue quartz calms children and animals. Animals prefer natural blue quartz for all forms of healing.

PSYCHIC PROPERTIES
Blue quartz is the crystal of visionaries and those who wish to see higher realms and communicate with evolved beings. Use it with prayer, when reciting a rosary, for chanting mantras, when walking a labyrinth or working with mandalas, to make a connection with the heart of life and with divine energies. Blue quartz is above all a stone for quiet meditation under blue skies: it will help you to merge momentarily with the cosmos.

RECHARGING ITS ENERGIES
Use clear quartz, an amethyst pendulum or a watermelon tourmaline wand to recharge.

PROPERTIES
TYPE: Quartz, natural. The clear blue is caused by tiny rutile tourmaline or zoisite inclusions that reflect blue light. Semi-transparent or deeply translucent, often stained by patches or veins of iron oxide. Also clear rock crystal dyed blue and the Siberian lab-grown deep, clear, bright-blue quartz
COLOUR: Bright to dark blue

SYMBOLIC ASSOCIATIONS
ZODIAC SIGN: Gemini
PLANET: Mercury
ELEMENT: Air
CANDLE COLOUR: Mid-blue
GUARDIAN ANGEL: Rahtiel
CHAKRA: Brow/throat
HERBS, INCENSES AND OILS: Fennel, bergamot, caraway, lavender and lemongrass
FLOWERS: Blue hyacinth, delphinium and lupin
ASSOCIATED CRYSTALS: Aqua aura, blue topaz and blue sapphire

KYANITE

MYTHOLOGY AND HISTORY
A relatively new stone to magic and healing, kyanite is believed to form a link with other kingdoms, animals, birds, plants, fish and insects as well as with humans. It provides a useful key to exploring and merging with their energies.

DIVINATORY SIGNIFICANCE
Kyanite is not used in divination.

HEALING AND THE ENVIRONMENT
Kyanite helps the healthy development of cells from womb to extreme old age. It allows us to develop our full potential, spiritually and mentally as well as physically. Kyanite draws

energies from the higher levels of our being to fill us with calm even at the most frustrating times or in the most difficult situations. Use it for responsible caretakership of the earth.

USES AT WORK AND HOME
A stone of connection, kyanite helps to strengthen family or friendship networks. It is very protective against negativity, dissipating hostility or spite. At work and personally it encourages creativity and is a stone for singers, dancers, composers, writers, painters, potters, sculptors and craftspersons.

CHILDREN AND ANIMALS
Kyanite makes reticent children more visible socially so that they get invited to parties. Place a small piece near any animal pens where an animal may be frequently disturbed.

PSYCHIC ASSOCIATIONS
Kyanite is one of the best stones for past-life recall, especially for a series of connected lives over time or if you are seeking to understand a present phobia or problem that seems to have no roots in your present world. The blades are also useful as a wand to repel negativity or whatever it is you wish to drive or cast away.

RECHARGING ITS ENERGIES
Leave it near plants for the hour after dawn.

PROPERTIES
TYPE: Aluminium silicate, flat mica-like layers, as blades or wands rather than rounded crystals. Sometimes grows with staurolite. Opaque to translucent, shiny almost pearly, sometimes with white
COLOUR: Mid-blue to sapphire or sky-blue

SYMBOLIC ASSOCIATIONS
ZODIAC SIGN: Pisces
PLANET: Jupiter
ELEMENT: Air/water
CANDLE COLOUR: Sky-blue
GUARDIAN ANGEL: Gediel
CHAKRA: Throat/brow
HERBS, INCENSES AND OILS: Balm of Gilead, fennel, lavender, yarrow and yerba santa
FLOWERS: Blue hyacinth, sea lavender and heather
ASSOCIATED CRYSTALS: Apatite, angelite and blue lace agate

LAPIS LAZULI

Lapis lazuli is associated with the brow chakra and helps to increase clairvoyant abilities. It is a good focus for meditation when placed in the centre of the brow and is a powerful crystal for healing.

PROPERTIES

TYPE: Silicate of sodium calcium and aluminium, with some sulphur. Opaque. With flecks of iron pyrites

COLOUR: Rich medium to royal blue, violet-blue and azure, even greenish-blue. Sometimes mixed blues

SYMBOLIC ASSOCIATIONS

ZODIAC SIGN: Libra

PLANET: Jupiter

ELEMENT: Air

CANDLE COLOUR: Royal blue

GUARDIAN ANGEL: Sahaqiel

CHAKRA: Brow / third eye

HERBS, INCENSES AND OILS: Cedar, frankincense, musk (artificial) sage and sandalwood

FLOWERS: Lupin, hollyhock and iris

ASSOCIATED CRYSTALS: Azurite, sodalite and turquoise

MYTHOLOGY AND HISTORY

The Sumerians believed that lapis lazuli contained the spirit of the deities; the Ancient Egyptians also regarded it as the stone of the gods. This was partly because it reminded them of the starry heavens, but also because, as shown in the Papyrus Ebers, lapis lazuli had medicinal properties that improve eyesight when worn in the form of the eye of Horus amulet or powdered around the eyes.

DIVINATORY SIGNIFICANCE

Stick to your principles and rise above any pettiness and attempted double-dealing.

HEALING AND THE ENVIRONMENT

Lapis relieves headaches and migraines, skin disorders and anxiety, and aids problems with the lymph glands, the ears and eyes. It calms the nervous system, reducing inflammation and pain. Lapis helps to heal the ozone layer.

USES AT WORK AND HOME

Around the home lapis brings contentment and a strong sense of family loyalty. At work it can help you gain promotion, maintain your integrity and inspire the trust of others.

CHILDREN AND ANIMALS

Lapis is very helpful with children who are very intelligent, who have Aspergers Syndrome or autistic tendencies, or who suffer from insomnia. It will calm highly strung animals, especially pedigree breeds, and will help them before a show.

PSYCHIC ASSOCIATIONS

Inspiring for all night magic, especially under the stars, and for psychic protection. Use it also for meaningful and prophetic dreams.

RECHARGING ITS ENERGIES

Use starlight to recharge lapis.

RIGHT Rough and polished lapis lazuli. Lapis is associated with divinity in a number of ancient cultures and is still used to contact the wisdom and protection of our personal spiritual guardians.

FAR RIGHT Lapis lazuli unites the different aspects of ourselves and our lives, to create harmony of mind, body and spirit.

IOLITE

PROPERTIES

TYPE: Silicate of
aluminium and
magnesium. Transparent

COLOUR: Pale
blue/purple

SYMBOLIC
ASSOCIATIONS

ZODIAC SIGN:
Sagittarius

PLANET: Jupiter

ELEMENT: Air/water

CANDLE COLOUR: Lilac

GUARDIAN ANGEL:
Shamshiel

CHAKRA: Brow

HERBS, INCENSES AND
OILS: Ferns, chamomile,
sandalwood

FLOWERS: Bluebell,
hibiscus and wisteria

ASSOCIATED CRYSTALS:
Blue sapphire, blue topaz
and violan

MYTHOLOGY AND HISTORY

Iolite was called the water sapphire because it was prized by Viking voyagers. They used a thin polarizing iolite filter lens to clear the haze so that they could see the direction of the sun on cloudy days for accurate navigation. This worked because of pleochroism, the property by which certain crystals can look clear, hazy or different colours according to the angle from which they are viewed. Iolite was sacred to Ran, Viking goddess of the sea, and after a safe journey the Vikings would cast gold into the sea as tribute.

DIVINATORY PROPERTIES

A new acquaintance or family addition may have hidden depths, so try a new approach if you are finding them difficult to warm to.

HEALING AND THE ENVIRONMENT

Iolite improves brain functioning and the efficiency of the metabolism. Iolite relieves headaches and prevents insomnia.

AT WORK AND IN THE HOME

Iolite brings joy and laughter into the home, so put it where light can shine on it. At work iolite will bring inspired solutions to problems that may have eluded the most logical brain. Set iolite on a table when brainstorming and to come up with alternatives to inefficient or unpopular working practices.

CHILDREN AND ANIMALS

This is a crystal to take on family outings and holidays to create a happy mood. Use iolite for an animal whom you find hard to love.

PSYCHIC ASSOCIATIONS

Called the stone of witches, iolite increases psychic and magical powers. It is potent for visualization work and goddess rituals.

RECHARGING ITS ENERGIES

Use natural light to recharge iolite.

SODALITE

PROPERTIES

TYPE: Lattice silicate

COLOUR: Deep blue with
white flecks of calcite,
occasionally indigo

SYMBOLIC
ASSOCIATIONS

ZODIAC SIGN: Cancer

PLANET: Moon

ELEMENT: Water/air

CANDLE COLOUR:
Indigo

GUARDIAN ANGEL:
Raziel

CHAKRA: Throat and
brow

HERBS, INCENSES AND
OILS: Hyssop, lavender,
myrrh, mugwort and
rosewood

FLOWERS: Bluebell,
cornflower and violet

ASSOCIATED CRYSTALS:
Amethyst, azurite and
lapis lazuli

MYTHOLOGY AND HISTORY

In modern spirituality, sodalite has become a stone of empowerment for older women. It is sacred to St Anne, the grandmother of Christ.

DIVINATORY SIGNIFICANCE

Be slow to speak and measure your words wisely in any situation where your opinion is asked or when making a decision.

HEALING AND THE ENVIRONMENT

Sodalite is a universal healing crystal, releasing gentle waves of power that spread through the system. Hold it before healing work to help you understand the underlying cause of the illness or distress and how best to heal it. A cooling stone, it calms physical or emotional overheating, a racing pulse, or high blood pressure. It gently balances blood-sugar levels and relieves inflammation, pain from burns, and problems with ears, throat, sinuses, mouth and thyroid. It helps the lymph and pituitary glands or glands in the mouth.

It is good for preserving old churches and places of worship that have become neglected.

USES AT WORK AND HOME

It helps those facing retirement or redundancy. It allows parents to move creatively to the next phase when children leave home. It helps teachers and all involved in the law to act wisely. Sodalite overcomes the fear of flying.

CHILDREN AND ANIMALS

Sodalite is good for children who have little contact with their grandparents. Sodalite soothes mother animals when their young are taken away after weaning.

PSYCHIC ASSOCIATIONS

More gently than lapis lazuli or turquoise, sodalite opens the third eye to see spiritual visions and the throat to tell of them. Sodalite will focus meditation if your mind is overactive and is useful in creative visualization when you imagine a desired scenario or object moving into your life. It is used in croning/wise woman ceremonies to welcome the wisdom of the later years.

RECHARGING ITS ENERGIES

Bury it in a plant pot of lavender or another fragrant herb for twenty-four hours.

SAPPHIRE

See also white sapphire (p42)

MYTHOLOGY AND HISTORY

In Judeo-Christian myth Abraham was said to have worn a magnificent sapphire around his neck. When he died it rose to the sun.

Star sapphires, which have a star formation inside them, are said to contain the angels of faith, hope and destiny, who were imprisoned in the stone for a minor misdemeanour. These special sapphires bring wisdom to the owners (see also star rubies, p132). Sapphire represents the forty-fifth wedding anniversary.

DIVINATORY SIGNIFICANCE

Sapphire is not used in divination.

HEALING AND THE ENVIRONMENT

Traditionally a stone of spiritual healing, a sapphire is especially effective if you are channelling healing powers from an angelic or higher source; it is a useful stone for Reiki healers. It also amplifies healing through the voice or through sacred music (for example, Buddhist or Gregorian chants).

USES AT WORK AND HOME

Sapphire is associated with purity of thought and purpose. This makes it an excellent counter in the home to the cynicism and less desirable aspects of modern culture. In the workplace, it inspires loyalty between work colleagues and discourages fraud and industrial espionage. It helps prevent workers from draining work resources for personal gain. Sapphire also encourages the resolution of legal entanglements.

CHILDREN AND ANIMALS

Sapphire is not used for children or animals, though a family sapphire can help children to contact their guardian angels.

PSYCHIC ASSOCIATIONS

Sapphire is a stone of new love, and of commitment and fidelity. Use sapphire in rituals to preserve constancy, especially if one partner is temporarily absent or regularly works away from home.

Star sapphire is strongly associated with clairvoyance, clairaudience and prophecy. It is especially good for scrying if you focus on the intersection of the lines within the crystal. Sapphires naturally increase all psychic and spiritual powers.

RECHARGING ITS ENERGIES

Leave your sapphire under blue skies or recharge it by the light of a sky-blue candle.

PROPERTIES
TYPE: Corundum. Sparkling
COLOUR: Pale to midnight blue, violet
SYMBOLIC ASSOCIATIONS
ZODIAC SIGN: Virgo
PLANET: Saturn
ELEMENT: Air
CANDLE COLOUR: Sky-blue
GUARDIAN ANGEL: Apollian
CHAKRA: Brow/throat
HERBS, INCENSES AND OILS: Benzoin, star anise, lemon verbena, sage, sandalwood
FLOWERS: Blue lotus, cornflower and delphinium
ASSOCIATED CRYSTALS: Aquamarine, blue zircon and blue tourmaline

CELESTITE / BLUE CELESTINE

See also orange celestine (p126) and angelite (below)

PROPERTIES

TYPE: Sulphate. Often in points or clusters. Semi-transparent

COLOUR: Pale to mid-blue, also white, occasionally green. Looks like ice crystals

SYMBOLIC ASSOCIATIONS

ZODIAC SIGN: Libra

PLANET: Jupiter

ELEMENT: Air

CANDLE COLOUR: Light blue

GUARDIAN ANGEL: Chadakiel

CHAKRA: Throat

HERBS, INCENSES AND OILS: Chamomile, eucalyptus, vervain, vetivert and vanilla

FLOWERS: Narcissus, periwinkle and starflower

ASSOCIATED CRYSTALS: Angelite, chrysocolla and blue topaz

MYTHOLOGY AND HISTORY

Celestite is the popular name given to blue celestine. It is called the Stone of Heaven, because it was created by angel song from the celestial choirs. Like angelite, it has gained popularity with the renewed interest in angels.

DIVINATORY SIGNIFICANCE

Do not fill your mind with worries about what might happen in the future as this may prevent you from enjoying and gaining full benefit from the present situation.

HEALING AND THE ENVIRONMENT

Celestite eases eye, ear, throat, mouth, headaches and speech problems. It relieves acute anxiety states, obsessive behaviour

patterns and digestive disorders caused or made worse by stress and protects against intestinal parasites or infections.

USES AT WORK AND HOME

Celestite prevents you from becoming locked in a loop of negative expectations and not hearing what is actually being said. It helps adult children accept their parents' choice of partner or stepfamily. Celestite is a stone for singers and actors, professional and amateur: it alleviates stage fright and nervous sore throats or loss of voice. Carry one if you work at or visit New Age fairs to protect you from less-than-spiritual vibes.

CHILDREN AND ANIMALS

Celestite allows ultra-cautious children to experience new activities and environments. It helps a rescued animal to trust again or an injured one to recover strength and optimism.

PSYCHIC ASSOCIATIONS

Meditate with celestite to achieve a total state of peace and unity with the universe and with divine powers. It fosters a gentle transition to the dream planes. It is also powerful for channelling angelic wisdom. Some crystals are said to contain angels – look for one when you choose yours.

RECHARGING ITS ENERGIES

Recharge it by wrapping it in blue silk and resting it in a drawer for forty-eight hours.

ANGELITE

See also celestite (above)

MYTHOLOGY AND HISTORY

Angelite is celestite that has been compressed for millions of years and so is the wiser stone. An ancient Peruvian healing stone, it has been adopted as an icon of angels and sacred sound.

DIVINATORY SIGNIFICANCE

You may be called upon to act as a peace-maker between those who are resorting to back stabbing or gossip to maintain their own position in an insecure situation.

HEALING AND THE ENVIRONMENT

Apply angelite to the palms of the hands or the soles of the feet to free the energy pathways between the chakras. Angelite amplifies healing with sound, whether a single voice or a group singing Buddhist or Gregorian chants. It is excellent for harmonizing the body, mind and spirit.

Angelite alleviates sunburn and throat and thyroid difficulties. It also helps the lungs, upper arms and shoulders and the skull.

It regulates fluid balances and aids a gentle weight-loss programme. Use it for peaceful action to alleviate suffering. It is an excellent stone to choose to send strength to prisoners or people living under harsh political systems or intolerant religious regimes.

USES AT WORK AND HOME
Angelite encourages sensitivity and kindness; it is an antidote to abrasive people at home or work. Angelite deflects cruelty and violence and protects against prejudice or intolerance.

CHILDREN AND ANIMALS
A beautiful gift, angelite connects children with their guardian angels. Place angelite in the ground when burying pets.

PSYCHIC ASSOCIATIONS
Use it when reciting mantras, for work with angels and for praying to Mother Mary and to female saints and goddesses. Angelite will return bad wishes as waves of compassion. It increases telepathic powers with loved ones.

RECHARGING ITS ENERGIES
In a place of spiritual power, pray for peace.

PROPERTIES

TYPE: Sulphate/anhydrite. Opaque. Veined with wings, but smooth when polished

COLOUR: Pale or mid- to celestial blue-lilac or violet

SYMBOLIC ASSOCIATIONS

ZODIAC SIGN: Aquarius

PLANET: Uranus

ELEMENT: Air

CANDLE COLOUR: Pale blue

GUARDIAN ANGEL: Raphael

CHAKRA: Throat/heart

HERBS, INCENSES AND OILS: Chamomile, cedarwood, lemon verbena, rosewood and vanilla

FLOWERS: Lily, lily of the valley and white lotus

ASSOCIATED CRYSTALS: Blue celestite, blue topaz and sapphire

BLUE CORAL

MYTHOLOGY AND HISTORY
Blue coral is sacred to Diwata ng Dagat, the goddess of the sea in the Philippines, one of the main areas from which blue coral comes.

DIVINATORY SIGNIFICANCE
Flow with events for the moment, for the tide will turn and you may find that what you wanted soon comes within your grasp.

HEALING AND THE ENVIRONMENT
Blue coral is a very gentle, though seemingly weatherworn, form of coral. It will relieve illnesses that return periodically or which are made worse by temperature or other climatic conditions. It is good for all orthopaedic conditions and microsurgery and for bone and cell regrowth, especially in old people or those who have been ill for much of their lives. Blue coral also regenerates skin and will soothe inflamed skin, rashes and burns. It is excellent for acne or scar tissue. Use in dolphin or whale conservation empowerments.

USES AT WORK AND HOME
Blue coral will assist regular shift workers to adapt their home and sleep patterns. It is protective for sailors and their families, ferry workers, fishermen, yachtsmen and women

and those who live, work or travel by sea. Blue coral also helps home workers and the self-employed to build in leisure time.

CHILDREN AND ANIMALS
Blue coral will establish a routine for chaotic children. It is good for all sea creatures.

PSYCHIC ASSOCIATIONS
It is wonderful for sea and water magic, for visualizations of underwater worlds and for shamanic journeys to the sea mother. Use it in wise woman/croning rituals. Carry blue coral to help you rebuild emotionally and psychically if it feels like the end of the world.

RECHARGING ITS ENERGIES
Sprinkle with seawater or sea-salted water.

PROPERTIES

TYPE: Organic calcareous skeletons of sea creatures. Pumice like, pock marked and rough

COLOUR: Light to mid-blue with white spots or smudges

SYMBOLIC ASSOCIATIONS

ZODIAC SIGN: Pisces

PLANET: Neptune

ELEMENT: Water

CANDLE COLOUR: Mid-blue

GUARDIAN ANGEL: Tamiel

CHAKRA: Throat

HERBS, INCENSES AND OILS: Gardenia, kelp (seaweed), rosewood, vanilla and vervain

FLOWERS: Bluebell, marsh marigold and sea lavender

ASSOCIATED CRYSTALS: Blue lace agate, blue chalcedony and angelite

AQUA AURA

MYTHOLOGY AND HISTORY

A New Age crystal, aqua aura combines magical gold (symbol of immortality, health, prosperity and perfection) and the pure energy of the crystal quartz, the light and life bringer. Aqua aura is the icon of the new era of spiritual knowledge, the Age of Aquarius.

DIVINATORY SIGNIFICANCE

You are evolving spiritually inside and may find that you need more personal time and space, which may not always be easy for those close to you to understand.

HEALING AND THE ENVIRONMENT

Aqua Aura puts your mind, body and spirit back on track if you have strayed (as most of us have) from the ideal blueprint of our potential. It re-activates a sluggish immune system and shields you from all kinds of harmful rays, pollution and negative people and situations. Aqua aura reminds us of our responsibility, by individual thoughts and actions, for the overall well-being of the planet.

USES AT WORK AND HOME

Aqua Aura enables us to flow with life and to find our own unique path to fulfilment. It stops us merely responding to life and puts us in control of our destiny. Aqua aura encourages us to take responsibility, to maximize what we can give and changes the emphasis from measuring success by material wealth to seeking a more ecological and spiritually focused lifestyle (while still recognizing that we have everyday responsibilities and still need to pay the bills).

CHILDREN AND ANIMALS

Aqua aura emphasizes the value and importance of children and the respect we should accord to all life forms.

PSYCHIC ASSOCIATIONS

Aqua aura creates a protective shield against psychic and psychological attack, against those who play mind or power games or seek to corrupt. It also kindles the divine spark or core within us all. Aqua Aura can be used in rituals to attract prosperity, especially if others will also benefit from good fortune.

RECHARGING ITS ENERGIES

Aqua aura does not need recharging very often, but benefits from being in the presence of a group of spiritually focused people and absorbing the positive powers of collective worship or ritual. Alternatively, carry aqua aura to the centre of a labyrinth and allow the spiralling energies to restore you both.

AQUAMARINE

PROPERTIES

TYPE: Beryl

COLOUR: Clear light blue or blue-green, the colour of a calm sea; occasionally a watery green

SYMBOLIC ASSOCIATIONS

ZODIAC SIGN: Pisces

PLANET: Neptune

ELEMENT: Water

CANDLE COLOUR: Turquoise

GUARDIAN ANGEL: Rahab

CHAKRA: Throat

HERBS, INCENSES AND OILS: Myrrh, eucalyptus, kelp (seaweed), tea tree and vanilla

FLOWERS: Honeysuckle, hydrangea and lemon blossom

ASSOCIATED CRYSTALS: Blue lace agate, emerald and jade

MYTHOLOGY AND HISTORY

In legend aquamarine was believed to contain the power of the sea and so was dedicated to a number of sea goddesses, including the Greek love goddess, Aphrodite, whose name means born of the foam. Sailors used it as an amulet to keep them safe from storms and bring them securely home.

DIVINATORY SIGNIFICANCE

A stone of travel, aquamarine indicates either the possibility of travel or that you will have an opportunity to widen your mental and spiritual horizons.

HEALING AND THE ENVIRONMENT

Aquamarine relieves sore throats, tooth and gum problems, fluid retention, digestive, bladder and kidney disorders, colds and upper respiratory difficulties, seasickness and all forms of travel queasiness. It eases pain and overcomes panic attacks and phobias, especially those connected with travelling by air or sea. It also takes away fears that arise about dental treatment.

Aquamarine is a useful stone for absent healing. Use aquamarine in rituals or empowerments to cleanse the seas and protect endangered oceanic species, especially dolphins and whales.

USES AT WORK AND HOME

Aquamarine enables couples who have grown apart to re-establish loving communication. At work aquamarine attracts overseas business or connections. Aquamarine helps to resolve legal matters favourably and, often, amicably.

CHILDREN AND ANIMALS

It is good for helping children to learn to swim or overcome a fear of water. Place one in a fish tank or pond for healthy marine life.

PSYCHIC ASSOCIATIONS

Aquamarine increases intuition, psychic awareness and clairvoyance. It is a good focus for meditation and visualizations about Atlantis, Lemuria and other lost worlds. Use also to make wishes on each seventh wave.

RECHARGING ITS ENERGIES

Leave it in sea water on the night of the full moon or in water with a pinch of sea salt in a blue glass bowl. Rinse in clear water after.

AZURITE

MYTHOLOGY AND HISTORY

In Ancient Egypt azurite was so sacred that only the priests knew and guarded its secrets; they used it in the inner sanctum to understand the will of the deities. It has been linked with the lost wisdom of Atlantis.

DIVINATORY SIGNIFICANCE

Listen to your dreams for guidance and trust your inner wisdom. If you do not already, you may soon feel ready to help others with your psychic and healing powers.

HEALING AND THE ENVIRONMENT

Azurite will help you to become a wise healer, amplifying your powers. It increases the flow of the life force through the body, oxygenating the blood and repairing brain cells. Azurite breaks chronic worry patterns.

USES AT WORK AND HOME

Azurite overcomes long-standing problems and breaks down communication blocks at home. At work it encourages professionalism, lessens gossip and brings out leadership qualities. It aids elder statesmen, professors, researchers, librarians and counsellors.

CHILDREN AND ANIMALS

Use azurite to communicate with children in the womb and to make the infant wise. It aids very old animals and long-living species.

PSYCHIC ASSOCIATIONS

Azurite brings creative and prophetic dreams, grants visions of other dimensions and helps communication with spirit guides. Azurite aids recall of actual past lives.

RECHARGING ITS ENERGIES

Use starligize azurite.

LARIMAR

MYTHOLOGY AND HISTORY

Also known as blue pectolite or dolphin stone, larimar is found in the Dominican Republic on the Caribbean island of Hispanola. Larimar was first used by the indigenous Tainos Indians for jewellery. When colonists came from the Old World led by Columbus, the stone fell out of use until it was rediscovered in 1916. Geologist Miguel Mendez named it after his daughter, Larissa, and mar, the Spanish for sea.

DIVINATORY SIGNIFICANCE

In a reading larimar can indicate either physical travel or change in a situation. This need not a spur-of-the-moment decision; what is required is calm reasoning to determine if the change is what you really want before you begin to take action.

HEALING AND THE ENVIRONMENT

Larimar is a stone of self-healing and should be carried to appointments with the doctor or therapist and at the hospital to promote clear, open communication. Larimar will also assist

with chemical imbalances and personality disorders and fight infections. Placed in the bath it will de-stress you. Associated with the throat chakra, larimar helps you to speak from your soul.

USES AT WORK AND HOME
An excellent stone for creating a calm atmosphere in a home or workplace where there are strong personalities, larimar facilitates successful business transactions. This stone should be carried by medical personnel and those who work in call centres, customer service and in public relations.

CHILDREN AND ANIMALS
Larimar helps children communicate with teachers and health professionals. Put larimar beneath an animal bed before visiting the vet.

PSYCHIC ASSOCIATIONS
Place larimar in water to create sacred water for ritual and for cleansing/empowering. Use it for increased telepathic communication, for accessing the Akashic wisdom and for working with healing dolphin energies.

RECHARGING ITS ENERGIES
Leave in moonlight in water for an hour.

BLUE CHALCEDONY
See also pink chalcedony (p104)

MYTHOLOGY AND HISTORY
Sometimes called sapphire in ancient times, blue chalcedony was sacred to the Classical moon and huntress goddess Diana. In Ancient Egypt, blue chalcedony was carved into scarab amulets, a symbol of rebirth that was placed with the mummy in the tomb. Among the Amerindians, blue chalcedony was made into arrowhead amulets to bring good fortune and protection.

DIVINATORY SIGNIFICANCE
Explain any difficulties you are having rather than bottling them up, which can lead to misunderstandings.

HEALING AND THE ENVIRONMENT
Blue chalcedony (especially banded blue) enables the fluids of the body to flow correctly, to avoid the building up of pressure, for example behind the eyes or in mucous membranes. It will ease hay fever and plant allergies that cause respiratory problems and may speed the dissolving/passing of gall and kidney stones. Pale blue increases lactation in nursing mothers (as does pink chalcedony).

USES AT WORK AND HOME
Blue chalcedony is the reality factor, replacing illusions and vague promises with practical plans and realistic timescales for any joint or collective venture, whether at home or work. It melts away blocks to learning new foreign languages and codes or technical information, such as understanding computer manuals.

Hold blue chalcedony and it will absorb stress and irritability, replacing them with a sense of calm and happiness.

CHILDREN AND ANIMALS
Blue chalcedony encourages children and animals to be playful and express their joy.

PSYCHIC ASSOCIATIONS
Blue chalcedony is the stone of telepathic psychic communication, whether with the essences of plants or animals, devas (higher spirits of nature), earth guardians, spirit guides, angels or life forms from other dimensions or planets. Paint an arrow head on a blue chalcedony and keep it in a charm bag to attract good fortune and protect you from psychic attack.

RECHARGING ITS ENERGIES
Revitalize blue chalcedony in running water.

PROPERTIES
TYPE: Cryptocrystalline quartz. Translucent or semi-translucent
COLOUR: Varying shades of soft blues. Can be banded
SYMBOLIC ASSOCIATIONS
ZODIAC SIGN: Cancer
PLANET: Moon
ELEMENT: Water
CANDLE COLOUR: Silver
GUARDIAN ANGEL: Yahriel
CHAKRA: Sacral/root
HERBS, INCENSES AND OILS: Lemon, coconut, gardenia, musk (synthetic) and sandalwood
FLOWERS: Mallow, marsh orchid and pansy
ASSOCIATED CRYSTALS: Aqua aura, blue topaz and blue celestite

RAINBOW OPAL

PROPERTIES

TYPE: Hydrated silica, non-crystalline, precious opal with curved bands of colour

COLOUR: All precious opals are called rainbow stones because of the rainbow flash of colour, but the rainbow opal refers popularly to the blue, brilliantly hued kind. Some blue opals do not have fire, but share properties with the rainbow opal

SYMBOLIC ASSOCIATIONS

ZODIAC SIGN: Cancer

PLANET: Moon, especially the blue moon

ELEMENT: Earth

CANDLE COLOUR: Any with more than one colour banded in the same candle

GUARDIAN ANGEL: Shekinah (or use Iris)

CHAKRA: Brow/throat

HERBS, INCENSES AND OILS: Jasmine, lemon, moonwort, orris and vanilla

FLOWERS: Lily of the valley, magnolia and peach blossom

ASSOCIATED CRYSTALS: Fire opal, rainbow moonstone and pearl

MYTHOLOGY AND HISTORY

Rainbow opal is sometimes found as boulder opal, hardened sandy clay with variable amounts of iron oxides and layers of precious opal. It is the stone of Iris, Greek goddess of the rainbow, symbol of hidden mysteries of the universe, momentarily revealed in all their beauty to humankind.

DIVINATORY SIGNIFICANCE

Rainbow opal is not used in divination.

HEALING AND THE ENVIRONMENT

Rainbow opal cleanses and gently energizes the aura and chakras. It alleviates depression and crankiness and will bring light and absorb pain anywhere in the body or mind. It is especially helpful for the eyes, for all glandular problems and for exhaustion.

USES AT WORK AND HOME

With rainbow opal the possibilities for your life widen and you become aware of all kinds of blessings in your life and avenues to be followed. Above all it prevents us from defeating our own efforts by stopping half way or unconsciously finding obstacles in the way of fulfilment.

CHILDREN AND ANIMALS

Rainbow opal will overcome disillusionment and early cynicism in children that has been caused by people letting them down (or, for

example, from the disappointment of finding there is no physical Santa Claus). Use rainbow opal for unresponsive animals.

PSYCHIC ASSOCIATIONS

Rainbow opal is the ultimate stone for all forms of wishes, for entering the world of the fey and for seeing beyond the physical and immediate reality to the wonders within nature and life.

RECHARGING ITS ENERGIES

Rainbow opal is very delicate and should be hydrated occasionally with a little water. Recharge it when you see a rainbow in the sky, or use a fibre-optic lamp.

CHRYSOCOLLA / GEM SILICA

MYTHOLOGY AND HISTORY

Native American medicine men and women used chrysocolla to improve the body's natural defences and increase resistance to disease. Their leaders utilized its powers to encourage peace between nations. Gem silica is a crystal of the goddess. It is traditionally the stone of musicians.

DIVINATORY SIGNIFICANCE

Be very gentle with yourself. It is an appropriate time to withdraw from activities or commitments you may no longer enjoy in order to allow yourself time for plenty of rest.

HEALING AND THE ENVIRONMENT

Chrysocolla is often called the women's stone, because it heals all female-specific problems, especially those related to hormones and reproduction, from puberty right through to the end of a woman's earthly life. It will ease the process of childbirth if held during labour.

However, for men as well as women, chrysocolla absorbs pain and fever, and regularizes the thyroid gland and blood-sugar levels. It effectively eases trauma of all kinds. It is a stone that is recommended for incest victims and for people who have suffered any form of sexual abuse.

USES AT WORK AND HOME

Chrysocolla will heal a home and family after a burglary, mugging or verbal or physical abuse. It can be used to erect a gentle but effective force field around the home against unpleasant or intrusive neighbours.

Chrysocolla helps promote open and positive communication with people who are abusive or unhelpful. This can be very useful if you have to deal with officials or those whose services you need who persistently refuse to answer messages. Chrysocolla is excellent for all creative work. It will also protect your computer from pornographic or unpleasant emails and guard your phone from malicious callers.

CHILDREN AND ANIMALS

Chrysocolla fosters a love of music in children. It will comfort a pregnant animal, especially a first-time mother.

PSYCHIC ASSOCIATIONS

Use chrysocolla for inducing psychic dreams that answer your questions. It is excellent for sacred earth rituals. It provides a focus when you want to attract love, and is useful to banish fear. Use it in rituals that honour the mother goddess.

RECHARGING ITS ENERGIES

Leave it with a copper ring or inside a copper bracelet overnight.

PROPERTIES
TYPE: Ring silicate. Crystallized gem silica is clearer and richly coloured. Semi-translucent
COLOUR: Bluey-green, turquoise, light blue or green
SYMBOLIC ASSOCIATIONS
ZODIAC SIGN: Taurus
PLANET: Venus
ELEMENT: Water
CANDLE COLOUR: Turquoise
GUARDIAN ANGEL: Pasiel
CHAKRA: Throat/heart
HERBS, INCENSES AND OILS: Balm of Gilead, clover, lemon verbena, strawberry and vervain
FLOWERS: African violet, eucalyptus and geranium
ASSOCIATED CRYSTALS: Copper, malachite and blue lace agate

BLUE TOPAZ

See also white (p43) and golden topaz (p118)

MYTHOLOGY AND HISTORY

Blue topaz was used in the tips of divining wands to find precious metals. Blue topaz was associated with Jupiter both in the Classical world and by the Hindus and so was a stone of justice and litigation.

DIVINATORY SIGNIFICANCE

Blue topaz is not used in divination.

HEALING AND THE ENVIRONMENT

Blue topaz is good for the regrowth of tissue and facilitates steady metabolic functioning. It is helpful for the thyroid, the throat, the eyes, the ears and the nasal passages. It calms panic attacks, and cools menopausal hot flushes. It promotes calm in a confrontation or crisis and keeps older people mentally alert.

USES AT WORK AND HOME

Blue topaz aids clear communication, allowing you to explain your point of view rationally, even under provocation, and helps you to give others a fair hearing. It defuses emotional undercurrents at home and clarifies situations at work when there are mixed messages. It is the stone of artists, writers and poets as well as public speakers, litigators, mediators and all who seek justice.

CHILDREN AND ANIMALS

Blue topaz will help a child or teenager who is being teased by siblings or peers to react

calmly, without resorting to reciprocal shouting or violence. Blue topaz is potent when bird habitats or bird species are under threat of extinction.

PSYCHIC ASSOCIATIONS

Use blue topaz in prayer to connect with saints and divinity. Wear blue topaz or focus on a crystal for meditation or for increasing your clairaudient powers.

RECHARGING ITS ENERGIES

Recharge with a soft blue candle or in the open air beneath a clear blue sky when the sun is still low in the sky.

PROPERTIES
TYPE: Island silicate
COLOUR: Light blue/green-blue. Sparkling
SYMBOLIC ASSOCIATIONS
ZODIAC SIGN: Libra
PLANET: Jupiter
ELEMENT: Air
CANDLE COLOUR: Light blue
GUARDIAN ANGEL: Zuriel
CHAKRA: Crown
HERBS, INCENSES AND OILS: Lilac, cedarwood, lavender, rosewood and vanilla
FLOWERS: Delphinium, gladioli and iris
ASSOCIATED CRYSTALS: Blue sapphire, lapis lazuli and turquoise

BLUE CALCITE

PROPERTIES

TYPE: Calcium carbonate, either polished smooth or as water ice. Semi-transparent to translucent

COLOUR: From pale to mid-blue, sometimes with white veins

SYMBOLIC ASSOCIATIONS

ZODIAC SIGN: Cancer

PLANET: Moon

ELEMENT: Water

CANDLE COLOUR: Silver

GUARDIAN ANGEL: Muriel

CHAKRA: Throat

HERBS, INCENSES AND OILS: Violet, ambergris (artificial), jasmine, mimosa, rose and yarrow

FLOWERS: Bluebell, sea lavender and speedwell

ASSOCIATED CRYSTALS: Angelite, blue lace agate and celestite

MYTHOLOGY AND HISTORY

Blue calcite is the crystal of water nymphs, especially those that live in underground rivers or rock-enclosed pools.

DIVINATORY SIGNIFICANCE

A soft answer, it is said, turns away wrath and you may need to hold your tongue under provocation in order to keep the peace with people who will never change but must be tolerated for the moment.

HEALING AND THE ENVIRONMENT

Like all calcite, blue is good for strengthening teeth and bones. It assists neuralgia, sore throats, the neck glands, headaches caused by hormonal fluctuations and menopausal hot flushes. It is excellent for fevers, burns and scalds and sunburn. Blue calcite promotes speedy healing, especially of wounds.

USES AT WORK AND HOME

In spite of its gentle nature, blue calcite is a deterrent against crime; placed on inner window ledges and near doors or valuable equipment it will help deter thieves or vandals. At work, blue calcite is helpful during delicate transactions. It is the stone of negotiators and mediators, priests of both sexes and all religions, race and equality officers and crime-prevention officers.

CHILDREN AND ANIMALS

Blue calcite gives confidence to children who are learning to swim. It steers teenagers away from bad company. Use blue calcite as an amulet for teething babies and for the emergence of second and wisdom teeth.

Blue calcite is good for snappy dogs or any other bad-tempered animals.

PSYCHIC ASSOCIATIONS

Blue calcite spheres are fabulous when polished and are excellent for all scrying work. Alternatively, scry by putting small unpolished pieces in water, lit after dark by a circle of silver candles. It is a good wish crystal to bring you peaceful but creative dreams of how to make your wishes come true in the everyday world. It is also a useful crystal for meditation.

RECHARGING ITS ENERGIES

Recharge blue calcite in running water, if possible in a stream.

HAWK'S EYE / FALCON'S EYE

See also cat's eye (p144)

MYTHOLOGY AND HISTORY

According to legend, the hawk is one of the birds that flies closest to the sun. It was a power animal in Native American spirituality and appears on several medicine wheels, often representing the south. It is known as the stone of the wise ancestors in Amerindian lore. In Celtic myth, Merlin is said to take the shape of a hawk to travel swiftly and the magical hawk of Achill is said to have acquired his wisdom before the beginning of the world and taught the poetic arts to druids.

DIVINATORY SIGNIFICANCE

Aim high, whether creatively, spiritually or in your work life, for you have the power to reach out for what would truly fulfil you.

HEALING AND THE ENVIRONMENT

Hawk's eye aids eye problems, especially those concerned with focus, and clears sinuses and congestion in the nasal passages. It relieves spine, neck and leg problems and aids mobility. Hawk's eye is protective for X-ray treatment and invasive medical tests.

USES AT WORK AND HOME
Hawk's eye is the crystal of expanding your horizons and is good for all forms of travel, especially journeys and holidays by air. At work, hawk's eye will likewise promote new opportunities within your existing work structure, or offer transfers or scope to work in a new location or area of expertize.

CHILDREN AND ANIMALS
Hawk's eye alleviates the fear of flying in children (and in adults) and prevents travel sickness. A wonderful stone for all birds, hawk's eye is especially good for bird of prey conservation and rescue work.

PSYCHIC ASSOCIATIONS
Hawk's eye is probably the best stone for remote viewing (seeing beyond the range of the physical eye), for clairvoyance and for astral travel.

RECHARGING ITS ENERGIES
Leave it open to the skies for a day.

PROPERTIES
TYPE: Quartz. Unoxidized brown tiger's eye

COLOUR: Blue, chatoyant, reflecting light in wavy bands that makes it gleam. Also greyish blue or green with the bands of colour that distinguish tiger's eye

SYMBOLIC ASSOCIATIONS
ZODIAC SIGN: Sagittarius

PLANET: Jupiter

ELEMENT: Air

CANDLE COLOUR: Mid-blue

GUARDIAN ANGEL: Barachiel

CHAKRA: Brow

HERBS, INCENSES AND OILS: Lemon balm, agrimony, aloe vera, rosemary and sandalwood

FLOWERS: Lupin, larkspur flowering bergamot, mint

ASSOCIATED CRYSTALS: Angelite, blue quartz and sapphire

BLUE GOLDSTONE

MYTHOLOGY AND HISTORY
Blue goldstone was created, it is said, to a secret formula by Italian monks in the seventeenth century. They were reputed to chant a magical formula over it to make it especially powerful.

DIVINATORY SIGNIFICANCE
You may find yourself getting unexpected positive attention or a chance to show hidden talents. It can also herald promotion at work.

HEALING AND THE ENVIRONMENT
Blue goldstone is helpful for migraines and visual disturbances, for assisting the flow of blood, for detoxifying the system and for recovering from surgery or intensive chemical therapies. It is also an energizer. It is good for land regeneration programmes and for cleaning the skies of fumes and pollution.

USES AT WORK AND HOME
All colours of goldstone are good for redecorating or renovating an old or unmodernized house, for converting other buildings into homes or for the ingenious adding of space to an existing home.

At work, goldstone will ensure that you gain recognition and a chance to develop your strengths. It will also attract a better salary or job opportunities. It is helpful for amateur

and professional actors and for those in the media, especially those who appear on radio or television, for PR and press officers and for all who want to become famous.

CHILDREN AND ANIMALS
A magical stone for children, it will help them lose fear of the dark as they hold a piece of the starry sky. Animals tend not to like it.

PSYCHIC ASSOCIATIONS
Goldstone is excellent for increasing telepathic powers and for all forms of star magic and channelling star guardians. Use it in charm bags to attract success and fame.

RECHARGING ITS ENERGIES
Leave goldstone by a window on a starry night.

PROPERTIES
TYPE: A man-made or treated stone. Usually tiny copper crystals suspended in translucent glass; sometimes dyed aventurine

COLOUR: Blue, red, black and brown, with sparkling golden copper flecks

SYMBOLIC ASSOCIATIONS
ZODIAC SIGN: Sagittarius

PLANET: Uranus

ELEMENT: Fire/earth

CANDLE COLOUR: Silver

GUARDIAN ANGEL: Sahaqiel

CHAKRA: Crown/brow

HERBS, INCENSES AND OILS: Copal, lavender, pine, sweet pea and star anise

FLOWERS: Iris, periwinkle and star flower

ASSOCIATED CRYSTALS: Iron pyrites, lapis lazuli and turquoise

CAVANSITE

PROPERTIES

TYPE: Calcium vanadium silicate. Very small crystals, needle like, sometimes as rosettes or attached to a more muted stone such as a zeolite-like white stilbite, a mineral with which it is closely associated. Also found as globules. Transparent, translucent or pearly

COLOUR: Brilliant ocean blue, bright vibrant turquoise, deep blue or greenish-blue

SYMBOLIC ASSOCIATIONS

ZODIAC SIGN: Aquarius

PLANET: Uranus

ELEMENT: Air

CANDLE COLOUR: Turquoise

GUARDIAN ANGEL: Shekinah

CHAKRA: Throat

HERBS, INCENSES AND OILS: Acacia, hyacinth, lilac, lotus and papyrus

FLOWERS: Delphinium, harebell and narcissus

ASSOCIATED CRYSTALS: Azurite, lapis lazuli and turquoise

PROPERTIES

TYPE: A rare form of zoisite, a group silicate. Clear

COLOUR: Blue-purple with flashing violet lights within

SYMBOLIC ASSOCIATIONS

ZODIAC SIGN: Sagittarius

PLANET: Uranus

ELEMENT: Air

CANDLE COLOUR: Violet

GUARDIAN ANGEL: Saritiel

CHAKRA: Crown / brow / throat

HERBS, INCENSES AND OILS: Fennel, feverfew, lavender, lemongrass and sandalwood

FLOWERS: Clematis, lilac and purple thyme

ASSOCIATED CRYSTALS: Iolite, purple fluorite, amethyst

HISTORY AND MYTHOLOGY

Found in Poona, India, in 1988, bright-blue cavansite is one of the wonders of the modern crystal world. It was cast up by Gaia at a time when the world's skies and the seas are at their most polluted.

DIVINATORY SIGNIFICANCE

Cavansite is not used in divination.

HEALING AND THE ENVIRONMENT

Cavansite is the stone of the spiritual healer who uses prayer to his or her personal divinity or source of goodness to send healing through their heart and their fingertips. Use it also to ask that an illness that has apparently been cured or is in remission will not return. It will assist those learning Reiki or other spiritual-healing techniques. It helps those who have speech, physical or learning disabilities to maximize their potential. Use it for rituals to cleanse the seas and skies and to ask the blessings of the earth mother.

USES AT WORK AND HOME

Cavansite is excellent for moving into a home that has bad memories or a dark atmosphere. Use it also for overcoming family tragedy or bereavement. It is a stone for conventional and alternative healers, for speech therapists, music makers, especially those working with disadvantaged people, and all who work with the seriously ill or disabled.

CHILDREN AND ANIMALS

Cavansite is helpful in the bedroom of a disabled or very sick child or teenager: it helps parents to love all children for what and who they are. It is beneficial for seriously injured or sick animals.

PSYCHIC ASSOCIATIONS

Cavansite enhances sacred chants from all traditions and is excellent for working with sacred forms, the magic circle, the labyrinth, the mandala, the Medicine Wheel and any crystal grid or formation.

RECHARGING ITS ENERGIES

Pray to the deity that has special significance to you to give your cavansite power.

TANZANITE

MYTHOLOGY AND HISTORY

Tanzanite is a relatively recent discovery. Legend says that about thirty years ago Masai cattle herders noticed a blue coloured stone after brown zoisite crystals on the ground were seared by a lightning fire that burned areas of the Merelani hills in Tanzania. Tanzanite can occur naturally in the blue-violet shade, but some that is sold is heat-treated brown zoisite and a number of blue stones are colour-enhanced.

DIVINATORY SIGNIFICANCE

Tanzanite is not used in divination.

HEALING AND THE ENVIRONMENT

Tanzanite restores vitality to the body, especially skin and hair, and encourages cell regeneration. It slows down the ageing process and increases the user's inner light, so they radiate health. It protects against the side effects of necessary powerful treatments.

USES AT WORK AND HOME

Tanzanite brings to the surface alternative aspects of the personality, so that a normally logical person will begin to develop their imaginative side quite spontaneously. This can open new avenues of employment.

CHILDREN AND ANIMALS

Let children weave stories about the stone. You may find they include quite detailed accounts of past worlds. Tanzanite lightens a cloudy aura in animals.

PSYCHIC ASSOCIATIONS

A very magical stone, tanzanite can connect you psychically with ancient wisdom, especially that of indigenous cultures whose spirituality has remained unchanged for thousands of years. It is good for creating guided visualizations, either alone or with a group, to explore other spiritual planes.

RECHARGING ITS ENERGIES

Leave it on any brown rock as a storm starts.

APATITE

MYTHOLOGY AND HISTORY

Because of its variety of colours and appearance, in the past apatite has been confused with other minerals. Hence it was given the Greek name apatao, which means to delude or deceive, in 1786, a time when minerals were being more closely categorized. It is a mineral closely connected with the human and animal kingdom since apatite formed in the human body gives strength to teeth and bones. It is also a major constituent in the tusks of elephants, walruses, hippopotamuses and rhinoceros.

DIVINATORY SIGNIFICANCE

You can draw strength from those around you, but sometimes need to ask for help, especially if you are usually strong.

HEALING AND THE ENVIRONMENT

Apatite will strengthen teeth and bones and help prevent bone thinning. It makes dentistry a more positive experience by calming fears and helping you to relax. Apatite is helpful for weight loss and for controlling appetite. It lifts apathy, helps to clear confused thoughts and improves memory and concentration. Apatite is beneficial for treating long-term illness. Use it in all earth awareness rituals.

USES AT WORK AND HOME

Apatite eases difficult relationships at work or home, helping you to communicate your feelings clearly without becoming over-emotional, however justifiable. It counters the stress overload that can lead to burnout.

CHILDREN AND ANIMALS

It eases teething problems and growing pains.

PSYCHIC ASSOCIATIONS

Apatite is good for meditation and for increasing clairvoyance, clairsentience, clairaudience and past-life recall. It is a very powerful stone for connecting with earth energies and earth spirits and for increasing psychic communication with animals, birds and sea creatures.

RECHARGING ITS ENERGIES

A delicate stone, place it near a vase of fresh flowers or on the soil near a herb or plant.

PROPERTIES
TYPE: Complex phosphate of calcium, chlorine and fluorine. Apatite is the most common phosphate. Opaque. Can be polished to a shine
COLOUR: Light to bright to dark blue, sometimes within the same crystal. Occasionally with white veins

SYMBOLIC ASSOCIATIONS
ZODIAC SIGN: Libra
PLANET: Jupiter
ELEMENT: Air/earth
CANDLE COLOUR: Deep blue
GUARDIAN ANGEL: Zuriel
CHAKRA: Throat
HERBS, INCENSES AND OILS: Ferns, lemongrass, laurel, lemon verbena, rosewood and vanilla
FLOWERS: Almond blossom, echinacea (purple coneflower) and anemone
ASSOCIATED CRYSTALS: Calcite, kyanite and jade

GREEN FLUORITE

See also purple (p49) and clear fluorite (p36)

Green fluorite transmits knowledge and is a gentle healer that detoxifies and harmonizes the whole system. Placed on the throat or heart centres, green fluorite will cleanse and energize all the chakras.

PROPERTIES

TYPE: Halide / fluorospar. Transparent or semi-transparent. Single crystals, two pyramid crystals fused together or as separate or interlocking octahedral clusters

COLOUR: Mid- to dark green

SYMBOLIC ASSOCIATIONS

ZODIAC SIGN: Pisces

PLANET: Neptune

ELEMENT: Water

CANDLE COLOUR: Lavender

GUARDIAN ANGEL: Nahaliel

CHAKRA: Throat / heart

HERBS, INCENSES AND OILS: Aloe vera, eucalyptus, lemon, lime and sarsaparilla

FLOWERS: Bog asphodel, sea aster and water lily

ASSOCIATED CRYSTALS: All forms of jade, serpentine and watermelon tourmaline

MYTHOLOGY AND HISTORY

Called fluorspar in the eighteenth century, fluorite really is a crystal of the New Age. It has come to represent the crystalline energy pyramids of Atlantis and individual pieces can transmit the stored wisdom and healing of past millennia. If you shine an ultraviolet light on fluorite it becomes fluorescent and glows in the dark.

DIVINATORY SIGNIFICANCE

Spend quiet time, preferably near water, alone or with friends and family and postpone any decisions or actions until you are fully in tune with your spiritual self again.

HEALING PROPERTIES

Green fluorite assists the absorption of vital nutrients, aiding the teeth and bones and the blood vessels, lungs and spleen. It promotes the healing of scars, both physical and emotional. Green fluorite is beneficial for arthritis, sore throats, ulcers of all kinds, heartburn, indigestion and insomnia. It regularizes hormonal, anxiety- or stress-based conditions. It is especially good for premenstrual syndrome and the menopause.

FAR RIGHT AND BELOW
Rough-cut and gem-quality green fluorite. Green fluorite is a gentle healer; it restores harmony to people, animals, plants and places. It provides subtle, soft but all-encompassing protection.

Use it when a person is tired of medical treatments, to strengthen their natural resistance to the condition and to quieten fears and frustration when results are slow.

USES AT HOME AND WORK

Use to create order out of chaos and to focus a group of people (the family or work colleagues) on a project that must be tackled. Green fluorite will improve and stabilize any partnership or cooperative venture, whether in personal or work life.

CHILDREN

Green fluorite is quietly encouraging for a reluctant student.

ANIMALS

Green fluorite is a lovely stone in the garden and will attract butterflies.

PROTECTIVE FUNCTIONS

Green fluorite brings resistance to disease and shields you against envy.

PSYCHIC ASSOCIATIONS

Green fluorite is wonderful for meditation in the open air and to channel the wisdom of nature essences, especially water spirits. It strengthens the value of herbs, flowers or flower and tree essences when used in healing or magic. A green fluorite wand will direct energies from nature into your heart and empower herbs for healing. Use the pyramid-shaped crystals for visions of Atlantis and other lands lost beneath the waves and to increase your psychic awareness. Use them also to heal damaged plants or other crystals that have lost their vitality or are cracked.

ENVIRONMENTAL WORK

Green fluorite will send healing energies to places that are no longer green and to threatened wildlife habitats.

SPECIAL PROPERTIES

Each green fluorite crystal will tell its own story, if you close your eyes. If you can, choose this crystal personally rather than by mail order, to get the one that is right for you.

RECHARGING ITS ENERGIES

Green fluorite is not a sunlight stone. To revitalize it, leave it in water overnight under the light of the moon. A stream would be perfect, otherwise use a bowl of water.

MOSS AGATE

<table>
<tr><td>PROPERTIES</td></tr>
<tr><td>TYPE: Oxide, chalcedony (quartz). Smoother and more translucent than tree agate. Translucent to opaque</td></tr>
<tr><td>COLOUR: Colourless with profusion of deep green tendrils inside of hornblende that may make it appear green; pale blue or a deeper green with pale blue or white inclusions</td></tr>
<tr><td>SYMBOLIC ASSOCIATIONS</td></tr>
<tr><td>ZODIAC SIGN: Virgo</td></tr>
<tr><td>PLANET: Earth</td></tr>
<tr><td>ELEMENT: Earth</td></tr>
<tr><td>CANDLE COLOUR: Moss or olive green</td></tr>
<tr><td>GUARDIAN ANGEL: Cathetel</td></tr>
<tr><td>CHAKRA: Heart</td></tr>
<tr><td>HERBS, INCENSES AND OILS: Ferns, moss, parsley, thyme and wintergreen</td></tr>
<tr><td>FLOWERS: Snowdrop, crocus and wood anemone</td></tr>
<tr><td>ASSOCIATED CRYSTALS: Amber, leopardskin jasper and tree agate</td></tr>
</table>

HISTORY AND MYTHOLOGY

Moss agate is frequently called the gardeners' crystal because of its long association with the accelerated growth of plants. To the Native Americans moss agate was a rain bringer and in Ancient Rome it was a talisman, believed to bring the good fortune and the blessings of the deities. In Europe it was placed in gardens, orchards and fields as an offering to the guardians of the land.

DIVINATORY SIGNIFICANCE

Let matters take their time and give new projects or relationships time to take root and to evolve naturally. This really is a case for gentle nurturing and patience.

HEALING AND THE ENVIRONMENT

Moss agate is a gentle gradual cleanser that can be worn next to the skin or used daily, to encourage new growth of healthy cells and tissue within the body, to relieve skin infections and to fight colds and flu.

Moss agate will also protect your aura by filtering out impurities and negativity. Moss agate is especially helpful in hot weather or climates to help prevent dehydration (drink water in which one has been soaking). Use this stone in rituals or empowerments for drought-ridden areas.

USES AT WORK OR HOME

Moss agate brings beauty to environments that are in less than ideal settings. It will slowly attract money or promotion. It is beneficial for all those who work in horticulture, botany or any form of alternative medicine, especially aromatherapy or herbalism. Plant moss agate in a flowerbed to promote the healthy growth of plants.

CHILDREN AND ANIMALS
Moss agate will attract friends to children who are lonely or are starting a new school. It helps animals in towns keep a link with the natural world. Moss agate encourages a balanced attitude in children and young animals and helps children and pets to bond.

PSYCHIC ASSOCIATIONS
Carry moss agate to increase your understanding of the magical properties of herbs, flowers and trees and to channel wisdom from devas and other nature spirits. In meditation, follow the pathways of a clear moss agate into other realms.

RECHARGING ITS ENERGIES
Leave moss agate with greenery for a night every month as it is a hard-working crystal and its energies become depleted.

MOLDAVITE
See also tektite (p151)

MYTHOLOGY AND HISTORY
Moldavite was formed in a meteor collision about fifteen million years ago in the Moldau River valley, in the Czech Republic. Used as an amulet from Palaeolithic times, moldavite is the fusion of meteor (extraterrestrial powers) with melted earthly rock (terrestrial). Because of this, moldavite is said to be the stone of those who feel that their spiritual roots or origins lie in the Sirius star system, the Pleiades, Orion or some other constellation or planet.

DIVINATORY SIGNIFICANCE
Do not worry if you sometimes feel alienated from the material world. You have unique gifts that can be developed if you follow your own unique path.

HEALING AND THE ENVIRONMENT
A powerful healer for body, mind and soul, moldavite is an excellent choice if the cause of an illness cannot be identified, conventional treatments are not responding or the problem is caused by the pollution or ills of the modern world (especially asthma and disturbances of electrical impulses in the brain). It is good for giving up smoking.

AT WORK AND IN THE HOME
Moldavite is a stone to wear if you live alone, whether by choice or necessity, or if you work or spend long periods in your own company: it will strengthen you and help you rejoice in your unique qualities. Moldavite can leave you feeling spaced out, so do not have it in the car when you are driving.

PROPERTIES
TYPE: Silica-based tektite. Transparent to translucent, some more opaque. Glassy, occasionally pitted
COLOUR: Deep bottle green when gem quality. Some blackish

SYMBOLIC ASSOCIATIONS
ZODIAC SIGN: Aquarius
PLANET: Uranus
ELEMENT: Fire
CANDLE COLOUR: Deep green
GUARDIAN ANGEL: Star system and planetary guardians
CHAKRA: Crown
HERBS, INCENSES AND OILS: Citron, mace, papyrus, pine and star anise
FLOWERS: Blue lotus, orchid and star flower
ASSOCIATED CRYSTALS: Lava/pumice, meteorite and tektite

CHILDREN AND ANIMALS
Moldavite connects children with the wider universe. Do not be surprised if they talk about other worlds or lives. It is good for spiritually evolved cats.

PSYCHIC PROPERTIES
Moldavite is called the Grail stone because it can show you the path to spiritual enlightenment. Use it to promote beautiful dreams and for star walking. It is also useful to channel wisdom from positive extraterrestrial sources.

RECHARGING ITS ENERGIES
Leave moldavite with a tiny piece of pumice and float the pumice away afterwards, or leave outdoors on the night of a meteor shower.

AMAZONITE

PROPERTIES

TYPE: Feldspar. Opaque

COLOUR: Blue-green or turquoise to darker greens with white lines

SYMBOLIC ASSOCIATIONS

ZODIAC SIGN: Virgo

PLANET: Uranus

ELEMENT: Earth

CANDLE COLOUR: Turquoise

GUARDIAN ANGEL: Voel

CHAKRA: Throat and heart

HERBS, INCENSES AND OILS: Basil, bergamot, fennel, mint and patchouli

FLOWERS: Hyacinth, hydrangea and tulip

ASSOCIATED CRYSTALS: Aventurine, bloodstone and green garnet

MYTHOLOGY AND HISTORY

Called the stone of courage, Amazonite is named after the Amazon women warriors because it is said to have originated in a land of women. Archaeological evidence suggests the Amazonians were a matriarchal society, possibly surviving from the Bronze Age.

DIVINATORY SIGNIFICANCE

You are in a strong position, so stand up for what you think is important, especially if fighting prejudice or injustice. You may need to assume leadership if others are divided or confused about priorities.

HEALING AND THE ENVIRONMENT

Amazonite helps both sexes to improve and maintain health and is especially good for breast problems. It assists the functioning of the passages of the throat, the thyroid gland, and nerve and neurological connections. It is good also for the upper spine and for encouraging a healthier lifestyle. A powerful crystal, amazonite fills the heart with courage and determination to do good in the world.

USES AT WORK AND HOME

Amazonite reduces anger and irritability in the home and prevents people bringing work or school-related problems home. It brings success at work by helping you to focus and makes sure you are in the right place at the right time. It also combats sexism.

CHILDREN AND ANIMALS

Amazonite will activate lazy teenagers and slovenly children. It also helps house-train young animals.

PSYCHIC ASSOCIATIONS

Amazonite is excellent for working with natural forces, including nature spirits. It is useful in weather and animal magic, and for contacting water and earth spirits. It works well with other crystals. Amazonite also increases clairvoyant and telepathic abilities. Use amazonite to attract good luck, especially when speculating.

RECHARGING ITS ENERGIES

Use a mint infusion to recharge amazonite.

GREEN AVENTURINE

See also red aventurine (p135)

MYTHOLOGY AND HISTORY

Green aventurine is sometimes called Indian jade, or the stone of heaven. It is known as the gambler's stone because it is the luckiest of all stones in games of chance. Green aventurine is often placed in charm bags to bring good fortune and money.

DIVINATORY SIGNIFICANCE

An excellent time to take a chance to gain what you want by speaking out, trying a new money-spinning idea or following a spur-of-the-moment inspiration.

HEALING THE ENVIRONMENT

Green aventurine is good for the eyes; it improves physical acuity and also enhances mental perception and the ability to discriminate between what is relevant and what is not. It calms free-floating anxiety, panic attacks and irregular heart rhythms. Green aventurine is a fertility stone and eases genito-urinary problems.

USES AT WORK AND HOME

Aventurine helps to prevent accidents owing to haste or carelessness and so is good for all

DIY. At work it increases opportunities by giving you belief in your own talents. Aventurine also protects your aura from psychic/psychological intrusion or draining by emotional vampires.

CHILDREN AND ANIMALS
Aventurine helps children to take more care with school work and handwriting. It is good for clumsy pets that live in a confined space.

PSYCHIC ASSOCIATIONS
Aventurine can be used to induce psychic dreams, to bring answers or to see into the future. It also increases clairvoyance. It is a good source of earth energy: hold it in the opposite hand from your pendulum when divining. Leave as a gift for nature essences.

RECHARGING ITS ENERGIES
Occasionally rest green aventurine in the leaves of a green plant during daylight.

TREE AGATE
See also moss agate (p78)

HISTORY AND MYTHOLOGY
Tree agate is quite coarse and knobbly even when polished. In earlier times, the white form of dendritic agate (really dendritic chalcedony) was called tree agate. Moss agate is very similar in mineralogical terms but tree agate is more translucent and the markings more feathery. Tree agate (or possibly dendritic agate) was considered a stone of abundance by the Ancient Greeks, and was buried in the fields at the time of sowing to ensure a good harvest. It was also much loved by Native Americans, who used it to help them connect with the power of the trees.

DIVINATORY SIGNIFICANCE
Go back to the roots of any problem or situation and you will find the answer. A good time for family reunions, especially with

people you have not contacted for a while, and for strengthening friendship and connections in your neighbourhood.

HEALING AND THE ENVIRONMENT
Tree agate relieves small bone, vein and capillary problems and obstructions within the body. It is very good for calming people who worry about their health. Use it in empowerments and rituals for reforestation.

USES AT WORK AND HOME
Tree agate strengthens family roots, links with places of origin and maintains family traditions. At work, it leads to gradual success and prosperity and helps networking. It protects you while travelling by air and car.

CHILDREN AND ANIMALS
It helps children to become more reflective, especially those who rush from disaster to disaster. It is good for wildlife in the garden.

PSYCHIC ASSOCIATIONS
Tree agate is a good focus for tree magic of all kinds, for channelling tree wisdom, for divination with tree or Ogham staves and as an amulet for druids.

RECHARGING ITS ENERGIES
Smudge tree agate with cedar or pine.

GREEN CALCITE

PROPERTIES

TYPE: Calcium carbonate, either as clear optical or translucent water ice

COLOUR: Pale to mid-green, occasionally emerald

SYMBOLIC ASSOCIATIONS

ZODIAC SIGN: Virgo

PLANET: Earth

ELEMENT: Earth

CANDLE COLOUR: Pale green

GUARDIAN ANGEL: Zuphlas

CHAKRA: Heart

HERBS, INCENSES AND OILS: Clary sage, honeysuckle, lemon balm, rosewood and wintergreen

FLOWERS: Cowslip, evening primrose and bee orchid

ASSOCIATED CRYSTALS: Jade, prehnite and serpentine

MYTHOLOGY AND HISTORY

Green calcite is the stone of the small benign earth spirits who live in woodlands or grassy fairy mounds, especially near water. It was used in ritual-giving ceremonies by the Amerindians, who honoured visitors with valuable gifts, knowing that the spirits would ensure abundance likewise came their way.

DIVINATORY SIGNIFICANCE

You may seem to be giving more than you receive but the balance will soon be redressed.

HEALING AND THE ENVIRONMENT

Green calcite will help to prevent and clear infections. It is good for directing absent healing to the recipient. Green calcite also helps with arthritic and bone discomfort and encourages bone health. Use it in empowerments against all forms of dumped waste.

USES AT WORK AND HOME

A wonderful stone for creating a calm home and workplace. Put a dish of green calcite in the bathroom to add to bath water to ease away the stress of the day (mix it with blue calcite for total relaxation). It is good for all philanthropists, charity workers and volunteers in any charitable or social work and anyone taking part in sports to guard against injuries. It also helps combat workaholic tendencies.

CHILDREN AND ANIMALS

Green calcite works well with hyperactive children and those with Attention Deficit Disorder. It also encourages children to be generous. Use it to cool children and animals in very hot weather.

PSYCHIC PROPERTIES

Bury pieces in your garden to ask the help of earth spirits to create you a beautiful garden. It is a lovely stone for meditation.

RECHARGING ITS ENERGIES

Hold it under running water, preferably beneath a fountain or small waterfall.

EMERALD

PROPERTIES

TYPE: Beryl. Sparkling

COLOUR: Brilliant green

SYMBOLIC ASSOCIATIONS

ZODIAC SIGN: Taurus

PLANET: Venus

ELEMENT: Earth

CANDLE COLOUR: Green

GUARDIAN ANGEL: Ashmodiel

CHAKRA: Heart

HERBS, INCENSES AND OILS: Lilac, avocado, lily of the valley, strawberry and vanilla

FLOWERS: Cyclamen, daisy and rose

ASSOCIATED CRYSTALS: Aquamarine, chrysoberyl and topaz

MYTHOLOGY AND HISTORY

According to the Book of Revelations, the throne of God is made of emerald. An early Christian bishop, Andreas of Caesarea, declared the emerald to be the stone of Saint John the Apostle and to have the power to release penitents from their sins.

In Ancient Egyptian myth, Thoth, the god of wisdom, gave emeralds to the world. The semi-divine Egyptian magician Hermes Trismegistos created the legendary Emerald Tablet, on which, it was said, were engraved all the secrets of magic and alchemy. Today, emerald is traditionally given to celebrate the fifty-fifth wedding anniversary.

DIVINATORY SIGNIFICANCE

Emerald is not used in divination.

HEALING AND THE ENVIRONMENT

Emerald assists eyesight and helps eye infections and conditions linked with the heart, lungs, thymus, pancreas and lymph nodes. It increases inner radiance and preserves youthfulness. Emerald is excellent for women in labour. It also improves the general health of older women and makes the transition through the menopause easier and more comfortable. Emerald helps to restore beauty to places that have been despoiled and promotes reforestation.

USES AT WORK AND HOME

Emerald protects women against all forms of domestic violence or abuse. In the workplace, emerald strengthens women and helps them to overcome prejudice and sexism. Even a very small uncut emerald will shield counsellors and care or social workers of both sexes and help them not to become weighed down by their responsibilities.

CHILDREN AND ANIMALS

It is not suitable for children or animals.

PSYCHIC ASSOCIATIONS

Emeralds are potent for older women in both magic and psychic development. Use emeralds for rituals for the gradual increase of prosperity and for preserving fidelity in a permanent relationship. Wear an emerald out of sight near your heart for attracting love, especially in later life. Wear an emerald openly for healing a relationship after infidelity or separation. Emerald can also be used in binding against psychic or emotional attack and for banishing nightmares and night phantoms. A symbol of rebirth in Egypt, emerald is useful for past-life recall.

RECHARGING ITS ENERGIES

Wipe emerald with a soft cloth and recharge its powers by the waxing moon.

AZURITE WITH MALACHITE

PROPERTIES

TYPE: Copper carbonate

COLOUR: Blue and green marbled effect, bright stone with large green flecks, turquoise or azure-blue and deep-green patches

SYMBOLIC ASSOCIATIONS

ZODIAC SIGN: Aquarius

PLANET: Uranus

ELEMENT: Air

CANDLE COLOUR: Turquoise

GUARDIAN ANGEL: Gediel

CHAKRA: Crown

HERBS, INCENSES AND OILS: Birch, bergamot, citronella, lemon verbena and sandalwood

FLOWERS: Delphinium, sea holly and sweet pea

ASSOCIATED CRYSTALS: Azurite, lapis lazuli and turquoise

MYTHOLOGY AND HISTORY

Azurite is often found growing with or on malachite in the same rock, forming a single crystal. These crystals can be a major source of copper. Like all combination stones, the combined power of azurite with malachite is different from and greater than that of the separate minerals.

When it is cut and polished it is sometimes called the planet stone, because it resembles the earth as seen from space, and so it has become a symbol of efforts to save the planet.

DIVINATORY SIGNIFICANCE

It is not used in divination.

HEALING AND THE ENVIRONMENT

Azurite with malachite is a powerful psychic and spiritual healer, especially when used with prayer. Azurite with malachite works on a spiritual rather than physical level, cleansing the higher aura levels that, if blocked, can suppress the body's natural immune system and cause illness. Some people reportedly have found it helpful during cancer treatment.

USES AT WORK AND HOME

Azurite with malachite crystals are the ultimate worry stone and, if held, will dispel panic or anger and restore a better sense of priority. Use it to dispel personal negativity and resentment that may be stopping you building on more positive aspects of the situation. It helps people who have been betrayed in love to forgive and either rebuild or move on.

CHILDREN AND ANIMALS

Azurite with malachite encourages children to become citizens of the world and to work against prejudice of all kinds, especially racial. It is not used for animals.

PSYCHIC ASSOCIATIONS

It is a stone of meditation and will connect you to cosmic and divine energies. However it may make you more sensitive to the suffering of others, so is not without a price.

RECHARGING ITS ENERGIES

Leave azurite with malachite overnight in moonlight around full moon.

MALACHITE

PROPERTIES

TYPE: Copper carbonate. Opaque

COLOUR: Emerald to grass-green with black or occasionally pale-green stripes, bands, swirls or marbling

SYMBOLIC ASSOCIATIONS

ZODIAC SIGN: Scorpio

PLANET: Venus

ELEMENT: Earth

CANDLE COLOUR: Emerald green

GUARDIAN ANGEL: Ausiel

CHAKRA: Heart

HERBS, INCENSES AND OILS: Cedar, fennel, parsley, pine and sage

FLOWERS: Gladioli, hollyhock and iris

ASSOCIATED CRYSTALS: Amazonite, aventurine and fuchsite

MYTHOLOGY AND HISTORY

Malachite is associated with strong love goddesses, who could be benign or vengeful, such as Our Lady of the Mountains in central Russia. She is a form of Venus who might protect miners if appeased. Freyja, the Viking goddess of love and beauty, was another patroness who could be cruel to cast-off lovers.

DIVINATORY SIGNIFICANCE

Follow your heart but do not be swayed by sentiment or pressurized by those who appeal to your emotions. A time for tough love.

HEALING AND THE ENVIRONMENT

Malachite is a cleansing and protective crystal for the industrialized world. It cleanses the auric field and aids the heart, stomach, liver and lungs. It eases migraines, kick-starts the immune system and makes body and mind feel refreshed each new day.

USES AT WORK AND HOME

It is good for cleansing and protecting workspaces against all the pollution and toxicity of noise, over-bright fluorescent lighting and harmful rays emitted by electrical equipment. Place near a computer or phone to filter out negative communication. At home, keep near white goods in the kitchen and by televisions and computers.

CHILDREN AND ANIMALS

Use at least two crystals per room if a child has a television or computer. Put beneath a pet bed if your animal lives in a town or near a radio mast or a power station.

PSYCHIC ASSOCIATIONS

A powerful crystal for protective magic, especially if travelling by air or on congested motorways, and for amplifying wishes in magic. It is useful for prosperity magic, especially concerning business matters, and as an amulet for all salespersons, especially at conferences and trade shows.

RECHARGING ITS ENERGIES

Cleanse regularly as it is so hard working. Wash it under running water, even though this weakens the stone. When it crumbles, bury your malachite as it has done its work.

NEPHRITE & JADEITE
See also bowenite (p88)

Nephrite, the most common jade, and Chinese jade are found in New Zealand, Europe and the Americas. Jadeite is virtually identical and is found mainly in the Americas, but also in China, Japan and Burma.

PROPERTIES

TYPE: Jadeite and nephrite / silicates

COLOUR: Pale to dark green. Transparent to opaque. Occasionally pink, purple, brown, black and white or even lavender or emerald green. Nephrite is creamier and less translucent than jadeite

SYMBOLIC ASSOCIATIONS

ZODIAC SIGN: Pisces

PLANET: Venus / Neptune

ELEMENT: Water

CANDLE COLOUR: All shades of green

GUARDIAN ANGEL: Anael

CHAKRA: Heart

HERBS, INCENSES AND OILS: Rose, chamomile, lavender, mugwort and patchouli

FLOWERS: Cherry blossom, orchid, and all marsh flowers

ASSOCIATED CRYSTALS: Green jasper, moss agate and rose quartz

FAR RIGHT AND BELOW Jade in all its forms brings good health and is associated with long life, faithful love and kindness.

MYTHOLOGY AND HISTORY

In the Neolithic period, the two mineral forms of jade were used for tools and weapons as well as amulets. Jade is the sacred stone of the Maoris, who call it greenstone.

In Ancient China food bowls were made of jade to energize the contents with life force and a piece of jade was placed on the eyelids or in the mouth of the dead to ensure the immortality of the spirit. Young men would present a bride-to-be with a jade butterfly as a symbol of faithful and eternal love. According to legend, a young man entered a wealthy mandarin's palace in pursuit of a rare green butterfly and saw the mandarin's beautiful daughter. Unusually the story ended happily with a wedding and with the youth presenting a jade butterfly to his new bride as a token of their meeting.

DIVINATORY SIGNIFICANCE

Respond gently and with compassion to those who are being difficult; they may be acting out of personal unhappiness and inadequacy.

HEALING PROPERTIES

Jade is a gentle healer that boosts the body's self-healing powers. It helps to resolve emotional or spiritual problems that may be lowering physical resistance. It is effective against lung, eye, bladder and kidney problems, fluid retention and blood-sugar imbalances. It aids arthritis and bone or joint pain or stiffness, especially of the hips. It calms and balances the mind and emotions and aids self-love and self-esteem.

USES AT HOME AND WORK

Jade will attract good fortune and prosperity to the home and workplace. At work, have jade in your pocket or on your desk when you are negotiating or trying to attract new business. Jade also helps to keep your mind sharp if other people are blinding you with facts and figures.

CHILDREN

All forms of jade attract friendship and so are good for lonely or shy children. Jade is a good stone during the teenage years, to help balance hormonal swings and unstable emotions.

ANIMALS

A natural transmitter of life energies, jade helps to keep pets healthy and encourages longevity. Use the softer opaque shades of jade and place crystals overnight in water bowls. It is very helpful for an animal giving birth.

PROTECTIVE FUNCTIONS

Jade repels negativity from others and is a good stone to have in your workspace to keep away intrusions from unfriendly colleagues or overcritical employers. Jade protects babies and women, especially pregnant women and new mothers.

PSYCHIC ASSOCIATIONS

Jade is excellent both for interpreting your dreams and for developing lucid dreaming. Jade brings out innate healing abilities.

ENVIRONMENTAL WORK

Like moss agate, Jade is a gardener's crystal and encourages the growth of beautiful gardens. Also known also as a rain bringer, jade can act as a focus for anti-drought rites.

SPECIAL PROPERTIES

Traditionally, jade is used in lovemaking to create a deeply spiritual as well as an erotic experience and to unite lovers at every level.

RECHARGING ITS ENERGIES

Cleanse and recharge jade under running water or with a sage or peppermint infusion.

BOWENITE (NEW JADE)

MYTHOLOGY AND HISTORY
Bowenite was much beloved in Russia before the Revolution. Fabergé created a bowenite clock in honour of the birth of Tsar Nicholas and also used it to adorn a number of his legendary ornamental eggs.

DIVINATORY SIGNIFICANCE
Sometimes the kindest thing you can do is to stand back and let other people make their mistakes without interference.

HEALING AND THE ENVIRONMENT
Bowenite resembles polished jade. However, psychically it has much more powerful energies. A powerful but user-friendly stone, it

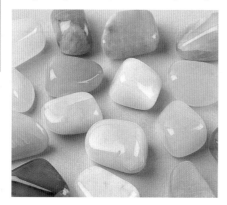

will ease skin disorders, strengthen the heart and help to stabilize blood-sugar levels. It also helps to balance hormonal swings and benefits nursing mothers who are having problems breastfeeding. Rub bowenite on the scalp to improve the health of both the scalp and hair. Also use it to help heal past traumas.

USES AT WORK AND HOME
A bringer of abundance to work and home, bowenite gives the confidence to try new activities and alternative methods. It redresses the balance if you have controlling partners at home or dominant colleagues at work.

CHILDREN AND ANIMALS
Bowenite is helpful for encouraging a child's independence, whether at school for the first time, changing schools or leaving home. It benefits habitually complaining children. It also motivates an inactive pet to explore.

PSYCHIC ASSOCIATIONS
Bowenite encourages you to become more spontaneous in divination and to trust your psychic powers. It is good in love rituals or as a gift to a lover who is reluctant to commit to a relationship through inertia or because his or her present life is very comfortable.

RECHARGING ITS ENERGIES
Smudge bowenite with cedar or sage.

SERPENTINE
See also bowenite (above)

MYTHOLOGY
Serpentine is so named because of its resemblance to snake skin (some kinds are scaly) and because of the associated belief that it protected against snake and other venomous bites. It was sacred to ancient snake goddesses: for example the Egyptian goddess Uadjet was pictured as a winged and crowned cobra, spitting poison at any who would do the pharaoh harm.

DIVINATORY SIGNIFICANCE
You may, like the snake, wish to shed your old skin and move on to a new beginning.

HEALING AND THE ENVIRONMENT
Serpentine directs its energies to the root of a problem or illness, even if this is not consciously known. Serpentine removes toxins and eases fatigue and illnesses that cause a lack of energy or muscle weakness. It calms nerves and soothes bites, stings, eczema and other skin disorders. It also balances hormones and mood swings.

USES AT HOME AND WORK
Serpentine will increase your self-confidence and teach you to trust your intuition in situations where there is no clear information

or others are trying to deceive you. It is protective against vicious tongues and scandalmongering.

CHILDREN AND ANIMALS
Serpentine encourages children to overcome fears of insects, snakes and lizards. It assists animals with skin complaints and helps to keep away fleas, ticks and mites.

PSYCHIC PROPERTIES
Serpentine strengthens connection with earth energies, especially at ancient sites and when working, through visualization, with energies of mythical creatures such as dragons.

RECHARGING ITS ENERGIES
Pass through the flame of a brown candle.

DIOPSIDE
See also violan (p57) and cat's eye (p144)

MYTHOLOGY AND HISTORY
This crystal is associated with the inner nature of people and the hidden mysteries of the universe. In its form as cat's eye and star diopside it holds secrets that must be explored by going within the stone – and ourselves.

HEALING AND THE ENVIRONMENT
Diopside will release deep-seated feelings that have been suppressed and cause headaches, raised blood pressure, eating disorders, addictions and obsessive behaviour. It is excellent for helping the elderly to cope with physical and mental disabilities and with degenerative conditions.

USES AT WORK AND HOME
Diopside is good for all forms of formal learning, for university and college courses for young adults and mature students and for retraining after redundancy or after a career change in later life. It also benefits those who are learning languages, and aids people who are taking their driving test. It helps authors and would-be authors to write more concisely and keep to schedules.

CHILDREN AND ANIMALS
Diopside will help a child with learning difficulties, especially dyslexia. It will effectively quieten excitable animals.

PSYCHIC ASSOCIATIONS
Diopside is a wonderful stone for meditation and exploring your inner world. The cat's eye and star forms are useful for scrying. Use it for discovering hidden places in nature and in towns. It will help you uncover forgotten knowledge in libraries and museums by allowing your intuition to guide you. Learn more about your essential self by holding the stone and sitting in darkness and silence until you can see colours in the darkness.

RECHARGING ITS ENERGIES
Use smudge to revitalize diopside.

PROPERTIES

TYPE: Serpentine, magnesium silicate. Gem-quality bowenite or new jade. Williamsite is softer

COLOUR: Olive to pale green. May be veined or spotted. Opaque green serpentine has brown or red inclusions. Rarely silvery

SYMBOLIC ASSOCIATIONS

ZODIAC SIGN: Scorpio
PLANET: Pluto
ELEMENT: Earth/water
CANDLE COLOUR: Brown
GUARDIAN ANGEL: Tubiel
CHAKRA: Solar plexus
HERBS, INCENSES AND OILS: Fennel, agrimony, dill, eau de cologne, lavender
FLOWERS: Flowering bramble, convolvulus and ground ivy
ASSOCIATED CRYSTALS: Amazonite, bowenite and leopardskin jasper

PROPERTIES

TYPE: Calcium-magnesium silicate or calcium-iron silicate

COLOUR: Light to greenish-brown to very dark green with a glassy or pearly lustre. Also white, transparent to translucent. Chromium-rich diopside is bright green. Sometimes found as a green cat's eye with tiny rutile inclusions. A much darker green diopside contains a shimmering four-pointed star

SYMBOLIC ASSOCIATIONS

ZODIAC SIGN: Gemini
PLANET: Mercury
ELEMENT: Air
CANDLE COLOUR: Silver
GUARDIAN ANGEL: Raphael
CHAKRA: Throat/heart
HERBS, INCENSES AND OILS: Clover, ferns, gum mastic, lavender and lemongrass
FLOWERS: Forsythia, impatiens and lilac
ASSOCIATED CRYSTALS: Cat's eye, rutilated quartz and violan

GREEN/ORBICULAR JASPER

See also yellow (p112), leopardskin (p142) and red (p128) jasper

See also yellow (p112), leopardskin (p142) and red (p128) jasper

PROPERTIES
TYPE: Chalcedony quartz. Opaque. Orbicular jasper can have gleaming green rhyolite with chalcedony inclusions
COLOUR: Light to dark green
SYMBOLIC ASSOCIATIONS
ZODIAC SIGN: Pisces
PLANET: Earth
ELEMENT: Earth/water
CANDLE COLOUR: Green or white
GUARDIAN ANGEL: Matariel
CHAKRA: Heart
HERBS, INCENSES AND OILS: Lotus, chamomile, kelp, lemon balm and water mosses
FLOWERS: Marsh marigold, sea lavender and water lily
ASSOCIATED CRYSTALS: Bloodstone, leopardskin jasper and moss agate

MYTHOLOGY AND HISTORY

Green jasper is the crystal of the rainmaker in a number of societies, including Eastern Europe and Native North America. The more exotic orbicular or ocean jasper comes from Madagascar and is given its name not only because of its appearance, but also because it can only be gathered at low tide. It is also called the moon gem because the orbs can resemble craters on the moon.

DIVINATORY SIGNIFICANCE

Green jasper signifies that new energies are coming into your life and is good for fertility in any way. Orbicular jasper reminds you to look for hidden meanings behind offers.

HEALING AND THE ENVIRONMENT

Green jasper helps the body to absorb nutrients from food, eases respiratory difficulties, especially those related to the weather, and prevents fluid build-up. Orbicular jasper relieves colds, flu and similar viral infections and restores the connection with biorhythms. Use orbicular or ocean jasper for healing polluted seas and protecting marine life; it is good when oil slicks occur.

USES AT WORK AND HOME

Green jasper balances different aspects of your life and prevents overwork burnout. Orbicular jasper takes the edge off competition and rivalry at work or home.

RIGHT Orbicular jasper is infused with the ebbs and flows of the sea and helps us to get in tune with our bodily and spiritual rhythms.

LEFT Green jasper is associated with the heart chakra.

CHILDREN AND ANIMALS
Both kinds of crystal will help a baby or young child establish proper sleep rhythms. It is good for both cold-water and tropical fish.

PSYCHIC ASSOCIATIONS
Green jasper gradually attracts money or good luck. Use orbicular jasper for working with the archetypal sea mothers and for visualizations or journeys beneath the sea.

RECHARGING ITS ENERGIES
Sprinkle with seawater or salted water.

GREEN GARNET

MYTHOLOGY AND HISTORY
Uvarovite and tsavorite are less common than grossular green garnet. The properties of all three types are almost identical. Use either the gem or rough form of garnet in healing, protective or magical work. Green garnet was a favourite gem of Fabergé, who used it to decorate his fabulous jewelled eggs.

DIVINATORY SIGNIFICANCE
It is a time when your heart is stirring, whether in love or a desire to travel or fulfil a dream. The feelings should be taken seriously even if the desire cannot be achieved at once.

HEALING AND THE ENVIRONMENT
All green garnets display anti-inflammatory properties and so are helpful for rheumatism, arthritis, mucous-membrane swelling, areas of irritation, boils, swollen scar tissue and wounds. They also help to detoxify the kidneys and the blood.

USES AT WORK OR HOME
Green garnets are excellent for bringing feelings and matters into the open in a positive way. At work green garnets will lessen the power of factions and reduce politicking. It is an excellent stone for protecting rural homes.

CHILDREN AND ANIMALS
It is not a stone for children or animals.

PSYCHIC ASSOCIATIONS
Use green garnet in rituals to find your twin soul, for helping secret love to become accepted by others and for protective rituals against emotional or psychic vampires.

RECHARGING ITS ENERGIES
Polish your stone carefully with a green silk cloth and speak a continuous chant for cleansing and empowerment.

PROPERTIES
TYPE: Island silicate. Uvarovite is calcium chromium silicate. Tsavorite, a sparkling grossularite garnet, contains vanadium and chromium. All are brilliant

COLOUR: Uvarovite is bright to emerald green, transparent to translucent. Andradite, called Demantoid, the green variety, used for gems, is light to medium green with horsetail, fibrous inclusions. Tsavorite is light, emerald or deep green

SYMBOLIC ASSOCIATIONS
ZODIAC SIGN: Taurus

PLANET: Venus

ELEMENT: Water/fire

CANDLE COLOUR: Green

GUARDIAN ANGEL: Anael

CHAKRA: Heart

HERBS, INCENSES AND OILS: Mimosa, neroli, rose, rosemary and ylang ylang

FLOWERS: Cyclamen, freesia and rose

ASSOCIATED CRYSTALS: Serpentine, emerald and red garnet

LEFT Uvarovite has the power to heal dissension or bad feelings in the workplace or at home.

DIOPTASE

PROPERTIES

TYPE: Hydrated copper silicate. Usually too soft for a gemstone. Transparent and shiny or slightly translucent

COLOUR: Emerald to deep, rich green

SYMBOLIC ASSOCIATIONS

ZODIAC SIGN: Taurus

PLANET: Venus

ELEMENT: Earth

CANDLE COLOUR: Deep pink

GUARDIAN ANGEL: Hagiel

CHAKRA: Heart

HERBS, INCENSES AND OILS: Lemon balm, geranium, rose, tansy and vanilla

FLOWERS: Lobelia, pink roses and wisteria

ASSOCIATED CRYSTALS: Chrysocolla, copper and emerald

MYTHOLOGY AND HISTORY
Called the copper emerald, like the emerald it is a stone of Venus and the love goddesses, but in their most gentle, benign aspects, displaying platonic love and compassion to humankind, the earth and its creatures.

DIVINATORY SIGNIFICANCE
Gracefully let go of what cannot be mended and above all forgive yourself for being only human after all.

HEALING AND THE ENVIRONMENT
Dioptase promotes a healthy cardiovascular and central nervous system, aids the heart and helps maintain stable blood pressure. It will ease ulcers of all kinds and stomach upsets,

especially those caused by stress. Above all, dioptase stops us from abusing our own bodies carelessly or through a lack of self-love. Healers should keep one with them to make sure they do not absorb their patients' illnesses through over-empathizing.

Use to heal hatred between nations and within nations and to soften prejudices and bigotry of all kinds.

USES AT WORK AND HOME
If you have had a hard time lately, dioptase will bring good things back into your life, though they may not be what you thought you wanted. Dioptase helps to mend family quarrels (send tiny pieces with a note of reconciliation). Use it also to return to employment without bitterness if you were unfairly dismissed or demoted.

CHILDREN AND ANIMALS
Dioptase teaches children to be forgiving, especially when they discover that their parents or best friends are not perfect. Use it for small birds and tiny animal pets. Dioptase encourages children to handle them gently.

PSYCHIC ASSOCIATIONS
Use dioptase in abundance rituals and when banishing old sorrows.

RECHARGING ITS ENERGIES
Dioptase is very delicate: pass an amethyst or rose quartz pendulum over it.

RAINBOW OBSIDIAN

MYTHOLOGY AND HISTORY
Rainbow obsidian is volcanic glass/magma, formed when lava hardens so fast no crystalline structures are created. Like all rainbow stones, it is said to be found at the end of the rainbow and has the power to grant wishes. Rainbow obsidian spheres are highly prized for scrying.

DIVINATORY SIGNIFICANCE
Make sure you take time for personal fun and happiness if you have experienced a difficult or labour-intensive period.

HEALING AND THE ENVIRONMENT
Rainbow obsidian draws out pain and absorbs negative energies, both physical and mental. It is an excellent stone for healers to use to cleanse the atmosphere and their own aura after giving healing. It may also bring about an unexpected sudden improvement in a chronic condition.

USES AT WORK AND HOME
Rainbow obsidian relieves fears over problems at home or work that can leave you paralyzed in inaction. This stone will also turn around

misfortune or a run of bad luck and attract happiness and prosperity instead.

CHILDREN AND ANIMALS
Rainbow obsidian is a lovely crystal to give a child as a present because it will continue to be a lucky charm throughout their life. Rainbow obsidian improves the well-being of all aquatic creatures.

PSYCHIC ASSOCIATIONS
Rainbow obsidian is potent for all transformation rituals and is excellent for scrying and for night magic. It strengthens prophetic abilities and it is a wonderful focus for wish magic and visualizing what it is you need. Hold your obsidian to sunlight so you can see the rainbows; name your fear and plunge the obsidian in a bowl of water, scattering rainbows of hope as you pull it out.

RECHARGING ITS ENERGIES
Revitalize rainbow obidian whenever there is a rainbow in the sky, or use a rainbow transfer on a window which catches the light.

PROPERTIES	
TYPE: Volcanic glass/magma. It has an iridescent chatoyant gleam, caused by trapped water bubbles	
COLOUR: Characterized by the rainbow sheen. Some is green with flashes of purple, red and blue, others are blacker with a blue sheen	
SYMBOLIC ASSOCIATIONS	
ZODIAC SIGN: Cancer	
PLANET: Moon	
ELEMENT: Fire/water	
CANDLE COLOUR: Silver	
GUARDIAN ANGEL: Zachariel	
CHAKRA: Sacral	
HERBS, INCENSES AND OILS: Apricot, ambergris (synthetic), eucalyptus, lemon and lemon balm	
FLOWERS: Jasmine, sea holly and water lily	
ASSOCIATED CRYSTALS: Rainbow opal, rainbow quartz and moldavite	

UNAKITE

MYTHOLOGY AND HISTORY
In magic unakite has become associated with the harmonious union of Mars and Venus and can be given as a token between married couples or long-term partners, as a symbol of their union. Sometimes at handfastings (Wiccan weddings) unakite is bound with yarrow, a herb of marriage.

HEALING AND THE ENVIRONMENT
Unakite can be used during labour to promote an easy birth. It triggers the body's self-healing processes and balances bodily fluids and metabolism. Unakite can also be used to encourage a regular breathing rhythm. It relieves obsessions or compulsions that have their roots in the past, even helping with childhood trauma.

Above all, for both self-healing and when healing others, unakite uncovers the roots of a problem and gently releases any blockages that may be preventing healing energies from flowing throughout the system.

In the environment, unakite is good for protecting endangered plant species.

USES AT WORK AND HOME
The stone of partnerships, unakite promotes harmonious relationships, both in love and in business. Use it for taking calculated risks and for making wise investments.

CHILDREN AND ANIMALS:
Unakite creates a safe place for children to talk about their problems. Use unakite when you are breeding animals.

PSYCHIC PROPERTIES
Unakite is the stone of rebirthing and for communicating with unborn children: a stone for fathers- and mothers-to-be. It is a joy to work with in fidelity rituals and wish magic.

RECHARGING ITS ENERGIES
Sprinkle unakite with a drop of olive oil and then carefully wash in running water.

PROPERTIES	
TYPE: A mixture of epidote or pisctacite and feldspar	
COLOUR: Moss or olive green and salmon pink or red	
SYMBOLIC ASSOCIATIONS	
ZODIAC SIGN: Scorpio	
PLANET: Mars/Venus	
ELEMENT: Fire/water	
CANDLE COLOUR: Pink	
GUARDIAN ANGEL: Theliel	
CHAKRA: Heart	
HERBS, INCENSES AND OILS: Apple blossom, marjoram, moss, rose and yarrow	
FLOWERS: Hibiscus, lily of the valley and passionflower	
ASSOCIATED CRYSTALS: Moss agate, rhodonite and tree agate	

PROPERTIES

TYPE: Silicate/zeolite. Transparent; or, more usually, translucent and lustrous with inclusions or ghost crystals within. Broken surfaces shine like mother-of-pearl

COLOUR: Pale or mint green to yellowy- or browny-green

SYMBOLIC ASSOCIATIONS

ZODIAC SIGN: Virgo

PLANET: Venus

ELEMENT: Earth

CANDLE COLOUR: Pale green

GUARDIAN ANGEL: Hamaliel

CHAKRA: Heart

HERBS, INCENSES AND OILS: Bergamot, moss, peppermint, rosemary and thyme

FLOWERS: Almond blossom, clover and lavender

ASSOCIATED CRYSTALS: Bowenite, peridot and serpentine

PREHNITE

See also apophyllite (p35)

MYTHOLOGY AND HISTORY

Named after Major Prehn, who discovered it at the end of the eighteenth century in South Africa, prehnite was previously used as a stone of prophecy and shamanism by indigenous sangomas (medicine men and women). In modern magic it is known as the prophecy stone.

DIVINATORY SIGNIFICANCE

Do not be afraid to acknowledge your negative feelings and to express them in a non-aggressive way.

HEALING AND THE ENVIRONMENT

Prehnite removes toxins from the system, helps the metabolism and bloodstream to function more efficiently, balances the meridians in the body and calms high blood pressure and hypertension. It is excellent for relieving claustrophobia and agoraphobia and is good for absent healing.

USES AT HOME AND WORK

Prehnite is probably the best stone for helping you to say no to unreasonable requests at home and work. It is especially good for women who find it difficult to express anger or to make demands of others, especially in a male-dominated environment. Leave one to protect your home when you go on holiday.

CHILDREN AND ANIMALS

Prehnite is useful as it effectively calms hyperactive children or animals.

PSYCHIC PROPERTIES

Prehnite is used to induce lucid dreaming. Hold the crystal when you wake to help you to recall your dreams. Place one next to tarot cards, a crystal ball or any other divinatory tool to increase your prophetic abilities.

RECHARGING ITS ENERGIES

Surround it by greenery for twenty-four hours.

PROPERTIES

TYPE: Island silicate. Transparent: olivine is more translucent

COLOUR: Olivine is olive; peridot is pale to bottle-green

SYMBOLIC ASSOCIATIONS

ZODIAC SIGN: Taurus

PLANET: Venus

ELEMENT: Earth

CANDLE COLOUR: Olive or dark green

GUARDIAN ANGEL: Achaiah

CHAKRA: Heart

HERBS, INCENSES AND OILS: Ivy, lavender, olive, patchouli and pine

FLOWERS: Hyacinth, lilac and orchid

ASSOCIATED CRYSTALS: Emerald, green topaz and serpentine

OLIVINE/PERIDOT

MYTHOLOGY AND HISTORY

The gem form of olivine is called peridot or chlorite. It is found in meteorites and in deep rock that may be brought to the surface during volcanic activity.

It was regarded as a wondrous stone in many ancient cultures, including that of the Ancient Egyptians, who mistakenly called peridots emeralds. Along with golden topaz, peridot was found on the Serpent Isle, a snake-infested island in the Red Sea. Again like golden topaz, peridot was believed to be visible only after dark. Olivine crystals are said to be the tears of the Hawaiian volcano goddess Pele.

DIVINATORY SIGNIFICANCE

One of the most fortunate stones, peridot indicates an in-flow of money, love, luck and peace into your life.

HEALING AND THE ENVIRONMENT

A general healer, olivine and peridot will cool fevers and ease liver and gall bladder problems. It effectively relieves insect bites, swellings, asthma and allergic reactions. It also helps to remedy breast, heart or lung problems. Use peridot to flood your mind, body and spirit with a sense of peace and well-being. It will also set up a protective shield around your aura.

USES AT WORK AND HOME
Olivine, as sand or tiny crystals, will attract money and good fortune into your home. A peridot in your purse or with your mobile will deter pickpockets and muggers. At work, olivine and peridot are helpful for businesses that involve direct selling or money exchange. Add one to a prosperity charm bag.

CHILDREN AND ANIMALS
Olivine and peridot help a child to mend a broken friendship and to become less anxious about peer pressures. They will de-stress a hyperactive pet.

PSYCHIC ASSOCIATIONS
As well as drawing money and luck, olivine and peridot are good for marriage and fidelity. They reflect negativity back to the sender.

RECHARGING ITS ENERGIES
Leave them under the light of a full moon.

BLUE GOLDSTONE

HISTORY AND MYTHOLOGY
Verdite, which comes only from South Africa and Zimbabwe, is called the green stone of Africa. It is of great antiquity: the oldest form of exposed rock dates back more than three and a half million years. It has been used by indigenous craftsmen for carving animals and sacred ancestral statues throughout the millennia and it is still used in sculpture today. Small pieces can be bought for healing and magical uses.

DIVINATORY SIGNIFICANCE
Look to traditional knowledge or wise older family members to guide you at the moment

HEALING AND THE ENVIRONMENT
Verdite acts as a cleanser and oxygenator for the blood. It relieves all genito-urinary problems and is good for sexual dysfunction, especially that caused by anxiety. In its native South Africa it is traditionally used to enhance both fertility and potency.

USES AT WORK AND HOME
Verdite will soften impatience, sarcasm, abrasiveness and irritability, whether your own or that of a family member, colleague, employer or employee.

CHILDREN AND ANIMALS
Verdite puts children in touch with their family and cultural heritage. Use verdite when breeding pedigree animals.

PSYCHIC ASSOCIATIONS
Verdite can be used for positive encounters with ghosts, for channelling the wisdom of the ancestors, for visualization work with the archetypal qualities of wild animals, especially those from South Africa, and for past-life work. Make verdite part of a fertility or abundance charm bag.

RECHARGING ITS ENERGIES
Place verdite among the leaves of any tropical greenery or near to an indoor plant.

PROPERTIES

TYPE: Silicate; found close to gold deposits. Opaque

COLOUR: Often deep green, other shades of green, rich emerald and golden brown. It may be mottled with white, red, or yellow or lighter green

SYMBOLIC ASSOCIATIONS

ZODIAC SIGN: Virgo

PLANET: Earth

ELEMENT: Earth

CANDLE COLOUR: Green or gold

GUARDIAN ANGEL: Zachariel

CHAKRA: Heart / root

HERBS, INCENSES AND OILS: Orange, avocado, mimosa, patchouli and sunflower

FLOWERS: Amaranth, hydrangea and schizostylis

ASSOCIATED CRYSTALS: Bloodstone, green jasper and serpentine

FUCHSITE

PROPERTIES

TYPE: Hydrous potassium aluminium silicate. Opaque

COLOUR: Dark emerald green

SYMBOLIC ASSOCIATIONS

ZODIAC SIGN: Libra

PLANET: Venus

ELEMENT: Air

CANDLE COLOUR: Metallic

GUARDIAN ANGEL: Hadakiel

CHAKRA: Throat / heart

HERBS, INCENSES AND OILS: Aloe vera, avocado, magnolia, marjoram and violet

FLOWERS: Apple blossom, fuchsia and sweet pea

ASSOCIATED CRYSTALS: Green aventurine, iron pyrites and moss agate

MYTHOLOGY AND HISTORY

Because it shimmers, fuchsite was considered a gift from the earth spirits, the Virgin Mary or Iemanjá, the Sea Goddess, in its homeland of Brazil. It is thought to grant blessings and the promise of better fortune.

DIVINATORY SIGNIFICANCE

This is a creative period; you can develop new interests or emerging psychic or healing talent.

HEALING THE ENVIRONMENT

Fuchsite aids recovery from illness or exhaustion, restores energy levels and brings

continued health; its healing powers will penetrate deep within the body. It also eases problems with the larynx, the throat and the arteries. Perhaps most importantly, it increases the will to get better.

USES AT WORK AND HOME

Fuchsite will generate a sense of beauty and grace in your home. At work it is a stone both of inspired thinking and also a diplomatic approach to resolve long-standing irritations. In both spheres fuchsite encourages cooperation and teamwork and so can be a stabilizer if the family members rarely meet because of different schedules. It also brings fun back into your life.

CHILDREN AND ANIMALS

Fuchsite helps children appreciate beautiful things and the importance of conservation in a throwaway society. It is good for exotic birds, such as parrots.

PSYCHIC ASSOCIATIONS

Fuchsite is a stone of astral projection and a focus for contact with angelic beings and spirit guides and fairy magic. Use a small piece (wrapped very carefully as it is brittle) in a good luck charm bag.

RECHARGING ITS ENERGIES

Use starlight, a fibre optic lamp or fairy lights.

CHINESE TURQUOISE

MYTHOLOGY AND HISTORY

Chinese turquoise is often greener than that from the Near and Middle East and the Americas and feels much gentler and smoother. Although popular for carvings and jewellery, turquoise was not mined in China itself until the thirteenth century. However, neighbouring Tibet had a rich source of turquoise. Both the stone and the powder or ointment made from it was valued in Tibet and China for its curative properties.

DIVINATORY SIGNIFICANCE

Chinese turquoise is the power stone, but it represents the power of love. It signifies that

love will win through eventually and your happiness will be well worth waiting for.

HEALING AND THE ENVIRONMENT

Chinese turquoise is soothing for eyes, for stomach and intestinal problems, especially those resulting in internal bleeding and for skin complaints, stings, bites and rashes. It is good for preventing mood swings and repetitive behaviour patterns that are not related to the actual situation.

USES AT WORK AND HOME

Chinese turquoise is a bridge-builder among stepfamilies, friends and neighbours and work

colleagues. It is especially potent where you need to work as part of a team. It is good for all situations where people live together, for example colleges and for house sharing.

VARISCITE

MYTHOLOGY AND HISTORY
Variscite is named after the Latin word for Vogtland in Saxony, where its colour matched the costumes of the traditional spring festivals (these may still be seen today). Because of its resemblance to tracks across the land, it was also a focus in sacred earth awareness ceremonies among the Native Americans and Australian Aboriginals.

DIVINATORY SIGNIFICANCE
Seek new contacts and friends through your existing network. You may enjoy a new group activity or holiday more than you think.

HEALING AND THE ENVIRONMENT
Variscite calms and balances both the body and the nervous system and acts as a preventative as well as a healing crystal. It revitalizes the blood, the main arteries and the vessels of the heart. Use it as a focus for the conservation of ancient sites and sacred waters.

USES AT WORK AND HOME
Variscite will increase your social confidence if you are in a new environment or are naturally shy. It also attracts abundance to the home and will stabilize an uncertain work situation. Variscite is also effective for networking, redeployment or relocation.

CHILDREN AND ANIMALS
Since Chinese turquoise is softer than ordinary turquoise, it is especially protective for babies and young children, whom it will help without overwhelming them with its energies. Chinese turquoise is similarly useful for small or baby animals.

PSYCHIC ASSOCIATIONS
Chinese turquoise is excellent for creating psychic dreams. It is useful for all forms of love and fidelity magic, especially young love or love that has to rebuild trust.

RECHARGING ITS ENERGIES
Leave it in moonlight under an early waxing moon phase, from when you first see the moon in the sky (that may be during the daytime) until you go to bed. Then place it under your pillow for the night.

CHILDREN AND ANIMALS
Variscite gives children a sense of history and of the sacred in nature. It settles animals living in a different habitat or climate from that of their species.

PSYCHIC ASSOCIATIONS
It is one of the best earth-energy stones for working with sacred earth sites, stone circles, turf labyrinths, barrows and holy wells. Use it for dowsing and for channelling the wisdom of earth guardians, for vision quests, spiritual journeys and for following ley lines.

RECHARGING ITS ENERGIES
Rest it on a standing stone or in a stone circle.

PROPERTIES

TYPE: Phosphate of aluminium with copper and traces of iron

COLOUR: Green, soft turquoise or blue, sometimes with a spider web of brown, grey or black veins or patches

SYMBOLIC ASSOCIATIONS

ZODIAC SIGN: Libra

PLANET: Venus

ELEMENT: Air

CANDLE COLOUR: Turquoise

GUARDIAN ANGEL: Zuriel

CHAKRA: Throat/heart

HERBS, INCENSES AND OILS: Rose, chamomile, rosewood, sandalwood and ylang ylang

FLOWERS: Blue hyacinth, harebell and narcissus

ASSOCIATED CRYSTALS: Apatite, jade and orbicular jasper

PROPERTIES

TYPE: Hydrated aluminium phosphate. Translucent

COLOUR: Most commonly light green. Also apple to bright green, bluish-green or turquoise or colourless. It usually has patterned light and darker brown veins across the surface

SYMBOLIC ASSOCIATIONS

ZODIAC SIGN: Virgo

PLANET: Earth

ELEMENT: Earth

CANDLE COLOUR: Bright green

GUARDIAN ANGEL: Aragael

CHAKRA: Heart/solar plexus

HERBS, INCENSES AND OILS: Almond, bistort, cedarwood, lemon verbena and tea tree

FLOWERS: Anemone, primrose and sweet tobacco

ASSOCIATED CRYSTALS: Apatite, Chinese turquoise and jade

WATERMELON TOURMALINE

PROPERTIES

TYPE: Complex silicate of boron and aluminium V. Transparent, translucent or opaque. Pleochroic (it can appear transparent when viewed from the side and almost opaque by looking down the long axis from either end)

COLOUR: Green outer core with inner red or pink. Striated in its natural form

SYMBOLIC ASSOCIATIONS

ZODIAC SIGN: Sagittarius

PLANET: Venus/Mars

ELEMENT: Water/fire

CANDLE COLOUR: Pink

GUARDIAN ANGEL: Raphael

CHAKRA: Heart

HERBS, INCENSES AND OILS: Rose, cardamom, geranium, liquorice and vanilla

FLOWERS: Apple blossom, orange blossom and all tiny roses or rosebuds

ASSOCIATED CRYSTALS: Green calcite, pink calcite and ruby in zoisite

MYTHOLOGY AND HISTORY

Watermelon tourmaline is one of the banded and most highly prized tourmaline forms. Tourmaline is named from the Singhalese word turamali (coloured stone) because it is found in every colour of the rainbow and has more colour varieties than any other crystal. Perhaps for this reason, in Arabia it was called the stone of the sun (or light), because white light contains the rainbow colours.

DIVINATORY SIGNIFICANCE

What would make you happy? Take time to find out and do something, however small, to give you pleasure every day.

HEALING AND THE ENVIRONMENT

The blending of red and pink or green makes it the perfect stone for reconciling conflicts of physical and emotional energies within the body that may be the underlying cause of illness or discomfort.

USES AT WORK AND HOME

Watermelon tourmaline is a good stone for merging different personalities and factions at work and home. It is also useful for large gatherings, such as Christmas parties, weddings, office parties and conventions. It is a very healing stone when a relationship is going through a difficult period, and will deflect quarrels or bitter words.

CHILDREN AND ANIMALS

Watermelon tourmaline will heal stressed and distressed children and animals. It is especially useful at a time of domestic upheaval or unhappiness.

PSYCHIC ASSOCIATIONS

The crystal of healers and apprentice healers, it is wonderful as a wand or as a double-terminated crystal – one end will be positive and energizing, the other receptive and calming. Try holding different crystals until you find your special healer. It will cleanse and energize chakras and auras and can substitute for a quartz crystal pendulum.

RECHARGING ITS ENERGIES

Revitalize watermelon tourmaline at twilight on three consecutive nights.

CHRYSOPRASE

See also lemon chrysoprase (p119)

MYTHOLOGY AND HISTORY

Associated with the sign of Taurus, in medieval times chrysoprase was engraved with the image of a bull to give strength and protection to the wearer. Chrysoprase is said to have fallen from the apple trees in heaven. The medieval mystic Hildegard von Bingen recommended chrysoprase for turning anger into soft words of forgiveness.

DIVINATORY SIGNIFICANCE

A stone of spring, chrysoprase represents a change of heart by others or a new opportunity for you concerning situations that have seemed hopeless or avenues that you thought closed.

HEALING AND THE ENVIRONMENT

If you or the people you are working with are new to healing, chrysoprase will make the body, spirit and mind receptive to healing energies. It is good for stomach ulcers and other digestive disorders and skin perforations or infected areas. Chrysoprase will fill the mind and spirit with optimism and give the impetus to get back into the mainstream of life after illness or despair.

USES AT WORK AND HOME

At any time of the year, open all the windows and doors at home and place a chrysoprase near the front and back or patio doors. This will give your home a psychic spring clean and attract all types of abundance – of health, happiness and enthusiasm as well as materially. At work, chrysoprase is excellent for beginning a new job, venture or project.

CHILDREN AND ANIMALS

It is excellent for helping to mend a heart broken by first love. It also aids children who fear failure and who are stressed by exams, unfamiliar subjects or coursework. Animals welcome chrysoprase during a long winter.

PSYCHIC PROPERTIES

A money and fertility charm, chrysoprase is an excellent stone for meditation, especially outdoors to connect you with natural energies, nature spirits and magical animals. Keep a piece with tarot cards to help you see the unexpected in a reading.

RECHARGING ITS ENERGIES

Revitalize chrysoprase in a light rain shower.

PROPERTIES
TYPE: Chalcedony (quartz) with nickel. Opaque
COLOUR: Apple green and lighter greens but always with even-colour quartz
SYMBOLIC ASSOCIATIONS
ZODIAC SIGN: Taurus
PLANET: Venus
ELEMENT: Earth
CANDLE COLOUR: Mint or apple green
GUARDIAN ANGEL: Tual
CHAKRA: Heart
HERBS, INCENSES AND OILS: Apple blossom, lemon balm, rose, vervain and vetivert
FLOWERS: Anemone, evening primrose and daisy
ASSOCIATED CRYSTALS: Green aventurine, green calcite and jade

ROSE QUARTZ

The crystal of gentle love, rose quartz has an affinity to the heart chakra. It is the crystal of peacemaking and is associated with practical gestures of concern. Rose quartz is lucky for those born under the sign of Taurus.

PROPERTIES

TYPE: Rose quartz

COLOUR: Pink

SYMBOLIC ASSOCIATIONS

ZODIAC SIGN: Taurus

PLANET: Venus

ELEMENT: Earth

CANDLE COLOUR: Pink

GUARDIAN ANGEL: Ashmodiel

CHAKRA: Heart

HERBS, INCENSES AND OILS: Vervain, echinacea, feverfew, geranium, mugwort, strawberry and ylang ylang

FLOWERS: Apple blossom, daisy, lilac and rose

ASSOCIATED CRYSTALS: Amethyst, moonstone and jade

MYTHOLOGY AND HISTORY

Adonis, lover of the Greek goddess Aphrodite (Venus in Roman lore), was attacked by Ares, god of war, in the form of a boar. Aphrodite rushed to save him and caught herself on a briar bush. Their mingled blood stained the white quartz pink. Zeus took pity on them and restored Adonis to Aphrodite for six months of the year. Because of this myth, rose quartz has become a symbol of reconciliation in love. It later became an appropriate gift to signify love among Roman youth.

Rose quartz is associated in modern ritual with Isis. An astrologer dropped a piece into the waters surrounding Isis's temple at Philae, Upper Egypt, as a way of maintaining contact with this place when she was back in England.

DIVINATORY SIGNIFICANCE

The 'heart stone', rose quartz is the crystal of reconciliation. It indicates you may become a

peacemaker either within your family or at work. But be sure not to be hurt by the combatants. It also indicates blossoming love and friendship or a gentler enduring love after the first passion of a relationship has faded or after a betrayal, again indicating the possibility of reconciliation.

HEALING PROPERTIES

Rose quartz is essential for healers: it will ease pain or tension, cuts or bruises, and emotional wounds, such as grief, stress, fear or anger.

USES AT WORK AND HOME

Rose quartz is an excellent stone for bringing peace. If a phone call unexpectedly becomes confrontational, circle a rose quartz anti-clockwise around the phone as you speak to absorb negativity.

It is also good for ongoing protection against intrusion or spite. Place a large piece of unpolished rose quartz with a pointed end in your personal work space. You can normally have the point facing a wall, but when an unwelcome intrusion comes your way, turn the crystal toward the unwanted visitor. The crystal will not harm, but merely act as a barrier. The intruder may stop, look puzzled as if trying to remember why he or she wanted to bother you and go off.

CHILDREN

Rose quartz is known as the children's stone because youngsters will instinctively choose this crystal out of a number of different ones if they have a headache. An unpolished chunk of rose quartz beneath a baby's cot will soothe restlessness and fretfulness. It is also good for teenage angst; a rose quartz can help a girl through the early stages of blossoming womanhood as it is very good for increasing healthy self-love and self-esteem.

ANIMALS

Rose quartz is an excellent stone for animals

who have been obtained from a rescue centre, who may be traumatized, or for strays. It is also useful for pregnant animals and their young. Water in which a rose quartz crystal has been soaked for eight hours can be given to calm a hyperactive animal.

PROTECTIVE FUNCTIONS

Rose quartz keeps away nightmares and helps to avoid addictive behaviour, especially food disorders associated with a poor self-image.

PSYCHIC ASSOCIATIONS

This is excellent for grounding after psychic work. Spheres are good for love divination. In love magic, it can act as a talisman to attract a lover or for deeper commitment. Rose quartz is used in fertility magic: place one in half an eggshell and leave on a window ledge from the crescent to the full moon. On the night of the full moon, prick the rose quartz with a tiny silver pin prior to love-making. Leave the rose quartz and pin in the eggshell until noon the next day, then wrap them all in white silk and keep in a drawer until the next crescent moon, when the spell is repeated.

ENVIRONMENTAL WORK
Circle a picture of a war-torn place with a piece of rose quartz while you recite a prayer for peace. Bury a piece in a polluted area.

SPECIAL PROPERTIES
Rose quartz can, initially, release suppressed emotions. If you can allow these feelings to flow from you, perhaps symbolically casting very tiny rose quartz shards into flowing water, you will experience a sense of freedom.

RECHARGING ITS ENERGIES
Cleanse and recharge rose quartz frequently if the colour begins to fade by sprinkling it with a few drops of rose water.

PINK TOURMALINE
See also verdite (p95) and watermelon tourmaline (p98)

MYTHOLOGY AND HISTORY
Pink tourmaline was the favourite crystal of Tz'u Hsi, the last Empress of China. When she died, her head was supported by a pillow made of pink tourmaline. Pink tourmaline is also called rubellite.

DIVINATORY SIGNIFICANCE
Though you are by nature caring, you may have heard one too many hard luck stories from a particular individual. You may need to show tough, rather than unconditional, love.

HEALING AND ENVIRONMENTAL
Pinker shades of tourmaline are excellent for a person who has not experienced healing before, to allow the power to flow via their heart. Pink tourmaline steadies the heart and is effective for chronic lung complaints. It is good also for allowing female/anima energies to find expression in both women and men.

The redder the stone, the more powerful its energies. Redder shades will unblock a sluggish root centre, allowing the life force to flow freely. Red tourmaline energizes the whole system and relieves chills, coughs and colds, muscle spasms and weakness. Use it for empowerments to translate good intentions into practical action in charity work.

CHILDREN AND ANIMALS
Pink tourmaline in all shades is helpful for girls and also boys approaching puberty. It helps broody animals that cannot have young.

USES AT WORK AND HOME
Pink tourmaline increases self-image so that we are able to open ourselves to friendship,

love and praise. At home or work, pink tourmaline will help you to make difficult decisions or deliver bad news with compassion. It is associated with all forms of learning, training and study.

PSYCHIC PROPERTIES
It is an effective block against powerful negativity. Use pink tourmaline for channelling from higher planes, especially from wise teachers who have chosen to work with humankind from the spirit world.

RECHARGING ITS ENERGIES
Revitalize pink tourmaline with still mineral water or by burning a barberry candle.

PROPERTIES
TYPE: Pink or red tourmaline. Complex silicate of boron and aluminium, composition varies
COLOUR: Pink to red
SYMBOLIC ASSOCIATIONS
ZODIAC SIGN: Taurus
PLANET: Venus/Mars (for redder shades)
ELEMENT: Water
CANDLE COLOUR: Dark pink
GUARDIAN ANGEL: Ashmodiel
CHAKRA: Heart/root
HERBS, INCENSES AND OILS: Aloe vera, barberry, valerian, vetivert and ylang ylang
FLOWERS: Amaryllis, hydrangea and rhododendron
ASSOCIATED CRYSTALS: Green fluorite, ruby in zoisite and pink spinel

CORAL
See also blue coral (p65)

PROPERTIES

TYPE: Organic, calcareous skeletons of sea creatures

COLOUR: Red, orange, salmon to paler pink and white

SYMBOLIC ASSOCIATIONS

ZODIAC SIGN: Scorpio

PLANET: Neptune

ELEMENT: Water

CANDLE COLOUR: Orange

GUARDIAN ANGEL: Rahab

CHAKRA: Heart

HERBS, INCENSES AND OILS: Allspice, cloves, cumin, kelp, pine and sweetgrass

FLOWERS: Sea lavender, hibiscus and oleander

ASSOCIATED CRYSTALS: Red jasper, amber and carnelian

MYTHOLOGY AND HISTORY
The Ancient Greeks believed coral was formed from the severed head of Medusa. Other legends say the mother goddess may be found in a tree of coral in the ocean. Highly polished coral can shine with a translucent beauty and is often used in jewellery.

DIVINATORY SIGNIFICANCE
Coral is not used in divination.

HEALING AND THE ENVIRONMENT
Primarily a fertility stone for women, coral also eases menstrual cramps and aids a regular monthly flow. In older women, coral warms arthritic bones and joints and aids tissue and bone regrowth. Use coral in rituals for less polluted seas.

USES AT WORK AND HOME
Coral brings luck to the home and protects it from inclement weather. It is the stone of all who work on or near water, bringing good fortune and guarding them from harm. It also helps all who rely on the land for a living.

CHILDREN AND ANIMALS
Traditionally worn by children to prevent falls, coral is a good amulet against accidents, especially in the early years and near water. It was used in rattles to ease children's teething pains, but can be used as an amulet rather than to bite on. Some modern Wiccans and goddess devotees hang coral on an infant's cradle to ask for the protection of the Goddess.

PSYCHIC ASSOCIATIONS
Coral is central to all sea rituals and is important in love and sex magic. Brighter shades of coral will attract passionate love. It is good also for creating psychic invisibility when you need to keep a low profile and for discovering the intentions of others. Coral is an effective fertility charm.

RECHARGING ITS ENERGIES
Recharge under the crescent moon at night.

PINK CHALCEDONY
See also blue chalcedony (page 69)

MYTHOLOGY AND HISTORY
Since the sixteenth century, magicians have worn chalcedony as an amulet to banish dark phantoms and visions, especially at night. White chalcedony is used by new mothers to increase their milk supply, and pink to protect the baby from harm in the early days of life. Pink chalcedony is a Goddess stone.

DIVINATORY SIGNIFICANCE
Pink chalcedony signifies that the secret fears that may keep you awake are unfounded and that you should talk about them to a trusted friend. They will then begin to lose their power over your life.

HEALING AND THE ENVIRONMENT
Pink chalcedony relieves shock and trauma. It is an excellent stone for helping first-time mothers when they are giving birth. It is helpful also for post-natal problems, especially after a prolonged birth or one involving medical intervention, such as forceps or Caesarean section.

organization: it will help you to settle in more easily and create a home base for yourself.

CHILDREN AND ANIMALS
It can ease the tensions of children who feel unloved, such as at a time of divorce. It will help a foster, step or adoptive child who has conflicting loyalties or is afraid to love again.

PSYCHIC ASSOCIATIONS
It can be used in rituals to increase self-love and self-esteem. Use it in gentle banishing magic: allow the stone to absorb your regrets and then hold it under flowing water.

RECHARGING ITS ENERGIES
Use running water to recharge chalcedony.

USES AT WORK AND HOME
Pink chalcedony will make it easier to cope with difficult children or relations. Use it if you work for a large or impersonal

PROPERTIES

TYPE: Cryptocrystalline quartz

COLOUR: Ferrous oxide impurities give varying shades of pink

SYMBOLIC ASSOCIATIONS

ZODIAC SIGN: Pisces

PLANET: Moon

ELEMENT: Water

CANDLE COLOUR: Mauve

GUARDIAN ANGEL: Varchiel

CHAKRA: Heart

HERBS, INCENSES AND OILS: Lemon verbena, lily of the valley, mimosa, rosewood and violet

FLOWERS: Crocus, cyclamen and pink roses

ASSOCIATED CRYSTALS: Milky quartz, pink moonstone and rose quartz

KUNZITE

MYTHOLOGY AND HISTORY
Discovered at the beginning of the last century, kunzite has rapidly become known as the woman's stone and is loved particularly by goddess worshippers.

DIVINATORY SIGNIFICANCE
Kunzite suggests it is important to flow with life and to allow events to unfold and resolve themselves, rather than confronting issues.

HEALING AND THE ENVIRONMENT
For women, kunzite relieves hormonal problems – premenstrual, menstrual and menopausal. It eases pregnancy, the early days of motherhood and lingering post-natal depression. Kunzite relaxes tense muscles and relieves tension headaches, panic attacks, mood swings and psychosomatic illnesses. It is beneficial for addictions, phobias or compulsions linked with low self-image. Kunzite counters man-made pollutants, and is useful against both chemical toxicity and that from the unwise use of radiation.

USES AT WORK AND HOME
Put kunzite in a charm bag when travelling by car, both to counter road rage in others and to calm your own tensions in traffic. At work, place kunzite in your workspace as an effective counter against undue pressure. It will also relieve the effects of noise, harsh lighting and inefficient air conditioning.

CHILDREN AND ANIMALS
Kunzite helps girls and boys to contact their gentler side. Give it to adolescent girls to assist them through early menstrual problems and fears. It helps babies to get used to the world after life in the womb. It aids animals pregnant for the first time and counters potential aggression towards new offspring.

PSYCHIC ASSOCIATIONS
Good for developing intuition in men and women, kunzite helps to make contact with angels, spirit guides, nature devas and the spirits of nature. Use it to work with power animal energies, especially creatures of the night or those that live underground.

RECHARGING ITS ENERGIES
Kunzite fades in sunlight, so recharge it under the light of the early waxing moon.

PROPERTIES

TYPE: Spodumene with lithium. Flat crystals with deep striations, occasionally colourless from some angles. Semi-transparent

COLOUR: Pink to lilac or pinky violet, streaked with white

SYMBOLIC ASSOCIATIONS

ZODIAC SIGN: Taurus

PLANET: Venus/Pluto

ELEMENT: Earth

CANDLE COLOUR: Pink

GUARDIAN ANGEL: Amatiel

CHAKRA: Heart

HERBS, INCENSES AND OILS: Lilac, chamomile, lavender, rose and ylang ylang

FLOWERS: Crocus, primrose and violet

ASSOCIATED CRYSTALS: Amethyst, purple fluorite and sugilite

DANBURITE

HISTORY AND MYTHOLOGY

Danburite is a relatively recent discovery. Under the Gaia hypothesis, the earth is a living entity that serves the needs of every age and provides healing for all ills of the mind, body and psyche from the plants and minerals on her surface. A crystal of the New Age, danburite addresses modern problems.

DIVINATORY SIGNIFICANCE

Look at any experience as part of a wider pattern in order to maximize opportunities and minimize problems. Few things happen by accident or cannot be redeemed.

HEALING AND THE ENVIRONMENT

Use danburite to draw spiritual healing powers through your body from angelic or divine sources. An all-body healer and gentle energizer, danburite will help detoxify the body, calm the mind and increase self-esteem. You need only a small piece, as its energies, though gentle, are very concentrated.

USES AT WORK AND HOME

Danburite dramatically increases tolerance levels and so is helpful if you live or work with difficult people or situations. It creates a spirit of cooperation and helps you to stay calm and to complete the task at hand with the minimum of personal stress. A piece by the phone seems to deter unwelcome salespeople as well as nuisance-callers.

CHILDREN AND ANIMALS

Danburite helps children to play together and is good for play-school and after-school play scheme organizers. It also helps maintain a harmonious atmosphere among animals and humans in kennels, stables or catteries.

PSYCHIC PROPERTIES

A focus for channelling angelic and spirit guide energies and wisdom, danburite also increases the ability to see other dimensions.

RECHARGING ITS ENERGIES

Wrap danburite in a piece of pink silk and leave in a drawer for twenty four hours.

RHODOCHROSITE

MYTHOLOGY AND HISTORY

Rhodocrosite is sometimes called the Inca rose because the Native Americans in the Andes believed it contained the blood of ancestral great rulers. Therefore it is the stone of power and of powerful love.

DIVINATORY SIGNIFICANCE

Drawing rhodocrosite in a reading signifies that in love or in family relationships you may have to fight for what you want and need. This will bring greater happiness in the end than accepting second best.

HEALING AND THE ENVIRONMENT

It is a powerful healing stone, especially for problems that result from emotional causes or low self-esteem, such as food or alcohol abuse, anorexia or bulimia, or over-reliance on tablets or drugs. It relieves asthma and aids detoxification of the liver and blood. It is also used in IVF and artificial insemination to help the body to accept the implant.

USES AT WORK AND HOME

Buy one to strengthen the love ties if you move in with or marry your lover. Also use it to call

PROPERTIES

TYPE: Manganese carbonate. Opaque

COLOUR: Rose pink with white or paler pink banding. Can be lighter pink or almost red. Rarely, transparent pink crystals

SYMBOLIC ASSOCIATIONS

ZODIAC SIGN: Sagittarius

PLANET: Mars

ELEMENT: Fire

CANDLE COLOUR: Bright pink

GUARDIAN ANGEL: Sandalphon

CHAKRA: Heart/solar plexus

HERBS, INCENSES AND OILS: Anise, cedarwood, copal, orange, rose and nutmeg

FLOWERS: Pink carnation, sweet pea and hibiscus

ASSOCIATED CRYSTALS: Rhodonite, rubellite and garnet

back a partner who has moved out or who works away. When you begin college or work at a new place, rhodochrosite can help you make friends and feel less lonely.

CHILDREN AND ANIMALS

Rhodochrosite is reassuring for children who are fostered or adopted. If children are away from home, it will encourage self-reliance and independence while maintaining links with home. Put it in the sleeping place of a missing animal; it may call them to return.

PSYCHIC ASSOCIATIONS

Use it to draw back an errant lover, to deepen love ties and to increase telepathic communication with lovers, family and pets.

RECHARGING ITS ENERGIES

Smudge the crystal with rose-scented incense.

LEFT Rhodocrosite with pyrites and quartz crystal.

RHODONITE

MYTHOLOGY AND HISTORY

The fire of rhodonite is tempered by the softening influence of Venus and the grounding power of the earth, so it is a slow-burning fire that can defuse stronger, less controlled forces. For this reason, rhodonite has come to be called the burning rose (rhodon is Greek for rose).

DIVINATORY SIGNIFICANCE

Let go of the past; forgive what you can and try to forget the rest. Your peace of mind is more important than trying to please those who may never be content.

HEALING AND THE ENVIRONMENT

Recommended for healing wounds and scar tissue, relieving autoimmune conditions, ulcers, lesions and skin conditions, especially allergies. It is also good for mental scars. It prevents you from repeating old mistakes that

hurt you before and will do so again. Rhodonite can be used as a focus for sending positive energies to people injured or made homeless by war or hurt by buried landmines.

USES AT WORK AND HOME

Rhodonite can help to heal family bitterness and serious rifts with the wider family. It encourages patience when others are being inefficient or unusually slow. At work, carry rhodonite to ensure that your abilities are given due credit. It is a stone associated with musicians and singers and with peacemakers and peacekeepers. It is for people in service industries and also helps shift workers to harmonize their rhythms.

CHILDREN AND ANIMALS

It helps a child to shine and develop their unique talents. It can be useful for children and teenagers who have trouble controlling their temper or are prone to swearing. It is soothing for any creature with a skin condition and for lizards and snakes.

PSYCHIC ASSOCIATIONS

Rhodonite keeps away negativity, both psychic attacks and the spite of others.

RECHARGING ITS ENERGIES

Revitalize rhodonite with the light of a pink candle, a fibre optic or lava lamp.

MANGANO/PINK CALCITE

MYTHOLOGY AND HISTORY

If you shine ultraviolet light on mangano, it will glow bright pink in the darkness. Mangano is associated with fairies and with gentle earth spirits who care for damaged plants or wounded animals.

DIVINATORY SIGNIFICANCE

Manganocalcite says be gentle with yourself; let go of guilt for matters you could not have changed. Pink calcite says you spend so much time helping others they may not realize your vulnerabilty. Ask for support: you will realize your value and others will feel needed.

HEALING AND THE ENVIRONMENT

Mangano fosters both self-esteem and compassion towards others. One of the gentlest stones, manganocalcite (along with all pink calcite) is effective for chronic problems or illnesses. It is particularly helpful for people who have been inadequately mothered or whose mother has died, even years later. Use when healing babies and children, for post-natal depression and for anyone who is physically or emotionally traumatized. Pink calcite will relieve a place that has been vandalized: bury pieces in the soil or circle them around the area on a map.

USES AT WORK AND HOME
Mangano helps to restore emotional security after a burglary or crisis in the home. At work it will lower stress if you are under pressure.

PINK SPINEL

MYTHOLOGY AND HISTORY
The name spinel derives from spina, the Latin for spine, because of its sharp, eight-sided crystals. Red spinel is often mistaken for a ruby and pink for a pink sapphire. The famous Black Prince's Ruby in the Imperial State Crown is in fact a spinel. Henry V wore it on his helmet at Agincourt; the helmet shielded him from an axe blow by the Duke of Alençon.

DIVINATORY SIGNIFICANCE
All may not be as it appears, so check carefully before signing up for any deals or making major commitments.

HEALING AND THE ENVIRONMENT
Pink spinel eases anxiety conditions, phobias or obsessions, especially those connected with low self-esteem or childhood trauma. The stone provides a gentle consistent energy, so is helpful for people who tire easily or who have chronic debilitating illnesses. Use pink spinel for pre-conceptual care and health of both would-be parents. The paler the pink, the gentler its properties.

USES AT WORK AND HOME
More protective than it might appear even in gentler shades, pink spinal should be worn by quiet, kind people whose opinions or wishes are sometimes ignored or overridden.

CHILDREN AND ANIMALS
Both crystals ease fretful babies and help mother-child bonding and small children overcome fears. With animals, they encourage mothers to care for their young.

PSYCHIC ASSOCIATIONS
Use all pink calcite for fairy magic and for working with mythical creatures, especially the unicorn. Manganocalcite is useful as a focus in mother-goddess rituals and those to release our inner child. Pink calcite also strengthens rituals for first love and self-esteem after betrayal.

RECHARGING ITS ENERGIES
Use crescent moonlight or play music of natural sounds, especially the ocean, to revitalize both crystals.

CHILDREN AND ANIMALS
A good-fairy crystal, pink spinel makes an excellent present at a naming ceremony as it endows the child with the continuing love and protection of the giver. The crystal is not suitable for animals.

PSYCHIC ASSOCIATIONS
Pink spinel is a powerful love token that carries the love of the giver. Therefore it is a wonderful emblem if love is relatively new and the couple must spend time apart or live a distance away.

RECHARGING ITS ENERGIES
Polish pink spinel very carefully with a pink cloth, rubbing away all negativity. Pass a clear crystal pendulum over it to energize.

PROPERTIES

TYPE: Calcium carbonate. As mangano semi-transparent to translucent. Optical or icicle calcite is transparent, with inner rainbows

COLOUR: Pink of varying shades, mainly pale. Mangano has white bands

SYMBOLIC ASSOCIATIONS

ZODIAC SIGN: Taurus

PLANET: Venus

ELEMENT: Water

CANDLE COLOUR: Pale pink

GUARDIAN ANGEL: Achaiah

CHAKRA: Heart

HERBS, INCENSES AND OILS: Lemon balm, chamomile, lavender, lily of the valley and rose

FLOWERS: Lily, pale-pink roses and snowdrop

ASSOCIATED CRYSTALS: Amethyst, pink chalcedony and rose quartz

---

PROPERTIES

TYPE: Magnesium aluminium oxide. Usually transparent and sparkling. Some spinel is artificial

COLOUR: From pale to bright pink, including a bright pink with orange

SYMBOLIC ASSOCIATIONS

ZODIAC SIGN: Scorpio

PLANET: Pluto

ELEMENT: Fire

CANDLE COLOUR: Deep pink

GUARDIAN ANGEL: Riehol

CHAKRA: Throat

HERBS, INCENSES AND OILS: Acacia, cedarwood, mimosa, deerstongue and gardenia

FLOWERS: Dog rose (pink), freesia and rosebay willowherb

ASSOCIATED CRYSTALS: Pink chalcedony, ruby and sapphire

CITRINE

Associated with the crown and solar plexus chakras, citrine releases joy and brings spiritual powers into the everyday world. Citrine was supposedly a powerful transmitter of solar healing energy in Atlantis.

MYTHOLOGY AND HISTORY

Until the sixteenth century, citrine was an umbrella term for all sparkling yellow stones, including stones such as topaz. Called the sun stone, citrine is said to hold pure sunlight and never to absorb any negativity. As a stone of Mercury, the Roman messenger god, it holds the clear sunlight of early morning, not the heat of noon. Regarded as the merchant's stone, citrine has been famed for improving communication, increasing selling power (owing to the influence of Mercury) and for attracting money or business. A citrine was placed in the cash register or put with the accounts; now it is put near the computer.

Above and right This sparking yellow sun crystal will melt away pain, doubt, sorrow and tension.

DIVINATORY SIGNIFICANCE

Heralding joy in every aspect of your life, citrine says it is time to communicate your ideas and needs clearly, especially at work. Try new activities and visit new places. Make time for any creative talents you have, as they may prove lucrative.

HEALING PROPERTIES

Citrine is excellent for the liver, spleen, gall bladder and digestive system. It reduces toxicity in the body, relieves back pain and eases skin problems and allergies. It is an effective remedy for depressive illnesses or phobias; it will help you to think clearly and put your problems in perspective.

USES AT WORK AND HOME

Citrine will clear any dark spots at home caused by restless ghosts or negative earth energies. Keep a citrine inclusion (tiny crystals in rock) in a room that seems dark, cold or unfriendly. Citrine is excellent for workers in the media and the arts.

CHILDREN

Citrine helps children and teenagers to feel loved and is good for blending together the tangled relationships that can arise in stepfamilies. It also helps keep open channels of communication with teenagers.

ANIMALS

Citrine helps pets, particularly rescued animals, settle into a new environment or temporary accommodation.

PROTECTIVE FUNCTIONS

The positive energy of citrine drives away darkness and night fears and protects against negative people.

PSYCHIC ASSOCIATIONS

Citrine is excellent for prosperity rituals. Charge a citrine with energies of abundance by burning a yellow candle next to it at dawn. Keep the energized crystal in your purse to attract money to you.

Citrine will make you more intuitive and help you distinguish between free-floating anxiety and your inner voice that advises you as to the right action. It is also very good for automatic writing (where you ask a question and allow your hand to write freely). It draws wisdom from the collective memory bank via your own psychic powers.

Use citrine in creative visualization to help bring a desired object or goal from your thoughts into the everyday world. Hold the citrine in your power hand (the one you write with) while picturing in your mind the desired result coming nearer. Carry the charged citrine with you as a reminder as you put your plans into action.

ENVIRONMENTAL WORK

A crystal of hope, citrine can be placed on an image of children in need or of an area of intense poverty or famine. Leave the citrine on the picture from dawn until noon, then wrap

---

PROPERTIES

TYPE: Quartz. Some citrine is heat-treated amethyst or smoky quartz

COLOUR: Pale to golden yellow, honey, dark orange

SYMBOLIC ASSOCIATIONS

ZODIAC SIGN: Gemini

PLANET: Mercury

ELEMENT: Air

CANDLE COLOUR: Lemon

GUARDIAN ANGEL: Raphael

CHAKRA: Crown and solar plexus

HERBS, INCENSES AND OILS: Almond, bergamot, lemon verbena, lily of the valley and papyrus

FLOWERS: Daffodil, peach blossom and primrose

ASSOCIATED CRYSTALS: Yellow diamond, golden topaz and yellow zircon

the crystal and picture in yellow or white silk and leave it covered until the next dawn. Repeat this process for three consecutive days. As you set the crystal on the photograph, name the positive energies you wish to send to the place. You may also wish to use citrine to bless any material gifts you send to such places.

SPECIAL PROPERTIES

Citrine does not absorb negativity but transforms it into positive energies. Therefore it is a crystal that can keep on energizing and protecting for a long time. This makes citrine useful if you are under a lot of pressure or are away from home and feel vulnerable.

RECHARGING ITS ENERGIES

Leaving citrine in sunlight from dawn till noon will fill it with extra radiance, especially on the summer solstice (21 June in the northern hemisphere and 21 December in the southern hemisphere). However, do not expose citrine to intense sunlight too frequently as it may start to crack.

YELLOW JASPER

See also Dalmatian (p148), green/orbicular (p90), red (p128) and leopardskin jasper (p142)

PROPERTIES

TYPE: Chalcedony quartz. Opaque

COLOUR: Yellow, often mustard or burnished colour through sandy and brown. Sandy picture jasper is mottled and looks like an abstract landscape

SYMBOLIC ASSOCIATIONS

ZODIAC SIGN: Capricorn

PLANET: Saturn/earth

ELEMENT: Earth

CANDLE COLOUR: Sandy yellow

GUARDIAN ANGEL: Sofiel

CHAKRA: Root

HERBS, INCENSES AND OILS: Hyssop, chamomile, fennel, hops and patchouli

FLOWERS: Cactus, tulip and wallflower

ASSOCIATED CRYSTALS: Lemon chrysoprase, leopardskin jasper and mookaite

MYTHOLOGY AND HISTORY

These earth-coloured jaspers are among the most revered among indigenous peoples and have entered the modern spiritual world as icons of earth awareness and the inter-connectedness of all life.

DIVINATORY SIGNIFICANCE

Yellow jasper signifies that others may be envious of what you are and have achieved: do not let any pettiness stop you from doing what you want. Brown or sandy jasper suggests you take the practical point of view and are not tempted by short cuts.

HEALING AND THE ENVIRONMENT

Yellow jasper helps the digestive system, especially the liver, gall bladder and large intestine. It relieves nausea, fat intolerance, chronic indigestion and bloating after eating. All jaspers effectively absorb pain.

Use brown and sandy pieces to protect you against and clear your body of environmental toxins and impurities, especially if you live in

a town. They are helpful for problems with balance and for chronic back pain. Jasper will empower earth-awareness work and acts as a deterrent to litter louts.

USES AT WORK AND HOME:

Yellow jasper protects you against spiteful neighbours and work colleagues. Place it near your workspace to prevent others from gossiping about you in your absence. Use

brown jasper to improve your skills and to keep calm when carrying out any DIY, home renovation or car maintenance. It is good for established businesses and to keep you on track for completing work that is detailed without making small errors.

CHILDREN AND ANIMALS
Yellow jasper reduces sibling rivalry and protects sensitive children against jealousy. Brown and sandy jasper relieve chronic conditions in animals and help animals from hot places settle in a temperate clime.

PSYCHIC PROPERTIES
Use brown jasper in magic to keep your feet on the ground while your spirit is in the air. All types of jasper are good for Native American rituals and for learning from other indigenous traditions. Jaspers are also earth energy transmitters and are effective even in a high apartment or office building. Yellow jasper can be used as a psychic barrier against a gossiping or bitchy colleague or relation.

RECHARGING ITS ENERGIES
Leave in sunlight in a tray of sand or earth.

RUTILATED QUARTZ

MYTHOLOGY AND HISTORY
The gold rutiles within the quartz were believed to be crystallized sunlight or gold belonging to dragons. Rutilated quartz was also regarded as an angel stone because it was said to contain the spirits of angels. The rutiles are sometimes called the hair of Venus.

DIVINATORY SIGNIFICANCE
This stone represents your inner treasure store of resources and experience that can help you if starting over again or seeking to make life changes. Believe in yourself and look for the hidden benefits in any situation.

HEALING AND THE ENVIRONMENT
Rutilated quartz helps to slow the progress of chronic diseases such as bronchitis or asthma. It assists regenerating tissues and brain cells and improves the condition of blood vessels and veins. Nursing mothers can benefit from rutilated quartz.

In older people it increases sexual desire and power and will ease mid-life crises in both sexes. Placed on the solar plexus chakra, it will unblock sluggish centres or energies and help to balance the entire system. Environmentally it is good for healing areas affected by nuclear waste or pollution.

USES AT WORK AND HOME
Rutilated quartz protects those who live in or near town centres. It helps counter ageism in the workplace and strengthens older people who are unemployed or forced into early retirement, encouraging them to explore new avenues of employment.

CHILDREN AND ANIMALS
This crystal eases loneliness in only children and also helps children to cope with family crises and reversals in fortune. Use rutilated quartz to bring love to those who are physically unattractive. It is an excellent crystal for crossbred animals.

PSYCHIC ASSOCIATIONS
Rutilated quartz is good for contacting guardian angels and channelling angelic wisdom. It encourages telepathy between people and increases clairvoyance. Use rutilated quartz for scrying in intense sunlight. It is a useful stone to convert wishes into reality. Place a crystal under the pillow to bring creative solutions in dreams. It is an excellent stone for past-life focus.

RECHARGING ITS ENERGIES
Leave for twenty minutes on a stone circle or on a stone in an ancient hillside. Otherwise, keep it with gold objects in a bag overnight (a tiny gold earring would suffice).

PROPERTIES
TYPE: Quartz with golden rutiles inside
COLOUR: Clear, occasionally smoky, quartz with golden-yellow to brownish-red needles that can form patterns within the crystal

SYMBOLIC ASSOCIATIONS
ZODIAC SIGN: Leo
PLANET: Sun
ELEMENT: Fire
CANDLE COLOUR: Gold
GUARDIAN ANGEL: Galgaliel
CHAKRA: Solar plexus
HERBS, INCENSES AND OILS: Basil, frankincense, garlic, nutmeg and orange
FLOWERS: Aster, broom and heather
ASSOCIATED CRYSTALS: Iron pyrites, obsidian and tektite

YELLOW CALCITE

See also orange (p126), pink (p108), green (p82), and blue calcite (p72)

Despite its various colours, all calcite has common properties, although the different colours can be used with their own chakras. Yellow calcite works through the sacral chakra, melting rigidity and calming fears.

MYTHOLOGY AND HISTORY

Calcite was used in Ancient Egypt for ritual bowls, cups and ritual objects, to pass the gentle healing power into the food, drink or offerings. It was believed to amplify the power of prayer. Stalactites and stalagmites are formed from calcite and their fabulous shapes in different caverns have led to legends growing up of animals or witches turned to stone. The most famous is the Witch of Wookey Hole Caves, in Somerset, England.

ABOVE AND RIGHT
Yellow calcite's slow, gentle healing powers are good for absent healing.

DIVINATORY SIGNIFICANCE

Calcite in all its colours and forms, except for clear calcite, indicates the need for patience and for allowing life to take its course. Golden yellow/honey calcite tells you to believe in yourself and maximize every opportunity to influence others quietly: your success and influence will grow each day.

Pale yellow calcite means you may find yourself having to accept put-downs of others temporarily, but time will vindicate you. White or cloudy calcite reminds you to take a step each day towards what would make you happy or any changes you desire.

HEALING PROPERTIES

Calcite, especially in its warmer shades, helps hormonal imbalances and painful muscles and joints. It also heals abuse and sorrow from the past that may linger, clouding the present and future. Calcite, especially golden yellow and cloudy white, is good for absent healing rituals. Yellow calcite helps the spine, bones, pancreas and spleen, the detoxification of kidneys and decalcification of joints and bones.

USES AT WORK AND HOME

As a stone of balance and integration, calcite in all its colours can ease tensions in close relationships and help the user to blend different priorities and demands on time harmoniously. Calcite gradually releases gentle energies in the home and workplace that keep conflict to a minimum and enable people to work and live together tolerantly.

CHILDREN

Pale yellow or honey calcite helps teenagers to study and calms exam nerves.

ANIMALS

Honey calcite, like green, is good for chronically sick animals and for those who have been ill-treated.

PROTECTIVE FUNCTIONS

Calcite releases and clears personal negativity and so makes the user resistant to the hostile vibes of others. Honey calcite will deflect spite and gossip. Optical spar also helps the user to see through deceit.

PSYCHIC ASSOCIATIONS

Because of the double refractive powers (if you draw a straight line and look at it through a clear or optical calcite, you see two wavy lines), calcite has long been regarded as a magical crystal that would double existing power, strength, health, prosperity and good fortune: it is often called the wish stone.

ENVIRONMENTAL WORK

Calcite will help with the slow transformation of a run-down urban area or war-torn city.

SPECIAL PROPERTIES

All forms of calcite, especially the clearer ones, have the power to help the user to break out of patterns of action that can see him or her repeating mistakes or being constantly attracted to the wrong kind of person.

RECHARGING THE ENERGIES

It can be brittle, so recharge by smudging.

PROPERTIES

TYPE: Calcium carbonate. Semi-transparent

COLOUR: Yellow/gold or honey

SYMBOLIC ASSOCIATIONS

ZODIAC SIGN: Pisces

PLANET: Neptune

ELEMENT: Water

CANDLE COLOUR: Yellow

GUARDIAN ANGEL: Barakiel

CHAKRA: Sacral

HERBS, INCENSES AND OILS: Lemon balm, eucalyptus, kelp (seaweed) and star anise

FLOWERS: Honeysuckle, sea lavender and water lily

ASSOCIATED CRYSTALS: Fluorite, sugilite and aragonite

CHRYSOBERYL / ALEXANDRITE

PROPERTIES

TYPE: Aluminium oxide

COLOUR: Chrysoberyl is clear yellow, honey or yellow green or brown; Alexandrite is deep or emerald green in daylight and ruby red in artificial light

SYMBOLIC ASSOCIATIONS

ZODIAC SIGN: Leo

PLANET: Sun / Venus (alexandrite)

ELEMENT: Fire / earth

CANDLE COLOUR: Gold / emerald green (alexandrite)

GUARDIAN ANGEL: Seratiel

CHAKRA: Crown (alexandrite); solar plexus (chrysoberyl)

HERBS, INCENSES AND OILS: Neroli, avocado, aloe vera, bergamot and sagebrush

FLOWERS: Daffodil, poppy and yellow iris

ASSOCIATED CRYSTALS: Topaz, emerald and ruby

MYTHOLOGY AND FOLKLORE

Yellow chrysoberyl, discovered in Brazil in the seventeenth century, became regarded as the stone of great leaders, especially in Spain and Portugal. Alexandrite was first found in the Ural Mountains in Russia on the birthday of Tsar Alexander II in 1830. Because it displayed the colours of imperial Russia, it became an icon of Russian sovereignty.

DIVINATORY SIGNIFICANCE

These stones are not used for divination.

HEALING AND THE ENVIRONMENT

Yellow chrysoberyl will relieve exhaustion. It is also excellent for diarrhoea, stomach ulcers and other intestinal disorders. It will assist a gentle weight-loss programme.

Alexandrite soothes problems with the head. It is also good for inner-ear problems and for relieving tinnitus and seasickness or any motion sickness.

USES AT WORK AND HOME

Yellow chrysoberyl prevents others from manipulating you, whether psychically or psychologically. It fosters a strong work ethos in a workplace and is good to set near a colleague who is idle or constantly chatters.

Alexandrite is good for regenerating enthusiasm and will protect you if you are travelling in mountain or hill country. Both crystals can help healers not to become overloaded by the troubles or negative energies of others.

CHILDREN AND ANIMALS:

Chrysoberyl can help older children to retain information. The crystals are not used with animals in these forms. A formation that resembles a cat's eye occurs in chrysoberyl, the original cat's eye (see cat's eye, p144).

PSYCHIC ASSOCIATIONS:

Yellow chrysoberyl seems to have some of the magical properties of the more ancient and now little-used yellow beryl. It can be used to make mirror rituals or divination more powerful. Use alexandrite for channelling wisdom from devas, the higher nature essences and from the guardians of mountains. Alexandrite helps you to use flower and gem essences more effectively.

RECHARGING ITS ENERGIES

Recharge both kinds with a sage smudge or incense or in a green place on a sunny day but out of direct sunlight.

AMETRINE

MYTHOLOGY AND HISTORY

Ametrines were given as tribute to the Queen of Spain during the seventeenth century by a conquistador who received the Anahi Mine in Bolivia as a dowry. However, ametrine has become popular in magic and healing only fairly recently.

DIVINATORY SIGNIFICANCE

Trust your intuitive faculties. You may need to negotiate on behalf of yourself or others and tread a middle way for a while.

HEALING AND THE ENVIRONMENT

Ametrine will cleanse and balance the aura, replacing negativity with positive energy. This two-in-one stone is good for all healing work as it can remove pain or blockages – physical,

psychic or psychological. It infuses the body with light and life. Ametrine helps to break bad habits and reduce cravings, especially smoking. It is good for repairing the ozone layer and rebalancing the ecosystem, also for bringing hawks and doves closer when there is threat of war or unrest.

USES AT WORK AND HOME

Ametrine helps workaholics to rebalance their lives to make room for personal and spiritual needs. It also eases a return to work after a break.

CHILDREN AND ANIMALS

The adolescent's stone, ametrine helps to get teenagers out of bed and keeps them out of trouble. It is good also for adolescent animals.

PSYCHIC ASSOCIATIONS

Ametrine makes it easier to contact angels, spirit guides and power animals. It helps draw these higher energies into our lives without becoming overwhelmed or losing our balanced view of the world. Ametrine is also helpful for the early stages of astral projection or out-of-body experiences; it allows you to retain connection with and awareness of the everyday world. In full moonlight, visualize a door in your ametrine. Walk through that door into other dimensions, whether the starlit sky, deep forests of myth or into a past world.

RECHARGING ITS ENERGIES

Revitalize ametrine on the night of the full moon around sunset.

PROPERTIES
TYPE: Quartz. Combination of amethyst and citrine. Transparent, sparkling
COLOUR: Natural mix of yellow and purple
SYMBOLIC ASSOCIATIONS
ZODIAC SIGN: Gemini
PLANET: Mercury
ELEMENT: Air
CANDLE COLOUR: Pearl grey
GUARDIAN ANGEL: Ambriel
CHAKRA: Crown
HERBS, INCENSES AND OILS: Lavender, lemongrass, lemon verbena, lime and sweetgrass
FLOWERS: Lilac, wild rose and Michaelmas daisy
ASSOCIATED CRYSTALS: Amethyst, citrine, smoky quartz

SUNSTONE

MYTHOLOGY AND HISTORY

Believed to have a piece of the sun, sunstone was prized by magicians, who used it to attract the strength of the sun and its associated power and wealth. It is associated with the legendary phoenix that appeared at the first sunrise and every five hundred years was said to become flame and rise anew from the ashes.

DIVINATORY SIGNIFICANCE

You can be optimistic that everything will turn out well in the near future. You may have an unexpected chance to take the lead.

HEALING AND THE ENVIRONMENT

An energizer, sunstone is good for cell

regeneration. It is effective against Seasonal Affective Disorder, all winter ills or chills, depression and despair. It increases sexual potency in men. It is excellent for reducing anxiety, fears and phobias of all kinds: it helps distinguish real danger from imaginary fear.

USES AT WORK AND HOME

Sunstone will bring sunshine into the home on a cold or wintry day or when there has been unhappiness. At work, sunstone is the crystal of leadership and is good if you have a sudden chance to deputize for someone in a higher position. It will foster unselfishness in a group situation and reduce rivalry.

CHILDREN AND ANIMALS

Sunstone helps shy or fearful children to be more outgoing and calms those with an overactive imagination. It helps to maintain the health of tropical birds, fish and reptiles.

PSYCHIC ASSOCIATIONS

It is an excellent charm to attract good fortune, prosperity and promotion. In weather magic it helps to bring sunshine. Use sunstone to represent the god or animus energies and a moonstone for goddess or anima energies.

RECHARGING ITS ENERGIES

Revitalize sunstone for an hour on either side of the noonday sun. Leave it out on the summer solstice from dawn until noon

PROPERTIES
TYPE: Plagioclase feldspar / silicate. A translucent quartz form is sometimes called the Oregon
COLOUR: From gentle orange to a vivid tangerine. Feldspar type flashes opalescent golden yellow and orange; the more common kind is softer orange with a red or golden sheen
SYMBOLIC ASSOCIATIONS
ZODIAC SIGN: Leo
PLANET: Sun
ELEMENT: Fire
CANDLE COLOUR: Gold
GUARDIAN ANGEL: Galgaliel
CHAKRA: Solar plexus
HERBS, INCENSES AND OILS: Bay, frankincense, saffron, St John's wort and tangerine
FLOWERS: Dandelion, marigold and sunflower
ASSOCIATED CRYSTALS: Citrine, fire opal and topaz

YELLOW ARAGONITE

See also orange aragonite (p122)

See also orange aragonite (p122)

PROPERTIES

TYPE: Dimorphous calcium carbonate. Usually twin crystals in clusters

COLOUR: Yellow/honey-coloured

SYMBOLIC ASSOCIATIONS

ZODIAC SIGN: Virgo

PLANET: Earth

ELEMENT: Earth

CANDLE COLOUR: Honey

GUARDIAN ANGEL: Jehoel

CHAKRA: Heart/root

HERBS, INCENSES AND OILS: Caraway, clary sage, moss, ivy and thyme

FLOWERS: Evening primrose, greater celandine and honeysuckle

ASSOCIATED CRYSTALS: Coral, green fluorite and yellow calcite

MYTHOLOGY AND HISTORY

Aragonite is named after Aragon, Spain, where it was discovered. It is like the warm winter sun, especially in its yellow and honey shades. It is also found in hot springs and so is regarded as a stone of the earth mother, from whose womb the warm waters flow.

DIVINATORY SIGNIFICANCE

If you can find one the right shape, yellow aragonite indicates that you should for now be content with your life and/or relationships even if they do not seem exciting. They contain the seeds of true happiness that will unfold over the years.

HEALING AND THE ENVIRONMENT

It is good for bones, especially the spine and teeth, and for absorbing necessary nutrients,

notably calcium. Yellow aragonite will warm you in the winter and offers resistance against colds, flu or viral infections, especially respiratory ones, and against the super bugs that lurk in modern hospitals. It also seems to help restore natural immunity if you have taken a lot of antibiotics. Use to increase recycling activities in your neighbourhood.

USES AT WORK AND HOME

Aragonite helps you to avoid hasty words or actions, which you may regret. It helps you to feel secure within yourself and remain unaffected by the mood swings of others. Keep a cluster at work to defuse stress. Use aragonite when you feel overwhelmed by responsibilities at home or work.

CHILDREN AND ANIMALS

An aragonite cluster in the bedroom will keep away nightmares and night terrors. It is good for animals and birds who live in cities.

PSYCHIC ASSOCIATIONS

Use yellow or colourless aragonite in all outdoor rituals and to connect with nature. It increases knowledge in herbalism. It is also a good focus for Goddess rituals and for channelling higher energies.

RECHARGING ITS ENERGIES

Leave it in very gentle sunlight for an hour.

GOLDEN TOPAZ

See also white (p43) and blue topaz (p71)

See also white (p43) and blue topaz (p71)

MYTHOLOGY AND HISTORY

A stone of the sun and of royalty and master magicians, the finest golden topaz (known as chrysolites, along with peridots) were found on Serpent Isle in the Red Sea. Pliny called the island Topazos, after the Greek for conjecture. Earlier, the Ancient Egyptians had granted the islanders the sole right to gather the stones, which, it was said, could be seen only at night, when they shone brilliantly. The name means fire in Sanskrit. Topaz increases in power with the moon, being at its greatest potency at the time of the full moon.

DIVINATORY SIGNIFICANCE

Golden topaz is not used in divination.

HEALING AND THE ENVIRONMENT

As a stone of the sun, golden topaz will fill your body, mind and aura with light and warmth. It is especially helpful for arthritis and rheumatism and has an affinity to the gall bladder, pancreas and liver. It is beneficial for all digestive disorders, particularly those affected by stress. Associated with gradual and permanent weight loss, it reduces the desire to binge eat and/or crash diet. It also relieves nervous exhaustion. For insomnia, an hour before bedtime drink water in which a topaz has been soaked.

USES AT WORK AND HOME
Topaz will help guard a home against fire and burglary and its inhabitants from domestic accidents. It also deters others from envying

you and your achievements and so is protective against spiteful neighbours, jealous work colleagues and office intrigues.

CHILDREN AND ANIMALS
It helps to stop sleepwalking and sleep disturbances. It is not suitable for animals.

PSYCHIC ASSOCIATIONS
Golden topaz is used in prosperity rituals and as a money and love charm. Traditionally worn to attract a wealthy lover, today it is used to attract one who is spiritually rich. Psychically, golden topaz is also a stone of astral travel. It was believed to confer invisibility on its wearer in the Near and Middle East in ancient times.

RECHARGING ITS ENERGIES
Revitalize towards sunset at the full moon when sun and moon are both in the sky.

PROPERTIES
TYPE: Island silicate
COLOUR: Golden yellow, the finest is Imperial topaz
SYMBOLIC ASSOCIATIONS
ZODIAC SIGN: Leo
PLANET: Sun
ELEMENT: Fire
CANDLE COLOUR: Gold
GUARDIAN ANGEL: Uriel
CHAKRA: Solar plexus
HERBS, INCENSES AND OILS: Bay, frankincense, orange, St John's wort and desert sage
FLOWERS: Buttercup, marigold and sunflower
ASSOCIATED CRYSTALS: Chrysoberyl, citrine and tiger's eye

LEMON CHRYSOPRASE
See also chrysoprase (p99)

MYTHOLOGY AND HISTORY
Alexander the Great wore a chrysoprase on his belt to bring victory. While he was resting after a battle in Egypt, a cobra stung the stone, saving his life.

DIVINATORY SIGNIFICANCE
Be particularly alert to what is going on behind the scenes, especially at work or in your social life. Double-check what you are told and avoid listening to gossip.

HEALING AND THE ENVIRONMENT
Lemon chrysoprase sharpens physical vision and provides a mental focus, cleans the system of impurities, improves skin and muscle tone, helps with weight loss and increases mobility. It also reduces nausea, especially in pregnancy, and helps re-establish fertility and hormonal patterns after a long period of artificial contraception.

USES AT WORK AND HOME
It helps with legal problems, especially relating to property, and speeds up the paperwork in house moves. At work, it helps you to think fast and to argue eloquently under pressure and to see through deception.

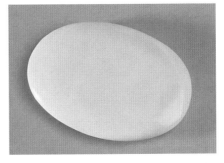

CHILDREN AND ANIMALS
It can break the cycle of night terrors in young children and counter bad influences in teenagers. It helps pets who are jealous.

PSYCHIC PROPERTIES
The more yellow shades of chrysoprase were used as an invisibility charm, so it can be a potent amulet if you need to keep a low profile. As a charm it seems to deter drunks from bothering you on late-night trains, buses and taxi ranks or in city centres.

RECHARGING ITS ENERGIES
Add it to your bath water; visualize negativity swirling away with the waste water.

PROPERTIES
TYPE: Chalcedony with nickel. Opaque
COLOUR: Lemon yellow to yellowy-green
SYMBOLIC ASSOCIATIONS
ZODIAC SIGN: Gemini
PLANET: Mercury
ELEMENT: Air
CANDLE COLOUR: Lemon yellow
GUARDIAN ANGEL: Raphael
CHAKRA: Solar plexus
HERBS, INCENSES AND OILS: Lemon, lemongrass, lime, mint and tea tree
FLOWERS: Lemon blossom, narcissus and primrose
ASSOCIATED CRYSTALS: Bowenite, pale citrine and prehnite

AMBER

Because insects, plants and even tiny animals are found petrified

inside its crystals, amber was thought to contain the essence of life

and so became known as the stone of the mother goddess.

Right and Above Amber is
a stone of courage,
personal power and
harmony.

PROPERTIES

TYPE: Organic gem made
from fossilized resin from
coniferous trees that grew
c. thirty million years ago

COLOUR: Translucent,
yellow or golden orange,
sometimes brown, often
containing fossilized insects
or tiny plants. Occasionally
black, violet, green or blue

SYMBOLIC ASSOCIATIONS

ZODIAC SIGN: Leo

PLANET: Sun

ELEMENT: Fire

CANDLE COLOUR: Gold

GUARDIAN ANGEL:
Verchiel

CHAKRA: Solar plexus

HERBS, INCENSES AND
OILS: Saffron, frankincense,
bay and St John's wort

FLOWERS: Sunflower,
dandelion, marigold

ASSOCIATED CRYSTALS:
Blood agate, carnelian and
sunstone

MYTHOLOGY AND HISTORY

Amber has been found in Palaeolithic graves and was the material for early amulets. Called the honey stone, or petrified sunlight, in China amber was thought to contain the souls of many tigers and the power of many suns. Another Oriental legend claims amber is drops of petrified dragon's blood. In the Classical world it was believed that amber was formed by the setting rays of the sun upon the sea. A Christian legend says amber was the solidified tears of birds at the crucifixion.

The Vikings called amber the 'tears of Freyja', after their goddess of love, who once sold her favours to the dwarves in return for an amber necklace. Thus amber became a symbol of passionate love, female sexuality and fertility. In Wicca and in shamanism it is used as a gateway to other realms.

DIVINATORY SIGNIFICANCE

Amber indicates that this is a time for deciding what you want. As a stone of prosperity, it indicates that your efforts may at last be recognized.

HEALING PROPERTIES

Amber stimulates the body's self-healing abilities. If you are working as a healer, it will stop you absorbing negative energies. It helps to improve short-term memory, relieves stomach ailments, soothes sore throats and inner-ear complaints and aids digestion. It strengthens the spine, lungs and central nervous system, and speeds cell regeneration. It is also good for speech problems.

On an emotional level, amber is an excellent crystal for relieving depression and anxiety. It increases inner radiance and strengthens a sense of self-worth.

USES AT HOME AND WORK

Amber attracts prosperity and success. It melts rigid or confrontational attitudes in others and is excellent if a workplace is fiercely competitive.

CHILDREN

The crystal helps shy children to relax in social situations. It will also protect them from spite and sarcasm in the class room and in the playground.

ANIMALS

Amber is useful to help older animals trigger their self-healing powers.

PROTECTIVE FUNCTIONS

Amber was used by Roman gladiators as an amulet to protect against both danger and fear. A stone of courage, it will help you to face opposition.

PSYCHIC ASSOCIATIONS

Amber provides a good focus for past-life work. Burn an orange candle after dark and gaze through half-closed eyes into the depths of the amber crystal.

For astral travel, hold amber up to sunlight, creating a doorway of radiance within the amber. Visualize yourself passing through it. Then lie down, placing the warm amber on top of your clothes in the centre of your stomach, a few inches above your navel, on the solar plexus chakra (see p10). Close your eyes and, in your mind, follow the amber path through the doorway.

In fertility magic, a rounded amber and pointed jet crystal are put in a red cloth bag, tied with three red knots and placed under the bed during lovemaking.

Carry amber in a charm or lucky bag to increase your psychic powers. Place a piece of amber on a magical altar for power and protection and when you are going to channel the wisdom of the Goddess.

PROPERTIES

TYPE: Dimorphous calcium carbonate that usually grows as twin crystals in clusters. Semi-transparent, translucent

COLOUR: Orange through orangey-brown to brown

SYMBOLIC ASSOCIATIONS

ZODIAC. SIGN: Capricorn

PLANET: Saturn

ELEMENT: Earth

CANDLE COLOUR: Orange or golden brown

GUARDIAN ANGEL: Sagdalon

CHAKRA: Sacral

HERBS, INCENSES AND OILS: Clary sage, cedar, pine, sagebrush and wheatgerm

FLOWERS: Clematis, honeysuckle and wisteria

ASSOCIATED CRYSTALS: Brown zircon, orange calcite and orange celestine

ENVIRONMENTAL WORK

Amber protects against modern technological pollution. It also helps to safeguard ancient sites from vandalism and from unscrupulous developers. Place your amber in the setting sun on top of a photograph of a site for a few minutes and send your wishes for the place through the crystal. Amber cleanses the seas and is valuable in rituals for areas that are under threat from erosion or from high tides.

SPECIAL PROPERTIES

Its magnetic properties have made amber an important stone for attracting love, and an amber necklace or pendant is said to attract lovers. On a more general level, it transforms negative into positive energy.

RECHARGING ITS ENERGIES

Charge amber in sunlight at noon for a few minutes, especially at the summer solstice.

ORANGE ARAGONITE

MYTHOLOGY AND HISTORY

The orange and brown shades of aragonite are symbolic spiritually and magically of underlying structures and connections. Some mollusc shells are made up of aragonite: it is layers of aragonite that give the abalone shell its pearl-like lustre and beauty. This shell is much loved by Native Americans for smudging or smoke magic.

DIVINATORY SIGNIFICANCE

You may feel that you have been waiting patiently for a long time. Maybe you were waiting for a lucky break or perhaps freedom after a time of heavy work or family responsibility. Persevere a little longer and you will find unexpected help or relief.

HEALING AND THE ENVIRONMENT

Healers benefit from holding an orange or brown aragonite before beginning a session, to allow their energies to centre and to shut out daily concerns. It is healing for many parts of the body, but especially for ovaries and the prostate gland, and for the central nervous system. It is excellent for jagged nerves, frayed tempers and unsettled stomachs, especially when caused by lack of rest or not taking regular meal breaks.

CHILDREN AND ANIMALS

Aragonite will encourage impatient children to wait and take their turn. Carry when training animals, especially horses. An aragonite cluster will improve timekeeping for family members and in the workplace. Use for procrastinating family members who put everything off until tomorrow.

PSYCHIC ASSOCIATIONS
Use orange or brown aragonite to make rituals environmentally friendly and focused and not just psychic shopping lists. Include aragonite in medicine-wheel ceremonies, smudging, earth-energy connections, dowsing and rituals to the earth goddess.

RECHARGING ITS ENERGIES
Bury in a pot of earth for twenty-four hours.

COPPER

MYTHOLOGY AND HISTORY
Copper is sacred to many of the love goddesses, including the Sumerian Innana, the Mesopotamian Queen of Heaven, Astarte and Ishtar, and the Greek goddess Aphrodite and her Roman counterpart, Venus.

DIVINATORY SIGNIFICANCE
Use a copper nugget for divination. You will experience a gentle but steady increase in your life of whatever it is that you need, whether money, love, health or happiness. Allow your heart to rule your head.

HEALING AND ENVIRONMENTAL
An all-purpose healer, copper has a natural ability to conduct electricity and so can harmonize the body's energies and clear any blockages or imbalances. Copper sends

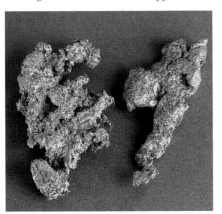

healing into the wearer's energy field. It detoxifies the system when worn next to the skin. It relieves rheumatism, arthritis, stiffness and swellings of hands and feet (use a copper ring or bracelet). Copper will maintain health and increase the metabolic rate to help weight-loss programmes. It also prevents travel sickness. Copper amplifies the energy of other crystals.

USES AT WORK AND HOME
Copper attracts money and good luck to both home and business. Traditionally, a pot filled with copper money was incubated in a warm place in the family home. (You can use copper discs or money from museum shops.) Copper also increases tact and balances extremes in emotion or points of view.

CHILDREN AND ANIMALS
Copper relieves carsickness in children. It is also beneficial to an animal that cannot settle in a new home.

PSYCHIC PROPERTIES
Wear a copper ring to attract love and fertility. Copper wands can be used to direct energies and attract power from the cosmos (sometimes copper wands are topped with clear quartz crystals).

Copper should be worn on the left side of the body by right-handed people and on the right by left-handed people.

RECHARGING ITS ENERGIES
Recharge copper under full moonlight.

PROPERTIES

TYPE: The metal is found as polished nuggets; copper oxide is orangey-red crystals or sparkling strands, sometimes with green. Cuprite is the name given to copper pyrites

COLOUR: Orangey red (with green), gleaming, sometimes also bronzed beautiful polished nuggets

SYMBOLIC ASSOCIATIONS

ZODIAC SIGN: Taurus

PLANET: Venus

ELEMENT: Water

CANDLE COLOUR: Emerald green

GUARDIAN ANGEL: Anael

CHAKRA: Crown / heart

HERBS, INCENSES AND OILS: Magnolia, mallow, mimosa, vanilla and yarrow

FLOWERS: Amaryllis, fuchsia and pink orchids

ASSOCIATED CRYSTALS: Emerald, malachite and schalenblende (zinc)

CARNELIAN

Associated with the solar plexus chakra, this crystal energizes your system and fills you with confidence and courage. Carnelian removes doubt and despair and reminds you of your unique strengths.

MYTHOLOGY AND HISTORY

Carnelians were used in Ancient Egyptian magic as protection for both the living and the dead. A carnelian in the form of the tjet, symbol of mother Isis, was placed on the neck of a mummy to ensure the protection and rebirth of the spirit in the afterlife. Another carnelian amulet was the Eye of Horus, which is still believed in parts of the Middle East to offer protection against the evil eye. A stone of courage, in Roman times a carnelian was engraved with the head of a lion or a great leader.

DIVINATORY SIGNIFICANCE

This may be a good time for independent action, whether emotionally or at work. Do not undervalue yourself or accept second-best treatment. Now is the time to work out what would make you happy and how this can be achieved. Carnelian is above all a crystal of personal happiness and fulfilment; if you believe in your unique talents and follow your personal goals rather than those set by others, you can achieve anything.

HEALING AND THE ENVIRONMENT

Carnelian warms and cleanses the blood and kidneys, stimulates a healthy appetite and increases physical energy. A stone both of fertility and male potency, carnelian can relieve PMS and menopausal symptoms and overcome sexual anxieties that prevent orgasm. Carnelian relieves addictions of all kinds, especially problems centring on food that may be linked with low self-esteem. It also alleviates arthritis, especially in men (coral is better for women).

Carnelian will aid in preserving ancient sacred sites and old buildings and reviving the energies if they have become derelict or forgotten. Bury carnelian in the soil or pour water in which carnelians have been soaked in sunlight on to the earth.

USES AT WORK AND HOME

Carnelian brings abundance in every way to the home and family. It aids decision making and all forms of buying and selling. It is good for builders and DIY enthusiasts and guards against falling masonry. Traditionally a protector against fire, storm and malevolence of all kinds, carnelian can be placed near entrances to the home, to garages and outbuildings, and on your desk at work to radiate positivity. Carnelian defines and strengthens your identity, so that your true self shines through without fear or the need to conform to the expectations of others.

CHILDREN AND ANIMALS

Carnelian inspires courage without aggressiveness, and acts as a balancer for sensitive children and teenagers. A carnelian attached to a collar or put in a pet's water will quieten an aggressive animal. Carnelians also encourage timid pets to make contact with humans. Add a carnelian to a goldfish tank to keep the fish healthy and to attract wealth.

PSYCHIC ASSOCIATIONS

Use carnelian as a focus for past-life work and for finding a twin soul. It is good for all love and sex rites, especially to rekindle or increase passion that has faded in an otherwise loving relationship. Place a carnelian under each corner of the mattress. Fire magic is also more effective if you circle a red candle with carnelians. Carnelian will act as a shield from attempted psychic intrusion into your thoughts.

RECHARGING ITS ENERGIES

Cleanse carnelian with sunlight or under running water. Keep carnelian with other stones to cleanse them of negative energies.

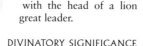

RIGHT AND ABOVE Carnelian fills the wearer with confidence.

PROPERTIES

TYPE: Chalcedony. Translucent

COLOUR: Orange to red, occasionally yellow or brown

SYMBOLIC ASSOCIATIONS

ZODIAC SIGN: Leo

PLANET: Sun

ELEMENT: Fire

CANDLE COLOUR: Orange

GUARDIAN ANGEL: Michael

CHAKRA: Solar plexus

HERBS, INCENSES AND OILS: Copal, frankincense, juniper, orange and rue

FLOWERS: Carnation, chrysanthemum, peony

ASSOCIATED CRYSTALS: Amber, coral and orange or red jasper

ORANGE CALCITE

PROPERTIES

TYPE: Calcium carbonate

COLOUR: Light orange through peach to rich orange

SYMBOLIC ASSOCIATIONS

ZODIAC SIGN: Leo

PLANET: Sun

ELEMENT: Earth

CANDLE COLOUR: Orange

GUARDIAN ANGEL: Zerachiel

CHAKRA: Sacral

HERBS, INCENSES AND OILS: Musk (synthetic), heliotrope, lemongrass, rosemary and tangerine

FLOWERS: Nasturtium, orange blossom and peach blossom

ASSOCIATED CRYSTALS: Aragonite, peach aventurine and orange celestine

MYTHOLOGY AND HISTORY

Orange calcite is said to have been cast from the chariot of the Baltic sun goddess, Saule, as she drove her chariot across the skies and began her long journey to overcome the powers of darkness on the Winter Solstice (21 December in the northern hemisphere).

DIVINATORY SIGNIFICANCE

Attitudes are softening and others may be warming to suggestions you made that were rejected earlier. So it is now well worth resubmitting or suggesting ideas or plans dear to your heart.

HEALING AND THE ENVIRONMENT

Orange calcite is very gentle for gallstones and any liver or spleen problems and is probably the best crystal for helping to relieve a gall-bladder attack. It is also helpful for any sexual dysfunction or fears and for healing the psychological scars of any sexual attack or abuse. Calcite helps to balance women's hormones and eases aching muscles.

FUNCTIONS AT WORK AND HOME

Create a warm, welcoming atmosphere at home by having dishes of orange calcite in areas where people sit. It also makes mealtimes and dinner parties congenial and friendly without destroying lively debate. At work, use orange calcite to break the ice with newcomers and create a relaxed atmosphere.

CHILDREN AND ANIMALS

Orange calcite makes children feel safer in what can seem to be a very frightening world.

Use it also for pet hens, ducks or rabbits, to help them become more domesticated and responsive to their owners.

PSYCHIC ASSOCIATIONS

Use orange calcite for very gentle love magic, especially for kindling a sexual relationship that begins later in life.

Orange calcite is good for relaxing people who have asked for a divinatory reading. If you are giving readings to others for the first time, orange calcite will allow your intuitive insights to flow. Orange calcite can help you to pray if you are angry or frightened.

RECHARGING ITS ENERGIES

Though calcite is brittle, you can recharge it and yourself by soaking it in your bath by candlelight. It is relatively cheap to replace and when it crumbles you know it is time to bury it a little prayer of thanks.

ORANGE CELESTINE/CELESTITE

MYTHOLOGY AND HISTORY

Orange celestine is sometimes called celestite. In India, powdered celestine was cast onto ritual fires in tribute to the fire god, Agni. When it burns, a bright-red flame flares up.

DIVINATORY SIGNIFICANCE

You should feel confident to increase any demands you are making or go up a gear in putting plans into action.

HEALING AND THE ENVIRONMENT

Orange celestine will fill your whole system with warmth and gentle energy, improve your general health and keep you healthy so that you have the confidence and strength to tackle any situation. Water in which orange celestine has been soaked will help the gall bladder, liver, spleen and pancreas and make you less prone to food allergies. It is helpful for breaking over-dependency on food, alcohol, cigarettes or medicines. It will also help you detach from a particular person who may be sapping your confidence.

USES AT WORK AND HOME
Orange celestine is good for all life changes, large and small, and will help you settle in to a new home, job or location. It will help you find your directions when visiting or driving to an unfamiliar place.

CHILDREN AND ANIMALS
Orange celestine helps a young child begin to become more independent, especially if he or she clings to their mother. It will benefit children who have school phobias or unusually strong fears about the mortality of their parents. Orange celestine is useful the first few times you leave a pet alone at home when you go to work.

PSYCHIC PROPERTIES
Orange celestine encourages intuition and the development of clairsentience (sensing information psychically from the atmosphere of a place). It is good also for work with aromatherapy oils. Hold orange celestine in each hand when you are trying to see auras.

RECHARGING ITS ENERGIES
Even orange celestine/celestite does not like sunlight that is too intense. Instead, sprinkle over it water in which the rays of the setting sun have been reflected.

PROPERTIES
Type: Sulphate. Transparent to semi-transparent

Colour: Orange and yellowish

SYMBOLIC ASSOCIATIONS

ZODIAC SIGN: Sagittarius

PLANET: Mars

ELEMENT: Fire

CANDLE COLOUR: Orange

GUARDIAN ANGEL: Sachiel

CHAKRA: Sacral

HERBS, INCENSES AND OILS: Neroli, chamomile, St John's wort and sagebrush

FLOWERS: Dahlia, marigold and wallflower

ASSOCIATED CRYSTALS: Amber, aragonite and orange calcite

MOOKAITE

HISTORY AND MYTHOLOGY
Mookaite is an Australian Aboriginal earth rainbow stone that has passed into general healing and magical use. It contains sacred earth energies akin to those found at sites such as Uluru (Ayers Rock). It is the stone of the universal earth mother, called Gaia after the ancient Greek earth mother, and a focus for the regeneration of the planet.

DIVINATORY SIGNIFICANCE
A wanderer's stone, mookaite channels any restlessness into plans to expand your horizons either physically or mentally. Welcome any opportunities for change, however unexpected, or a modification to your present lifestyle or location.

HEALING AND THE ENVIRONMENT
With all those earth energies flowing within it, mookaite is a very active crystal, helping the body to heal itself, purifying the blood, strengthening the immune system and speeding the healing of wounds. It also settles imbalances in the stomach, glands and fluid levels and eases hernias or ruptures. It helps to heal the planet and to conserve ancient rock sculptures and earth-energy sites.

USES AT WORK AND HOME
Mookaite shields against all negativity. It helps with house moves or major renovations. At work it helps us see opportunities for change

or improvement in working practices and reduces the impact of distractions or obstacles. It prevents worries about the future or past failures diverting us from the task at hand.

CHILDREN AND ANIMALS
Use mookaite to settle children or animals in new locations or situations.

PSYCHIC ASSOCIATIONS
Mookaite amplifies awareness of earth energies and spirits at ancient earth sites, while offering protection against being overwhelmed. Good to carry when dowsing, mookaite also protects the wearer from people who play mind games.

RECHARGING ITS ENERGIES
Recharge at sites of earth power, such as stone circles. Alternatively, use a sage infusion.

PROPERTIES
TYPE: Jasper (chalcedony quartz) and chert, sometimes with fossilized inclusions. Opaque

COLOUR: The colour ranges through large mottled patches of yellow, orange, brown, beige and white, and green

SYMBOLIC ASSOCIATIONS

ZODIAC SIGN: Virgo

PLANET: Earth

ELEMENT: Earth

CANDLE COLOUR: Dark orange

GUARDIAN ANGEL: Harabael

CHAKRA: Root, sacral and solar plexus

HERBS, INCENSES AND OILS: Almond, dill, honeysuckle, lavender and moss

FLOWERS: Heather, flowering banksia or golden wattle tree and brown chrysanthemum

ASSOCIATED CRYSTALS: Banded agate, brecciated jasper and leopardskin jasper

JASPER

See also yellow jasper (p112), leopardskin jasper (p142), green jasper (p90), Dalmatian jasper (p148) and mookaite (p127)

Jasper is the stone of warriors. In Teutonic legend, the hilt of the magical sword of Siegfried, dragon slayer and ill-fated lover of the mystic Brünhild, was inlaid with red jasper to give him courage.

ABOVE AND FAR RIGHT Red jasper protects against all forms of attack and malevolence and brings fertility and optimism.

PROPERTIES
TYPE: Chalcedony quartz. Opaque

COLOUR: Single colours and patterned. Varies from brick red through orange to brownish-red hue. Red includes poppy-coloured jasper and brecciated jasper (red with black or brown rock inclusions)

SYMBOLIC ASSOCIATIONS
ZODIAC SIGN: Aries

PLANET: Mars

ELEMENT: Fire

CANDLE COLOUR: Red and burgundy

GUARDIAN ANGEL: Samael

CHAKRA: Root

HERBS, INCENSES AND OILS: Cedar wood, dragon's blood, fennel, ginger and mint

FLOWERS: All bright-red flowers, especially tulip, poppy and carnation

ASSOCIATED CRYSTALS: Agate, bloodstone, tiger's eye

HISTORY AND MYTHOLOGY

Traditionally, jasper was one of the most popular stones for making seals and amulets because it is durable but easily carved. Mark Antony had a red jasper seal ring with which, according to romantic legend, he marked his letters to Cleopatra. The Ancient Egyptians used red jasper for their protective amulets, especially the tjet (the 'buckle of Isis'), which was an important fertility symbol and female power image. Some Native North American peoples call red jasper the blood of the earth and consider it particularly sacred.

DIVINATORY SIGNIFICANCE

Jaspers in any colour but especially red or orange indicate that you should tackle any problems head on, although without being aggressive. If you confront bullies or prejudice, opposition will melt away.

HEALING PROPERTIES

Red (and orange) jasper helps with menstrual problems and menopausal difficulties. It aids circulation and can warm cold limbs or aching joints and muscles. It also increases energy and stamina and is good for anaemia or toxicity in the blood. Jaspers are helpful for anyone who has been in hospital or convalescing for a long period or who has been chronically depressed. Use red jasper as a fertility crystal after a prolonged period of artificial contraception.

USES AT WORK AND HOME

Red jasper gets you going on cold winter mornings or when you are too tired to get out of bed. It helps to keep you cheerful and focused whatever the day throws at you.

CHILDREN

Give red jasper to older children and teenagers to help them resist prejudice or spite from their peers or over-dominant teachers. Though too powerful for young children, red jasper is very good for fighting for the rights of any disabled child.

ANIMALS

It stimulates timid animals such as cats to defend their territory from more predatory animals. Red jasper helps new animal mothers to feel maternal about their newborn, especially if they initially reject the babies.

PROTECTIVE FUNCTIONS

All jaspers, most powerfully in red, offer protection against physical threats and psychic attack and also stave off accidents or bad luck. Above all use, red jasper will return negative energies to the sender.

PSYCHIC ASSOCIATIONS

Red jasper is a powerful focus for sex magic and for increasing passion in lovers. It also sends out psychic defence vibes to keep you safe from all harm.

ENVIRONMENTAL WORK

Red jasper is good for rituals or empowerments against the effects of drought in different parts of the world. Pour water over your jasper and let the water fall on the ground, naming the place in which there is drought and asking for its end.

SPECIAL PROPERTIES

If possible, use jasper next to the skin either on a cord around your neck or on a belt.

RECHARGING ITS ENERGIES

Pass your red jasper through the flame of a red candle to revitalize it.

RED AGATE

See also banded agate (p140)

MYTHOLOGY AND HISTORY

Agates have been used for thousands of years and in many cultures for magic and healing. The Vikings used a red agate in axe divination: they heated an axe head and placed the agate on the red-hot blade – where it fell indicated the direction of lost objects or hidden treasure. Fire agate was used in alchemy because it was believed to contain the essence of fire.

DIVINATORY SIGNIFICANCE

If you draw red or blood agate, you may feel passionately about an issue – or maybe a person. This is a good time to speak or act. If you draw a fire agate you may need to get rid of destructive factors in your life that are sapping your energy.

HEALING AND THE ENVIRONMENT

All red agates are excellent for blood and colon disorders, for energizing the system, for speeding up the metabolism, improving the efficiency of bodily functions and for burns, scalds and acute skin inflammation. Fire agate burns away disease and promotes the resolution of lingering illnesses and debility.

USES AT WORK AND HOME

Red agate will bring desired or needed change to your life. It will galvanize you into action, providing a sudden but controlled surge of energy that will allow you to finish half-completed projects or chores. All agates are good for finding employment.

CHILDREN AND ANIMALS

It will empower a girl who is menstruating for the first time. Use when mating animals.

PSYCHIC ASSOCIATIONS

Red agate amplifies smudging, incense burning, fire and candle magic. All red agates will create a powerful shield around your aura and cleanse it of pollution. Carry a red agate if you feel spooked.

RECHARGING ITS ENERGIES

Pass red agate through the flame of a beautiful red candle to recharge its energy.

FIRE OPAL

MYTHOLOGY AND HISTORY

Arabian legend tells that opals fell from heaven in lightning flashes. In his novel Anne of Geierstein, Sir Walter Scott described how the heroine's opal glowed when she was happy, flashed red when she was angry and turned to grey ashes when holy water was splashed on it, soon after which she died. Opals were considered unlucky until Queen Victoria, who had opal mines in Australia, gave them as gifts at a royal wedding. Fire opals are called the stone of explorers, conquerors and great leaders. Red opals are exchanged by lovers so that passion will last.

DIVINATORY SIGNIFICANCE

Fire opal is not used in divination.

HEALING AND THE ENVIRONMENT

Fire opal is used to heal the intestines, abdomen and the kidneys and lower spine and back muscles. An energizer for the whole system, it is traditionally worn over the womb or genitals to increase potency, fertility and sexual desire. Fire agate can be used in rituals to prevent volcanic eruptions and large-scale forest fires in the dry season and to send strength to all who fight fires or work in the emergency services and face danger daily.

USES AT WORK AND HOME
A bringer of joy, fire opal keeps you in touch with your instincts, and is useful when you must make a decision without all the facts. Fire opals attract custom and money to business premises. Keep one in a cash register or credit card machine. When a new business opens, hide a tiny fire opal above the main entrance. They also defend against fire, storm and lightning strikes and arson attacks.

CHILDREN AND ANIMALS
It is too powerful for children and animals.

PSYCHIC ASSOCIATIONS
Fire opal aids sex magic and is effective in rituals to increase passion in a relationship. It is excellent for working with the four elements and channelling the energies of the fire spirits in a positive way.

RECHARGING ITS ENERGIES
Like all opals, fire opal is very delicate and should be washed in a little water regularly to keep it hydrated as well as energized.

PROPERTIES

TYPE:	Hydrated silica, non-crystalline, containing iron. Translucent and milky, occasionally colourless and more transparent. Fire opals are usually common. Flame opal has a flickering red streak
COLOUR:	Red, dark orange or yellow background colour

SYMBOLIC ASSOCIATIONS

ZODIAC SIGN:	Libra
PLANET:	Mars
ELEMENT:	Fire/water
CANDLE COLOUR:	Silver
GUARDIAN ANGEL:	Shamshiel
CHAKRA:	Solar plexus/sacral
HERBS, INCENSES AND OILS:	Barberry, cayenne, copal, hibiscus and rosemary
FLOWERS:	Amara, aubrietia and begonia
ASSOCIATED CRYSTALS:	Moonstone, rainbow obsidian and ruby

RED TIGER'S EYE

MYTHOLOGY AND HISTORY
Red tiger's eye is traditionally used in amulets to repel the evil eye and to give the wearer courage and invulnerability. It was the stone of Hephaestus, Greek god of fire and metalwork, who created armour, weapons and jewels for the gods in his workshop beneath the volcanic Mount Etna.

DIVINATORY SIGNIFICANCE
A wonderful period lies ahead when you can direct your energies into any activity and are assured of success. Matters of personal creativity are especially favoured.

HEALING AND THE ENVIRONMENT
Red tiger's eye helps tired blood to rejuvenate and restores natural rhythms to the female menstrual cycle. It also increases male potency. As with all tiger's eyes, it sharpens eyesight, especially night vision. A good stone to promote healing after surgical intervention, it also relieves psychosomatic and depressive conditions.

USES AT WORK AND HOME
Red tiger's eye brings both money and good luck to the home. It is a very powerful protective stone against attack and accidents both in the home and while travelling, especially on trains and late-night buses. A useful stone of protection for hospital workers and surgeons and those in dangerous occupations. Red tiger's eye is also beneficial for long-distance car, train and coach drivers.

CHILDREN AND ANIMALS
Red tiger's eye is a good survival stone against playground bullying. A tiger's eye attached to a cat's collar protects it from cat haters.

PSYCHIC FUNCTIONS
Red tiger's eye, like all tiger's eyes, increases clairvoyance. Use it as a charm for money, success and power when the need is urgent or the plan ambitious.

RECHARGING ITS ENERGIES
Leave the stone in sunlight from noon until the sun is low in the sky.

PROPERTIES

TYPE:	Oxide, quartz. Chatoyant, reflecting light in wavy lines that gives it the eye appearance
COLOUR:	Red with dark to light banding

SYMBOLIC ASSOCIATIONS

ZODIAC SIGN:	Aries
PLANET:	Mars
ELEMENT:	Fire
CANDLE COLOUR:	Deep red
GUARDIAN ANGEL:	Nathaniel
CHAKRA:	Root
HERBS, INCENSES AND OILS:	Cloves, angelica, marjoram, mandarin and peppermint
FLOWERS:	Chrysanthemum, geranium and scarlet sage
ASSOCIATED CRYSTALS:	Red aventurine, red jasper and golden tiger's eye

RUBY

MYTHOLOGY AND HISTORY

In ancient times the ruby was referred to as a carbuncle, though this also refers to garnet. Star rubies have a naturally occuring six-pointed star. The most valuable rubies are deep red with a slight blue tinge called, in folk tradition, pigeon's blood.

Rubies are called the tears of Buddha. In Burma, legend tells that all the rubies in the world come from an egg laid by the dragon Naga. The star ruby is said to contain three helpful angels or spirits (see also the star sapphire, p63). Rubies were said to darken if there was danger: Catherine of Aragon's ring darkened just before she was cast aside by her husband, King Henry VIII. However, rubies also signify lasting love and the fortieth wedding anniversary is called ruby.

DIVINATORY SIGNIFICANCE

Ruby is not used in divination.

HEALING AND THE ENVIRONMENT

Associated with the life force and life blood, ruby is a powerful energizer. It is good for the circulation and for increasing energy and stamina generally. Rubies will also release suppressed anger or negativity in a creative way. Ruby relieves impotence in men.

USES AT WORK AND HOME

Ruby guards the home and your possessions against fire, storms and intruders. It also protects the wearer against nightmares. At work a ruby increases your profile and will attract money and new orders to a business if you are self-employed.

Right Ruby protects the home. It is a stone of long-burning fire, whether in love or in the desire to make positive changes and achieve fame or fortune in tangible permanent ways.

CHILDREN AND ANIMALS
Ruby is too powerful for children or animals.

PSYCHIC ASSOCIATIONS
Use a star ruby for scrying. Focus on the place within the stone where the lines intersect and it is said you will connect with the Akashic records, the wisdom of humankind in all ages. Ruby brings prophetic dreams and it also provides a focus for prosperity rituals.

RECHARGING ITS ENERGIES
Wipe ruby carefully with a soft cloth and recharge under the light of the stars.

RUBY IN ZOISITE

MYTHOLOGY AND HISTORY
Ruby in zoisite is found in the African subcontinent, on rocky outcrops in the area of Mount Kilimanjaro, in Tanzania. The combination of these two magical and healing crystals – the ornate ruby of civilized beauty and adornment with the wild yet soothing power of nature expressed in zoisite – has made ruby in zoisite popular for healing and to provide insight.

Ruby in zoisite is also used to make fabulous modern carvings that express the synthesis of the tamed and free spirit.

DIVINATORY SIGNIFICANCE
At heart you are a free spirit and may need more time and space by yourself to express your individuality outside your present work or domestic world.

HEALING AND THE ENVIRONMENT
A stabilizing crystal, ruby in zoisite slows down a racing pulse and heartbeat. It directs energy into calm harmonious waves that enable your body and mind to maintain their equilibrium under stress. Protective against viruses and infections, especially bacterial ones, ruby in zoisite will soothe any inflammation.

Ruby in zoisite reduces over-acidity in the body and increases fertility in women and potency in men. It is also useful to counteract obsessions. In convalescence it helps to stop a person overexerting themselves or returning to the bad habits that may have contributed to the illness in the first place.

USES AT WORK AND HOME
Ruby in zoisite takes away excess emotional reactions, channelling enthusiasm into positive focused action at home or work. It is excellent for healing betrayal or lost love and at work prevents passions breaking out either as inappropriate anger or sexual feelings.

CHILDREN AND ANIMALS
Ruby in zoisite helps children and animals to learn social restraint while retaining their natural joy and spontaneity.

PSYCHIC ASSOCIATIONS
This crystal is wonderful for creating magical journeys in the mind and helps you produce visualizations either for your own psychic work or for leading a group.

RECHARGING ITS ENERGIES
Sprinkle ruby in zoisite with a rosemary infusion to revitalize its energies.

PROPERTIES
TYPE: Zoisite is a silicate and ruby a corundum
COLOUR: Red and black patches or swirls on bright green
SYMBOLIC ASSOCIATIONS
ZODIAC SIGN: Sagittarius
PLANET: Mars with Venus
ELEMENT: Earth and fire
CANDLE COLOUR: Green or green and red combined in a single candle
GUARDIAN ANGEL: Rampiel
CHAKRA: Heart / root
HERBS, INCENSES AND OILS: Cedar, fennel, ferns, pine, rosemary and mountain thyme
FLOWERS: Gentian, poppy and red valerian
ASSOCIATED CRYSTALS: Orbicular jasper, ruby and watermelon tourmaline

GARNET

See also green garnet (p91)

MYTHOLOGY AND HISTORY

According to myth, a garnet illuminated Noah's Ark day and night when the skies were black with rain. In Eastern Europe the garnet was said to protect against vampires. The garnet was worn by the Crusaders, who believed it would light the way home. In medieval times almandine garnets were used in jewellery and also in church and temple windows. Garnet represents the eighteenth wedding anniversary.

DIVINATORY SIGNIFICANCE

Use the cheaper, round, dark-red, almost opaque garnet in divination. If you draw this stone, avoid anyone who is critical or discouraging if you are trying to achieve a goal that may attract envy or opposition.

HEALING AND THE ENVIRONMENT

Associated with the root chakra, garnet is one of the best crystals for reawakening survival instincts. Garnet is a steady warmer: physically it heats cold fingers and toes, improves a sluggish circulation and relieves rheumatic joints. It also melts frozen feelings and paralyzing fear. Garnet can alleviate the acute pain of gallstones. Use it also for fertility and for stimulating healthy antibody growth against viruses and infections, especially winter illnesses.

USES AT WORK AND HOME

Garnet is protective against those who would steal your possessions, ideas or credit for work. It overcomes writer's block and lack of inspiration in any field.

CHILDREN AND ANIMALS

Garnets traditionally keep children safe when they go swimming or are near water. Use a garnet if a pet is unhappy about staying at home when its owners go to work.

PSYCHIC ASSOCIATIONS

Focus on a garnet to attain what you feel passionately about: a job or a creative venture. Wear one as a psychic shield in crowded places or when you are vulnerable.

RECHARGING ITS ENERGIES

Charge it on moonless or cloudy nights.

BLOODSTONE/HELIOTROPE

MYTHOLOGY AND HISTORY

Bloodstone gets its name from the myth that, at the crucifixion, the blood of Christ fell on green jasper. Engraved bloodstone was used by the Babylonians in divination and by them and the Ancient Egyptians to magically defeat enemies. A mother goddess stone, it is associated with mother-and-child images such as Isis and Horus and the Black Madonna.

DIVINATORY SIGNIFICANCE

You may need to stand up for the rights of someone who is temporarily vulnerable, perhaps against prejudice, or on behalf of a younger family member or colleague.

HEALING AND THE ENVIRONMENT

Bloodstone is primarily a cleanser, both of the blood and the whole system. It is especially recommended for the liver, kidneys, bone marrow and intestines and will help you stay on course if you are beginning a detox programme or a diet. An excellent women's stone, bloodstone relieves menstrual and menopausal symptoms and helps women keep up their strength in labour.

CHILDREN AND ANIMALS
Sew a bloodstone crystal in the lining of the coat of a child who is being teased or bullied at school. Bloodstone helps animal mothers, especially first-time mothers during labour.

PSYCHIC ASSOCIATIONS
Use bloodstone in goddess rituals and for exploring past lives, especially in dreams. In storms and in weather magic, use it to give you courage to shed destructive habits and people. Bloodstone also attracts money. It is a good charm for athletes and for anyone who wishes to win a competition. Make talking stones by casting five or six into a bowl of running water (use a tiny hose from a tap). Put the plug into a sink, close your eyes, ask a question and hear the answer in the water.

USES AT WORK AND HOME
Useful against bullies, emotional as well as physical, in the home and workplace. It will support you if you are a single parent or are the only carer of an elderly relation.

RECHARGING ITS ENERGIES
Use running water or sunlight.

PROPERTIES
TYPE: Chalcedony, a jasper variation
COLOUR: Dark green with red or orange or sometimes white spots
SYMBOLIC ASSOCIATIONS
ZODIAC SIGN: Aries
PLANET: Mars
ELEMENT: Fire
CANDLE COLOUR: Red
GUARDIAN ANGEL: Asrael
CHAKRA: Root/sacral
HERBS, INCENSES AND OILS: Basil, cinnamon, cumin, dragon's blood and ginger
FLOWERS: Scarlet pimpernel, red carnation and snapdragon
ASSOCIATED CRYSTALS: Amazonite, carnelian and red jasper

RED AVENTURINE
See also green aventurine (p80)

MYTHOLOGY AND HISTORY
A stone of balance, it was the talisman of the Mississippi paddle-boat poker players. Wise Native American chiefs carried red aventurine power stones to help their people survive long treks to reservations when all seemed lost.

DIVINATORY SIGNIFICANCE
You may need to act as an anchor on reality for those around you who may be taking extreme positions.

HEALING AND THE ENVIRONMENT
Red aventurine is helpful in encouraging the body to burn fat efficiently and also to lower cholesterol levels. As a stone of balance it is

especially helpful to anyone who is trying to lose weight permanently after years of fluctuating weight. It also relieves eczema and fungal infections of the skin. Aventurine comes in many colours: the softer the colour, the gentler the result.

USES AT WORK AND HOME
Red aventurine will redress the balance at home if one person does all the chores. At work this crystal will allow you to achieve your ambitions without upsetting the equilibrium of the workforce, to be successful without being ruthless.

CHILDREN AND ANIMALS
Aventurine prevents small boys being swept up in macho attitudes while helping girls to insist on equality of opportunity. It is good for overweight pets.

PSYCHIC ASSOCIATIONS
Use aventurine in fertility magic or in charm bags for an urgent infusion of money or to fast track your career.

RECHARGING ITS ENERGIES
Pass it through a candle of a similar colour.

PROPERTIES
TYPE: Oxide, quartz, with flecks of hematite, goethite or iron mica that make it glint. Opaque
COLOUR: Red, orange and peach
SYMBOLIC ASSOCIATIONS
ZODIAC SIGN: Aries
PLANET: Mars
ELEMENT: Earth
CANDLE COLOUR: Deep red
GUARDIAN ANGEL: Barakiel
CHAKRA: Solar plexus
HERBS, INCENSES AND OILS: Cedar, grey sage, rosemary, sweetgrass and white sage
FLOWERS: Columbine, red clover and tiger lily
ASSOCIATED CRYSTALS: Carnelian, red agate and red jasper

TIGER'S EYE

See also hawk's eye (p72) and red tiger's eye (p131)

Tiger's eye is said to contain the power of the sun and of earth and so can translate pure energy into material success. The Ancient Egyptians used it for amulets to transmit the power of Ra, the sun god.

RIGHT AND ABOVE Tiger's eye brings luck and good fortune.

PROPERTIES

TYPE: Oxide, quartz. Chatoyant (reflecting light in a wavy band)

COLOUR: Honey or golden-brown bands

SYMBOLIC ASSOCIATIONS

ZODIAC SIGN: Leo

PLANET: Sun

ELEMENT: Fire/earth

CANDLE COLOUR: Gold

GUARDIAN ANGEL: Uriel

CHAKRA: Solar plexus

HERBS, INCENSES AND OILS: Bay, blessed thistle, saffron, spearmint and walnut

FLOWERS: Buttercup, peony and sunflower

ASSOCIATED CRYSTALS: Amber, carnelian and golden topaz

MYTHOLOGY AND HISTORY:

Tiger's eye is associated with the tiger, the king of beasts in Eastern myths. In Japan, the tiger was believed to live for a thousand years. Roman soldiers carried tiger's eye so they would be brave in battle.

DIVINATORY SIGNIFICANCE

Lady luck is smiling on you. You may soon have more money, happiness, health and fulfilment. An excellent crystal to choose if you are involved in money-making ventures or planning a new project – if you keep your nerve.

HEALING PROPERTIES

Tiger's eye slows down a hyped-up system while gently energizing a weak or exhausted person. It reduces cravings for excess food, tobacco, alcohol or stimulants. It helps digestion and eases ulcers, bruises and stomach and gall-bladder problems. It warms rheumatic joints and bones. Above all, tiger's eye is an impetus for a balanced health, detoxification or exercise plan since it creates a steady, slow rhythm that is likely to lead to success.

USES AT WORK AND HOME

A natural luck and money bringer, tiger's eye keeps potential shopaholics in check as it injects a reality principle into finances. It helps those who work with stocks and shares and is good for estate agents, bankers and insurance staff. It balances money-generating skills with what will actually work and helps assess the reliability of would-be clients.

CHILDREN

Tiger's eye attracts success to a young person, especially in mid-teenage years, helping them not to be daunted by competition. It helps young entrepreneurs develop their computer and embryonic business skills that will bring them financial security. It counters stubbornness and deflects tantrums in toddlers.

ANIMALS

Tiger's eye is effective for overindulged pets that attempt to become domestic tyrants.

PROTECTIVE FUNCTIONS

Tiger's eye traditionally protects against the evil eye: carry one when you are facing a potential verbal, mental or psychic attack by someone in a position of power or who has emotional influence over you. Breathe in the golden light and allow it to create the aura of a tiger so all will turn back from attempting harm. It is also good for travellers.

PSYCHIC ASSOCIATIONS

Use tiger's eye in all prosperity rituals. As a money-attracting charm, keep a piece in a money pot and add a coin every day. Keep the pot in a warm place to incubate wealth. Use tiger's eye for scrying by candlelight or in sunlight; it is good for accessing past worlds and the wisdom of the cosmic memory bank. Tiger's eye stops you feeling spooked by powerful psychic energies or ghosts. Use one in a charm bag to prevent psychological or psychic vampires draining your energy.

ENVIRONMENTAL WORK

Use in empowerments to help conservation of tigers and other endangered big cats in the wild and for their care in conservation parks.

SPECIAL PROPERTIES

It is said that if you carry a tiger's eye, by the end of the day any deception or a person's untrustworthy nature will be revealed.

RECHARGING ITS ENERGIES

Tiger's eye loves late afternoon sunlight; use this to amplify its golden inner sun.

BROWN ZIRCON

MYTHOLOGY AND HISTORY

Romans prized the golden brown zircon that, like all orange and reddish zircons, was known as jacinth. According to the Roman writer Camillus Leonardus, jacinth increased ingenuity, glory and wealth and ensured travellers would not fall prey to diseases or attack. During the fourteenth century it was worn as a protection against the Black Death and it kept this role during the Great Plague of London in 1665. Brown zircon was believed to predict storms by glowing red.

DIVINATORY SIGNIFICANCE

Brown zircon is not used in divination.

HEALING AND THE ENVIRONMENT

An all-purpose healer, brown zircon will balance the pituitary and pineal gland. It eases bowel problems, especially those caused by stress or food allergies, for example irritable bowel syndrome, and also extreme constipation. Use it to relieve insomnia and also for delayed, irregular or scanty menstruation. It is very effective for chakra work: use it to activate the minor chakras on the soles of the feet (these chakras are ruled by the root chakra).

USES AT WORK OR HOME

A natural bringer of prosperity, brown zircon is primarily a stone of safe travel: use it for commuting, for holiday travel and for business trips. Keep it in the car to guard against road rage and reckless drivers. Keep a zircon crystal in your luggage to ensure that your accommodation will be welcoming and comfortable.

CHILDREN AND ANIMALS

Brown zircon gives children stability. Use it when an infant is learning to walk and to help older children become more agile. It helps animals to avoid picking up parasites, such as fleas and ticks.

PSYCHIC ASSOCIATIONS

This stone aids telepathy and helps to access the Akashic records, the collective wisdom of humankind, through meditation. Use it in rituals for the safe return of lost or stolen property.

RECHARGING ITS ENERGIES

Smudge zircon with sage or rosemary.

DESERT ROSE

MYTHOLOGY AND HISTORY

Legend tells that desert roses are formed by lightning that liquidizes sand, which then solidifies. Because of this, desert rose was long regarded as a gift from the deities and spirits of the desert places and as solidified fire.

DIVINATORY SIGNIFICANCE

Listen to your inner voice and, if necessary, step back and take stock of your life before making any concrete decisions. This is the stone of inner gold, which represents your as-yet-undeveloped potential.

HEALING AND THE ENVIRONMENT

This is an excellent crystal for healing grief and abuse and for letting go of what holds you back from experiencing life to the full. It is good for viral infections, especially skin ones, such as warts. Desert rose also relieves nausea and so is good for travel sickness and an unsettled stomach caused by tension. Desert rose will calm panic attacks and aid phobias, especially claustrophobia.

USES AT WORK AND HOME

Place a desert rose in the centre of the home for family unity. At work it is good to help you to develop a particular area of expertise or responsibility and for long-term training. Carry a desert rose crystal to keep a low profile at a time of possible redundancies, sackings or general tension in the workplace.

CHILDREN AND ANIMALS

Desert rose will help children who are shy to shine at a particular talent. It is a stone for very old and sick animals.

PSYCHIC ASSOCIATIONS

Desert rose can amplify fire magic, especially in transformation spells. It is good also for star magic, for accessing past lives and for contacting angelic or devic essences.

RECHARGING ITS ENERGIES

It is extremely delicate: cleanse by moonlight or by smudging with sage or sweetgrass.

PROPERTIES
TYPE: Gypsum that forms 'roses' in deserts
COLOUR: Pale brown or pinkish with silver/pearl glints
SYMBOLIC ASSOCIATIONS
ZODIAC SIGN: Scorpio
PLANET: Pluto
ELEMENT: Fire
CANDLE COLOUR: Pale brown
GUARDIAN ANGEL: Each desert rose contains its own guardian angel or deva. Close your eyes, hold the crystal, an image or a voice will form
CHAKRA: Root or heart (pink)
HERBS, INCENSES AND OILS: Copal, fennel, parsley, tarragon and witch hazel
FLOWERS: Flowering cactus, oleander and orchid
ASSOCIATED CRYSTALS: Petrified wood, fossils and banded agate

MAHOGANY OBSIDIAN

MYTHOLOGY AND HISTORY

Mahogany obsidian is called the blood of mother earth or Pele. Pele is the mother of volcanoes and is often described as sitting in her cave beneath the volcano by the light of a single blue flame. Some Hawaiians still claim descent from her, so this stone is sacred.

DIVINATORY SIGNIFICANCE

Do not set yourself too high standards or judge yourself critically. You should not hold back from opportunities because you doubt your ability to cope and to succeed with a new situation.

HEALING AND THE ENVIRONMENT

A powerful but warming crystal that will melt away energy blockages and improve your circulation. It is helpful for painful teeth and gums and will speed recovery after a debilitating illness or crisis. Wonderful for deep skin healing and for all hormonal problems with older women. It also helps you to enjoy your sexuality, rather than worrying about technique or about not having a perfect body. It helps in areas of land that suffer from erosion or subsidence.

USES AT WORK OR HOME

Mahogany obsidian is an excellent stone for helping you to make balanced decisions in any area of your life. It will guard the home from natural disasters such as floods, storm

damage, hurricanes, earth tremors or whirlwinds. It is a stone for grandmothers, young or old, and for any women over fifty.

CHILDREN AND ANIMALS

It helps children to resist dust mites. Place near an animal's bed to settle them.

PSYCHIC ASSOCIATIONS

Use mahogany obsidian for connecting with earth energies, for past-life work and all forms of fire or candle magic.

RECHARGING ITS ENERGIES

Recharge in late afternoon or autumn sunlight.

PROPERTIES
TYPE: Volcanic glass that has started to crystallize and contains high levels of iron
COLOUR: Mahogany, brownish-red or orange-brown with black spots or black with brownish spots, depending on the degree of crystallization
SYMBOLIC ASSOCIATIONS
ZODIAC SIGN: Scorpio
PLANET: Pluto
ELEMENT: Fire
CANDLE COLOUR: Burgundy
GUARDIAN ANGEL: Cassiel
CHAKRA: Solar plexus/root
HERBS, INCENSES AND OILS: Copal, dragon's blood, juniper, saffron and rosemary
FLOWERS: Blood rose, poppy and red nettle
ASSOCIATED CRYSTALS: Pumice, rainbow obsidian and tektite

BANDED AGATE

PROPERTIES

TYPE: Oxide, chalcedony, cryptocrystalline quartz

COLOUR: There are a vast number of banded agates. Browns and fawns of all shades are very common

SYMBOLIC ASSOCIATIONS

ZODIAC SIGN: Libra

PLANET: Mercury

ELEMENT: Air/earth

CANDLE COLOUR: Dark yellow or fawn

GUARDIAN ANGEL: Cassiel

CHAKRA: Root

HERBS, INCENSES AND OILS: Anise, ferns, lemongrass, sweetgrass and sagebrush

FLOWERS: Heather, lavender and pansy

ASSOCIATED CRYSTALS: Leopardskin jasper, moss agate and tree agate

MYTHOLOGY AND HISTORY

The 'earth rainbow', agate is a balancer. It celebrates the twelfth wedding anniversary.

DIVINATORY SIGNIFICANCE

Your dreams can come true if you take one practical step at a time, however small.

HEALING AND THE ENVIRONMENT

An all-healer, banded agate balances body, mind and spirit. It is good for the skin, stomach, colon, liver, spleen and kidneys. It shields the body from adverse side effects of X-rays and radiation. It benefits all plant life.

USES AT WORK AND HOME

Agate improves memory and concentration, increases stamina and encourages honesty. It is a stone of slow financial increase.

CHILDREN AND ANIMALS

Agates steady young children so they do not bump into objects, and reassures animals.

PSYCHIC ASSOCIATIONS

Carry or wear an agate for psychic protection and to prevent you absorbing others' negativity.

RECHARGING ITS ENERGIES

Bury agate in earth overnight.

PETRIFIED WOOD

PROPERTIES

TYPE: Fossilized trees in which the wood is replaced by a mineral, usually quartz or agate

COLOUR: Brown, grey, red or fawn. May be banded and include white

SYMBOLIC ASSOCIATIONS

ZODIAC SIGN: Virgo

PLANET: Earth/Saturn

ELEMENT: Earth/akasha

CANDLE COLOUR: Brown or grey

GUARDIAN ANGEL: Zuphlas

CHAKRA: Root

HERBS, INCENSES AND OILS: Burdock, echinacea, fennel, sage and thyme

FLOWERS: Polyanthus, poppy and snapdragon

ASSOCIATED CRYSTALS: Moss agate, rutilated quartz and tree agate

MYTHOLOGY AND HISTORY

Legends abound of forests that were turned to stone by witches or wizards or reclaimed by a mighty flood.

DIVINATORY SIGNIFICANCE

Look to traditional sources of wisdom and those who are truly wise to answer any questions you have. You may become interested in healing or ancient spirituality.

HEALING AND THE ENVIRONMENT

A stone of transformation, it is useful for illnesses that are difficult to diagnose or treat, for progressive illnesses, and those linked with age. It is useful for mobility problems and aids the spine, bones and skeleton.

USES AT WORK AND HOME

Petrified wood helps those living in old buildings and benefits homes with structural problems. At work it counters ageism and is good for archaeologists, librarians, historians, and those who study ancient religions. Use it

to protect woodlands and for reforestation.

CHILDREN AND ANIMALS

It helps children to value tradition. It relieves ailments and crankiness in old animals.

PSYCHIC PROPERTIES

Use it to connect with the wisdom of trees, to channel knowledge from wise spirit guides. It helps access past lives, to see into the Akashic records and to contact family ancestors.

RECHARGING ITS ENERGIES

Place near trees or tall plants for a few hours.

GEODES

MYTHOLOGY AND HISTORY
The Ancient Egyptians thought geodes were the eggs of a bird. They are Goddess symbols.

DIVINATORY SIGNIFICANCE
Place a geode in the four directions to amplify your intuition and protect you from negativity.

HEALING AND THE ENVIRONMENT
Set two halves of a geode or an amethyst and a citrine on your altar. They will amplify other healing crystals, herbs and oils and increase your spiritual powers. Use a pair as a fertility symbol or to help head problems.

USES AT WORK AND HOME
Every home should have a geode to absorb sorrow, anger and fear and release gentleness.

CHILDREN AND ANIMALS
Let a child choose a geode or buy one for a baby. They are good for nocturnal animals.

PSYCHIC ASSOCIATIONS
The ultimate shaman's stone, geodes bring visions and altered states of consciousness.

RECHARGING ITS ENERGIES
Allow candlelight to shine on to the geode.

PROPERTIES
TYPE: Stone hollow balls with crystal centres
COLOUR: Grey, brown or black with crystals within
SYMBOLIC ASSOCIATIONS
ZODIAC SIGN: Cancer
PLANET: Moon
ELEMENT: Water/earth
CANDLE COLOUR: Silver
GUARDIAN ANGEL: Gabriel
CHAKRA: Brow
HERBS, INCENSES AND OILS: Myrrh, eucalyptus, lemon, lotus and wintergreen
FLOWERS: Evening primrose, Michelmas daisy and petunia
ASSOCIATED CRYSTALS: Green garnet, moldavite and pietersite

PIETERSITE

MYTHOLOGY AND HISTORY
The Chinese called pietersite the eagle's eye, because of its blue gleam, or the tempest stone. It is named after Sid Pieters, who discovered it in Namibia in 1962.

DIVINATORY SIGNIFICANCE
Aim high: do not fear leaving what is safe and predictable. You are your own anchor.

HEALING AND THE ENVIRONMENT
Pietersite has positive effects on growth hormones and regulates blood pressure and body temperature. It aids the lungs and eyes.

USES WORK AND HOME
Pietersite is one of the best stones to help you to focus and prioritize if your home or work life is often interrupted. Use it if you work from home, job share or have a demanding family of any age. It is helpful also if you need to relocate home, work or both at short notice. It is beneficial if you have to travel by car in bad weather.

CHILDREN AND ANIMALS
Place in an older child's room to lessen chaos over lost items. It calms animals in storms.

PSYCHIC ASSOCIATIONS
A crystal to help you soar spiritually, especially if time for yourself is limited or too often cut short by other people's crises.

RECHARGING ITS ENERGIES
Leave it briefly in a storm or heavy rainfall.

PROPERTIES
TYPE: Oxide, quartz. Variation of tiger and hawk's/falcon's eye. Chatoyant
COLOUR: Dark brown or golden brown with blue/blue-black
SYMBOLIC ASSOCIATIONS
ZODIAC SIGN: Sagittarius
PLANET: Jupiter
ELEMENT: Air
CANDLE COLOUR: Blue
GUARDIAN ANGEL: Anpiel
CHAKRA: Crown/throat
HERBS, INCENSES AND OILS: Poppy, oakmoss, sagebrush, sandalwood and wintergreen
FLOWERS: Brown pansy, honesty and wallflower
ASSOCIATED CRYSTALS: Apatite, desert rose and hawk's eye

FOSSILS

See also petrified wood (p140)

PROPERTIES

TYPE: The preserved remains of creatures that over millions of years have been changed to stone

COLOUR: Brown, grey, fawn, green and black

SYMBOLIC ASSOCIATIONS

ZODIAC SIGN: Capricorn

PLANET: Saturn

ELEMENT: Earth

CANDLE COLOUR: Pale brown

GUARDIAN ANGEL: Semakiel

CHAKRA: Root

HERBS, INCENSES AND OILS: Aconite, amaranthus, barberry, moss and patchouli

FLOWERS: Foxglove, mimosa and red clover

ASSOCIATED CRYSTALS: Amber, jet and petrified wood

MYTHOLOGY AND HISTORY

The most common fossils are ammonites, fossilized sea animals, which are sometimes called snake or serpent stones. Fossilized sponges are known as witch stones. Fossils have been revered in the magical practices of many lands, and legends explain their origin. For example, the Celtic Christian saint, Hilda, said that the ammonites on Whitby Beach were snakes which she turned into stone whose heads had broken off when she cast them over the cliff. Fossils have been found in Neolithic burial mounds in various parts of the world, perhaps left there as a way of easing the passage to the afterlife.

DIVINATORY SIGNIFICANCE

Fossils are not used in divination.

HEALING AND THE ENVIRONMENT

A symbol of long life, fossils contain the life force, which is released in healing in a gentle but potent way. Ammonites especially were traditionally used in labour to relieve pain and to ease the birth.

USES AT WORK AND HOME

Fossils will help to bring tradition and character to a newly built house or apartment or one in a soulless area. They also create an organized home and increase domestic harmony. At work, fossils bring long-lasting success and stability to new or high-tech firms. All fossils are deeply protective.

CHILDREN AND ANIMALS

Fossils are not used for children or animals.

PSYCHIC ASSOCIATIONS

Use fossils in ritual to represent the earth element. It is excellent as a past-life and past-worlds focus, for Atlantean and Lemurian visualizations and for an increased intuitive understanding of crystals and stones.

RECHARGING ITS ENERGIES

Revitalize fossils in any ancient place, best of all within the sound of the sea.

LEOPARDSKIN JASPER / RHYOLITE

See also green/orbicular (p90) and red jasper (p128)

MYTHOLOGY AND HISTORY

A shaman's stone, leopardskin jasper is connected with the wisdom and the spiritual power of totem animals, especially fierce predators. The crystal (sometimes alternated with jaguar, panther or leopard teeth) was worn in a necklace for Otherworld travel.

DIVINATORY SIGNIFICANCE

Drawing leopardskin jasper promises that spring is in the air, whether an emotional rebirth or practical steps towards the tomorrow you want.

HEALING AND THE ENVIRONMENT

Leopardskin jasper is a stone of regeneration: it can make you look and feel younger and more energetic if you carry it with you. It is useful for all skin problems, for skin growths and blemishes, especially viral ones. It helps deal with infections and promotes the speedy healing of animal bites or insect stings. It speeds emotional healing after trauma or a nervous breakdown.

Leopardskin jasper is potent for the conservation of endangered big cats in the wild and ill-treated domestic ones.

USES AT WORK AND AT HOME

Leopardskin jasper brings what you need, not what you think you want. Use it for rekindling love that has become buried beneath domestic, career or financial concerns. It will help to lower your psychological and physical profile when you need to remain unobtrusive.

CHILDREN AND ANIMALS

Leopardskin jasper strengthens the link between animals and children; buy one when you first acquire a pet. It is the ultimate stone for contented cats.

PSYCHIC ASSOCIATIONS

Use leopardskin jasper in charm bags and altars to connect you with all kinds of magical powers, especially with the power of the four winds and archetypal animal strengths. Use it

for astral travel on the back of a wild cat, and for amplifying telepathic cat communication (try it at a wild cat conservation park as well as with your pet).

RECHARGING ITS ENERGIES

Leave it anchored outside on a windy day.

HOLEY STONES

MYTHOLOGY AND HISTORY

The most ancient and magical of all healing stones, holey stones are also called holy stones, or hag stones. The most famous is the huge pre-Celtic Men an Tol at Morvah in Cornwall, UK, through which children were passed for healing. Holey stones were also called the Stone of Odin, because, in Viking legend, the Odin turned himself into a worm in order to pass through a hole in the rock to steal the mead of poetry and inspiration.

DIVINATORY SIGNIFICANCE

Use a small round stone for divination. This is a magical time when anything can happen, but you can be sure it will be good. You may receive unexpected good news.

HEALING AND THE ENVIRONMENT

An all-healer which draws out illness and protects against disease, holey stone is helpful for childhood ills and infections, especially chicken pox. Holey stone relieves cramps, stomach and bone pains. You can direct absent healing to a person, animal or place through the hole if held up to sunlight or full moonlight (do not look directly at the sun).

USES AT WORK AND HOME

Holey stones will protect homes, workplaces, farms and farm buildings, warehouses and boats, if suspended on a red cord tied with three knots. Stones with three holes are especially powerful.

CHILDREN AND ANIMALS

Holey stones are especially protective for children and animals and will protect children from nightmares.

PSYCHIC ASSOCIATIONS

Gaze through the hole to see fairies and nature spirits and to glimpse the future. Use as a wish stone and use a pointed holey stone for dowsing.

RECHARGING ITS ENERGIES

Use flowing water, best of all the sea.

CAT'S EYE

PROPERTIES

TYPE: Chrysoberyl, the original cat's eye, and tiger's and hawk's eye. Also carnelian, diopside, selenite, tourmaline and moonstone. Translucent

COLOUR: Orangey-brown, yellow, golden, orange or green, but also creamy white

SYMBOLIC ASSOCIATIONS

ZODIAC SIGN: Leo

PLANET: Sun / Venus (green)

ELEMENT: Fire / earth

CANDLE COLOUR: Gold

GUARDIAN ANGEL: Seratiel

CHAKRA: Sacral

HERBS, INCENSES AND OILS: Apricot, benzoin, frankincense, neroli and Solomon's seal

FLOWERS: Freesia, oleander and peach blossom

ASSOCIATED CRYSTALS: Hawk's eye (blue tiger's eye), peridot and topaz

MYTHOLOGY AND HISTORY

From early times, cat's eye was believed to protect against the evil eye, to attract fabulous wealth and to make the wearer invisible or to take the form of a cat. It was sacred to the temple cats in Burma, who were believed to be reincarnated priests, and in Egypt to the cat goddess Bast. Cat's eye stones were made into thumb rings by medieval archers to give the bowman acute vision, especially at twilight.

DIVINATORY SIGNIFICANCE

Finances or fortunes are or soon will be on the increase, especially if you have suffered a loss or reversal. In the meantime, conserve your resources where possible.

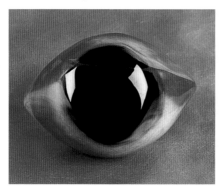

HEALING AND THE ENVIRONMENT

Cat's eye will increase your inner radiance and help you to love yourself. It can be used to aid vision, especially night vision, and mental clarity. It increases the healing effect of other stones.

USES AT WORK AND HOME

The prosperity bringer, use cat's eye at home and work to restore lost fortune or income or to find other sources of making money. It is a good stone for all those who work at night or travel after dark.

CHILDREN AND ANIMALS

Cat's eye is deeply protective of children, but younger ones sometimes find this crystal a little creepy. It is an excellent stone for cats, especially pedigree ones.

PSYCHIC ASSOCIATIONS

Cat's eye is good when you want to lower your psychological or physical profile. Gaze into the stone and visualize yourself surrounded by shimmering light. It is also good for scrying and for increasing your intuitive and clairvoyant powers.

RECHARGING ITS ENERGIES

Use a fibre optic lamp, twinkling Christmas tree lights or a brilliant starlit night.

SMOKY QUARTZ

PROPERTIES

TYPE: Quartz (also called Cairngorm). Translucent

COLOUR: Smoky brown or dark grey, tinted by natural radiation

SYMBOLIC ASSOCIATIONS

ZODIAC SIGN: Capricorn

PLANET: Saturn

ELEMENT: Earth

CANDLE COLOUR: Indigo

GUARDIAN ANGEL: Torquaret

CHAKRA: Crown / root

HERBS, INCENSES AND OILS: Cedar, cypress, ivy, mullein and patchouli

FLOWERS: Brown carnation, mimosa and pansy

ASSOCIATED CRYSTALS: Garnet, obsidian and rutilated quartz

MYTHOLOGY AND HISTORY

A guardian against all forms of bad luck, particularly in Alpine regions, smoky quartz was traditionally made into crucifixes and set on bedroom walls to keep away evil.

DIVINATORY SIGNIFICANCE

Smoky quartz promises a better tomorrow and light at the end of what may seem to be a very long tunnel.

HEALING AND THE ENVIRONMENT

Smoky quartz is excellent after a period of illness or depression for gently restoring energy and optimism. It will melt all energy blocks in limbs, in the adrenal glands,

pancreas and kidneys It is also beneficial for kidney stones. It reduces anxiety, relieves psychological sexual blocks and can aid insomnia. Stand on grass or earth, holding your smoky quartz pointing downwards in your receptive hand and negativity will drain out of your body and mind. It is an unusually gentle crystal for opening your kundalini energy if you have become very tired or dispirited. Use it to direct light from the crown chakra into your body.

USES AT WORK AND HOME

Smoky quartz protects the home and work premises. It guards vehicles from theft and breakdown and the driver against road rage.

CHILDREN AND ANIMALS

This is helpful at night for banishing children's nightmares and fears of the dark: let the child see the light of the moon or shine a tiny torch through the crystal. A pain reliever for older animals, it protects nocturnal creatures.

PSYCHIC ASSOCIATIONS

Use it by candlelight as a focus for astral travel: in your mind's eye, create within the the crystal a tunnel and doorway of light into other realms. It aids meditation if you find concentration difficult. Use it for channelling the wisdom of earth spirits at old sites. It is good for bringing peaceful dreams.

RECHARGING ITS ENERGIES

Leave it on a rock, preferably at a sacred site, for twenty minutes to absorb earth energies.

PUMICE / LAVA

MYTHOLOGY AND HISTORY

Pumice is formed when lava is filled with gas bubbles as it spews out of the volcano. Pele, the Hawaiian goddess of volcanoes, fire and magic, is the mistress of lava. Pumice is especially magical because it floats on water. Lava is magical because it involves the fusion of the four elements, the molten lava representing the element of water.

HEALING AND THE ENVIRONMENT

Pointed lava will draw out pain and illness: pass it anticlockwise round a candle and flick the pain in the lava towards the candle. Lava is good for chronic skin conditions, rashes and allergies of all kinds. Pumice is traditionally

held by women in labour to ease the pain of birth. It is also used to absorb menstrual cramps and will relieve cramp in any part of the body.

USES AT WORK AND HOME

Lava protects the home from lightning, fire and intruders. At work it will act as an amulet of protection against bad-tempered employers or colleagues and spiteful workplace gossip. Alternatively, have a pair of small pumice stones at home or work, one lighter coloured to attract good fortune, and a darker one near the door to absorb negative vibes. When the bad vibe stone feels heavy, float it away on water and replace it.

CHILDREN AND ANIMALS

It is too powerful for children and animals.

PSYCHIC ASSOCIATIONS

A magical stone used in protection rituals, candle and fire magic and to encircle your bed at night to ward off malevolence or psychic attack. Whisper your secret desires and wishes into the holes in pumice, or call a lover, and set it afloat on running water. Banish sorrows by telling your pumice.

RECHARGING ITS ENERGIES

Pass clockwise round a red candle flame.

PROPERTIES
TYPE: Volcanic rock. Rough (male) or smooth (female)
COLOUR: Brown or grey towards black, also blue

SYMBOLIC ASSOCIATIONS
ZODIAC SIGN: Aries
PLANET: Mars
ELEMENT: Fire
CANDLE COLOUR: Red
GUARDIAN ANGEL: Samael
CHAKRA: Sacral/root
HERBS, INCENSES AND OILS: Basil, coriander, ginger, nettle and peppermint
FLOWERS: Bracken, heather and thistle
ASSOCIATED CRYSTALS: Hematite and iron pyrites

OBSIDIAN

See also snowflake (p150), mahogany (p139) and rainbow obsidian (p92)

The more opaque obsidian is, the more concentrated its powers. In the polished form it is usually sold in, most obsidian is opaque, though shining. Apache tears, natural water-worn pebbles, are translucent.

MYTHOLOGY AND HISTORY

Apache tears are named after an incident in Arizona. Soldiers ambushed a group of Apaches. Many were killed and the rest leapt over a cliff, rather than be taken. The women of the tribe wept at the base of the cliff and their tears were embedded in obsidian. It is said that those who carry Apache tears will never know deep sorrow.

From early times obsidian was carved into arrowheads; obsidian arrows are still used for protection when set points facing outwards. Myth relates that the seven arrows of the Ancient Egyptian lion goddess Sekhmet were sometimes made of obsidian: she used them magically against wrongdoers.

Highly polished obsidian was used by the Mayans for magic mirrors. In Elizabethan times John Dee had a similar divining mirror. Obsidian is often called the wizard stone.

ABOVE Obsidian arrows are regarded as a protective amulet to repel harm.

RIGHT Obsidian is associated with thistles.

DIVINATORY SIGNIFICANCE

Let old sorrows go; happier times are ahead and there is a light at the end of the tunnel. You have a great deal of power you can use if you are not afraid to change the status quo.

HEALING PROPERTIES

A natural pain reliever, it improves circulation and is good for the arteries and the stomach. An excellent anti-shock crystal, obsidian lessens the power of phobias. It eases pain and blockages in the lower body, especially the lower spine and feet. Apache tears lift depression and relieve dark, stagnant energies.

USES AT HOME AND WORK

Black obsidian dampens inner anger and frustration at others' incompetence or stubbornness and creates the impetus for change.

Use obsidian spheres as stress absorbers at home and work. Obsidian helps things to run more smoothly. Apache tears lift the crippling inertia that comes from grief after loss.

CHILDREN

The Apache tear consoles a traumatized or grieving child. Hold it up to sunlight so that he or she can see that the light is still present. It likewise alleviates terrors of the dark.

ANIMALS

Black obsidian desensitizes a pet that overreacts to noise and traffic.

PROTECTIVE FUNCTIONS

All obsidian protects you from negative vibes and hostility at work or home. It is especially good for kind-hearted people who are innocent of the ways of the world. It is a traveller's stone, especially if you travel by night.

PSYCHIC ASSOCIATIONS

It is a stone of prophecy and amplifies magical powers. Use obsidian arrows for psychic self-defence, usually four, five or seven. Face them inwards round you or a central obsidian crystal to draw power. It is also excellent for labyrinth work and for rituals of the Black Madonna, Isis and her infant son Horus, the sky God. Apache tears are good for vision quests or spiritual pilgrimages, inner or outer.

ENVIRONMENTAL WORK

Apache tears help in the preservation and regeneration of indigenous spirituality, especially Native North American.

SPECIAL PROPERTIES

Obsidian is a personal stone and is generally kept by one person, not given as a gift.

RECHARGING ITS ENERGIES

Recharge obsidian under any light source.

PROPERTIES

TYPE: Volcanic glass/magma with no crystalline structures

COLOUR: Black. Apache tears are dark smoky grey

SYMBOLIC ASSOCIATIONS

ZODIAC SIGN: Scorpio

PLANET: Pluto/Saturn

ELEMENT: Fire/earth

CANDLE COLOUR: Burgundy

GUARDIAN ANGEL: Uriel

CHAKRA: Root

HERBS, INCENSES AND OILS: Basil, mint, parsley, pine and sandalwood

FLOWERS: Primula, thistle and tulip

ASSOCIATED CRYSTALS: Blue goldstone, moldavite and tektite

DALMATIAN JASPER

PROPERTIES

TYPE: Cryptocrystalline quartz with iron oxide impurities. Opaque

COLOUR: Black spots on a fawn or paler background

SYMBOLIC ASSOCIATIONS

ZODIAC SIGN: Virgo

PLANET: Earth

ELEMENT: Earth

CANDLE COLOUR: Brown

GUARDIAN ANGEL: Thuriel

CHAKRA: Root

HERBS, INCENSES AND OILS: Cedar wood, fennel, mint, parsley and thyme

FLOWERS: Dandelion, dog rose and Michelmas daisy

ASSOCIATED CRYSTALS: Banded agate, leopardskin jasper and mookaite

MYTHOLOGY AND HISTORY

The unusual appearance of this Mexican stone has led to it being adopted as a crystal for healing animals and for veterinarians who practice alternative healing. Perhaps its pattern was nature's clue to mortals, as it does work remarkably well in this sphere.

DIVINATORY SIGNIFICANCE

You may find loyalty from an unexpected source if a fair-weather friend has dis-illusioned you recently. Anything to do with animals is well aspected.

HEALING THE ENVIRONMENT

Dalmatian jasper will cleanse and gently energize the auric field. It also improves the

state of internal organs and counters both constipation and irritable bowel conditions.

Use as a focus to help animals kept in badly run zoos, battery animals, those in circuses and all dogs that are badly treated.

USES AT WORK OR HOME

Dalmatian jasper is the stone to strengthen family loyalties, tell true from false friends, and for seeing through financial scams. It encourages teamwork rather than rivalry in the workplace. It is excellent for all who work closely with animals, especially vets, alternative practitioners or those working in animal welfare.

CHILDREN AND ANIMALS

Dalmatian jasper will overcome a child's fear of animals. It is the ultimate stone for dogs and all pets. It is excellent for strengthening the effect of herbal and flower-essence remedies in animal treatment.

PSYCHIC ASSOCIATIONS

The best stone for telepathic communication with animals, for learning animal healing and as a protective amulet for animals.

RECHARGING ITS ENERGIES

Leave it in greenery or between the fronds of a pot of herbs for twenty-four hours.

JET

MYTHOLOGY AND HISTORY

Like amber, jet is of great antiquity. Jet is sacred to Cybele, mother of the Gods in Classical mythology. Since the Bronze Age, jet from Yorkshire has been used for ornaments and jewellery. It has been found among grave goods for thousands of years. It became popular when Queen Victoria wore it after the death of Prince Albert. Jet was carried by sailors' wives to keep their husbands safe at sea, a practice that dates back to Viking times.

DIVINATORY SIGNIFICANCE

Accept that you need to let a past sorrow or regret go. Protect yourself from anyone who drains your energies.

HEALING AND THE ENVIRONMENT

Jet is an excellent stone for all skin problems, bites and stings, tooth pains, neuralgia, migraines, stomach pains caused by irritations of the colon or bowel and for colds. Use it to relieve labour pains and all pains or swellings in the lower body, legs and feet. Psychologically it guards against nightmares and free-floating anxiety.

USES AT WORK AND HOME

Jet is naturally protective, especially if there has been bereavement or divorce in a family. In home and business, jet will stabilize finances and help you to take practical steps to overcome debt problems. At home or work,

CHILDREN AND ANIMALS
In earlier times jet was placed on the stomach of a newborn to provide lifelong protection from harm. Encourage a child to talk about any fears while holding a piece of jet and then bury the jet – and the fears. Jet will help ease an old animal into death.

place a piece of jet facing the outer door to keep negative people and vibes at bay. Leave a piece of jet in the hearth or near the centre of the home if you are going away, as an amulet and a sign of a safe return.

PSYCHIC ASSOCIATIONS
Though a mother goddess stone, jet often represents the God energies in witchcraft and a piece can be placed on the altar next to the amber that symbolizes the Goddess. Like amber, jet is used as a doorway into other dimensions, especially the past.

RECHARGING ITS ENERGIES
Bury jet in soil overnight. Jet jewellery is traditionally only worn by one person.

PROPERTIES
TYPE: Organic fossilized wood that has been turned into a dense form of coal. Opaque, glassy
COLOUR: Black or occasionally very dark brown

SYMBOLIC ASSOCIATIONS
ZODIAC SIGN: Capricorn
PLANET: Saturn
ELEMENT: Earth
CANDLE COLOUR: Very dark purple or black
GUARDIAN ANGEL: Cassiel
CHAKRA: Root
HERBS, INCENSES AND OILS: Cedar, cypress, ivy, hyssop and myrrh
FLOWERS: Asphodel, dark-red carnation and white lily
ASSOCIATED CRYSTALS: Black marble, obsidian and black onyx

BLACK ONYX
See also sardonyx (p153)

MYTHOLOGY AND HISTORY
Black onyx is either naturally black or has been heat treated. A stone associated with wizards and sorcerers, in the Middle East, onyx is believed to absorb sorrow. It was engraved with the image of Mars or Hercules in Classical times as an icon of courage.

DIVINATORY SIGNIFICANCE
Indicates the need to bring matters that have been dragging on to a satisfactory conclusion.

HEALING AND THE ENVIRONMENT
This stone has strong grounding properties. It is good for all problems with the ear, especially the inner ear, with balance and sensory and motor mechanisms within the body, for the health of the soft tissue and for feet. It is used to ease animal bites.

It is excellent for working against chemical and fuel emissions from factories and against chemical waste that pollutes rivers.

USES AT WORK AND HOME
This is a very useful stone for helping those who are easily distracted to concentrate, for stopping nightmares and for protection after dark, both in the home and while travelling. At work black onyx helps you to stand up for yourself in an argument or unfair criticism,

especially from someone senior, without losing your temper. Onyx will also lower the sexual temperature in workplace encounters.

CHILDREN AND ANIMALS
Older children may like this protective stone; some do not. It protects animals out at night.

PSYCHIC ASSOCIATIONS
Use it for grounding you in rituals and during astral projection. Used mainly in defensive magic to send back any form of negativity.

RECHARGING ITS ENERGIES
Leave your onyx to recharge in sunlight.

PROPERTIES
TYPE: Chalcedony
COLOUR: Black

SYMBOLIC ASSOCIATIONS
ZODIAC SIGN: Capricorn
PLANET: Saturn
ELEMENT: Earth
CANDLE COLOUR: White
GUARDIAN ANGEL: Semakiel
CHAKRA: Root
HERBS, INCENSES AND OILS: Aloe vera, ambergris (synthetic) copal, cypress and patchouli
FLOWERS: Wild cherry, edelweiss, Glastonbury thorn or blackthorn blossom and flowering ivy
ASSOCIATED CRYSTALS: Jet, sardonyx and black marble

NEBULA

PROPERTIES

TYPE: Unclassified as yet, a quartz pentellerite. Opaque

COLOUR: Black/very dark green with lighter green orbs

SYMBOLIC ASSOCIATIONS

ZODIAC SIGN: Scorpio

PLANET: Pluto

ELEMENT: Air

CANDLE COLOUR: Burgundy

GUARDIAN ANGEL: Raziel

CHAKRA: Crown

HERBS, INCENSES AND OILS: Mullein, frankincense, myrrh and mugwort

FLOWERS: Fuchsia, oleander and poinsettia

ASSOCIATED CRYSTALS: Moldavite, rainbow moonstone and tektite

MYTHOLOGY AND HISTORY

Nebula was found in a wild area of Mexico. The stone resembles the sky seen through a telescope.

DIVINATORY SIGNIFICANCE

You may need to reassess a situation, perhaps at work or with a new social group, and see how far you can go along with principles you may feel are not reconcilable with your own.

HEALING AND THE ENVIRONMENT

Nebula can connect us with cosmic energies and so enables us to tap into healing powers emanating from the more spiritually evolved parts of ourselves. It is valuable for unifying the whole self and is useful for all who feel alienated, fragmented or pulled in different directions by life. A mother earth stone found to heal modern ills, it may help those diseases created by environmental neglect. Nebula is a reminder of the sanctity of all life, including plants, rocks, insects and birds.

USES AT WORK AND HOME

Nebula is a reminder of our responsibility for our own actions and words. It reminds us that each individual contributes to the morality and caring attitude of the whole.

CHILDREN AND ANIMALS

Use nebula to explain to children their place in the universe. Nebula makes it easier to communicate telepathically with animals.

PSYCHIC ASSOCIATIONS

Use nebula for meditation, for astral travel and for channelling the wisdom of star guardians. We do not yet fully understand the healing properties of this new stone.

RECHARGING ITS ENERGIES

Use starlight to recharge nebula.

SNOWFLAKE OBSIDIAN

PROPERTIES

TYPE: Volcanic glass/magma in which grey feldspar inclusions appear as the obsidian crystallizes. Opaque

COLOUR: Black with white spots

SYMBOLIC ASSOCIATIONS

ZODIAC SIGN: Capricorn

PLANET: Saturn

ELEMENT: Earth

CANDLE COLOUR: White

GUARDIAN ANGEL: Shalgiel

CHAKRA: Crown/root

HERBS, INCENSES AND OILS: Cedar, cypress, lemongrass, sweetgrass and yarrow

FLOWERS: Sweet tobacco, snowdrop and white hyacinth

ASSOCIATED CRYSTALS: Apache tears, black onyx and sardonyx

MYTHOLOGY AND HISTORY

Snowflake obsidian is the equivalent of the Chinese yin/yang symbol, a representation of the unity of opposites that create life. It is valuable in the centre of medicine wheels and magic circles. It is a charm against hard winters.

DIVINATORY SIGNIFICANCE

A stone that indicates new beginnings, hope after a setback or despair and gentle gradual improvement in whatever area of your life has caused you pain in the past.

HEALING AND THE ENVIRONMENT

Snowflake obsidian, especially when held on the body at a major artery point, will improve circulation, assist the efficient processing of fat and encourage cells and skin to regrow healthily. Use it for warming frozen limbs, to help blurred vision, to soothe migraines and to dissolve deep-seated depression. It will remove pain and energize at the same time. Use in empowerments for a fairer distribution of world resources and wealth.

USES AT WORK AND HOME

A stone for spring-cleaning and clearing your mind. It clears away illusions and prevents daydreaming. Use it to acknowledge and express creatively your own negative feelings and unfulfilled needs without feeling guilty.

CHILDREN AND ANIMALS

It guides children who are liberal with the truth. It is useful for all slow-moving, cold-blooded or naturally nocturnal creatures.

PSYCHIC ASSOCIATIONS

Add to a charm bag to give you protection and good fortune. It increases clairaudient powers and can be used in ritual or when scrying to discover the truth about a person or situation. It assists accuracy when reading the I Ching.

RECHARGING ITS ENERGIES

Burn a tiny dark and a white candle in front of it until the candles are burned through.

BOJI STONE

MYTHOLOGY AND HISTORY
Smooth and round Boji stones are female, male stones are more angular, have pointed uneven surfaces, feel heavier and are more crystalline. They work best as a pair. Androgynous stones that combine both features can be used singly. Known to shamans in North America for hundreds of years, they have been introduced into crystal lore comparatively recently.

DIVINATORY SIGNIFICANCE
Boji stones are not suitable for divination.

HEALING AND THE ENVIRONMENT
Hold a boji stone in each hand to balance the chakras. Experiment to see if the male stone feels better in the right or left hand. With a single stone, hold the boji in your receptive hand. Use both, or the single boji, to cleanse and rebalance the aura. Hold your boji stone/s every morning to give you energy and fill you with harmony. They relieve discomfort if one is held over the painful spot and are good for cell and tissue regeneration, especially after an illness. Use them to send healing to the planet. They unbalance other crystals, so store separately.

USES AT WORK AND HOME
If you are very sensitive to atmospheres, boji stones will act as a protective barrier. They shield you against psychic or emotional vampires.

CHILDREN AND ANIMALS
They are too powerful for children or animals.

PSYCHIC ASSOCIATIONS
Good for past-life work and for astral travel, boji stones bring out innate healing powers.

RECHARGING ITS ENERGIES
Expose to the light, if possible the sun, once a week. They also love full moonlight. Charge through handling.

PROPERTIES
TYPE: Palladium and pyrite discs in layers or platelets
COLOUR: Black or grey / brown with a gold sparkle. May have a rainbow sheen

SYMBOLIC ASSOCIATIONS
ZODIAC SIGN: Scorpio
PLANET: Uranus
ELEMENT: Earth / fire
CANDLE COLOUR: Burgundy
GUARDIAN ANGEL: Cassiel
CHAKRA: Balances all the chakras
HERBS, INCENSES AND OILS: Clove, bergamot, hyssop, lemon balm and nutmeg
FLOWERS: Almond blossom, edelweiss and gardenia
ASSOCIATED CRYSTALS: None

TEKTITE
See also moldavite (p79)

MYTHOLOGY AND HISTORY
Tektites were associated with the gods of thunder and lightning. An otherworldly stone, tektite is associated with extraterrestrial forces and is carried by some people in areas of UFO activity to prevent alien abduction.

DIVINATORY SIGNIFICANCE
Tektite can signify a time of spiritual change or development, perhaps owing to a psychic experience or sudden illumination.

HEALING AND THE ENVIRONMENT
Use tektite for all skin disorders, problems with the autoimmune system and for illnesses such as ME that drain the body of strength.

USES AT WORK AND HOME
Tektite should be buried near your front and/or back doors, in a plant pot if you live in an apartment, to guard your home against fire, storms and hostility and to attract abundance. In your career, use tektite to kindle your inner power to make change.

CHILDREN AND ANIMALS
It is too powerful for children and animals.

PSYCHIC ASSOCIATIONS
Tektite is associated with extraterrestrial channelling and especially with the healing energies from the guardians of the Pleiades, a group of stars within the seasonal constellation Taurus. Some myths recount that the Mayans came from the Pleiades and were thereby guardians of the solar system. Tektite is excellent for all star magic, for lucid dreaming and clear dream recall.

RECHARGING ITS ENERGIES
Leave outside in stormy weather, particularly when lightning is flashing. Or leave out at night in late August, during the frequent meteor showers from the Pleiades region.

PROPERTIES
TYPE: Natural glass, formed where lightning or meteorites struck sand, fusing it into glass. Smooth and shiny outside, glassy inside
COLOUR: Black / dark grey

SYMBOLIC ASSOCIATIONS
ZODIAC SIGN: Sagittarius
PLANET: Jupiter / Pluto
ELEMENT: Fire
CANDLE COLOUR: Grey
GUARDIAN ANGEL: Jehoel
CHAKRA: Brow
HERBS, INCENSES AND OILS: Allspice, basil, dragon's blood, ginger, juniper and star anise
FLOWERS: Hollyhock, red thistle and blood-red roses
ASSOCIATED CRYSTALS: Moldavite, meteorite and obsidian

BLACK OPAL

See also rainbow (p70), white (p39), water (p40) and blue opal (p70)

PROPERTIES

TYPE: Hydrated silica, non-crystalline. Opaque
COLOUR: Grey/blue to black; red, orange, green, blue flashes

SYMBOLIC ASSOCIATIONS

ZODIAC SIGN: Cancer
PLANET: Saturn/Mars
ELEMENT: Fire/water
CANDLE COLOUR: Silver
GUARDIAN ANGEL: Gabriel
CHAKRA: Root/crown
HERBS, INCENSES AND OILS: Cypress, ivy, mugwort, myrrh and sandalwood
FLOWERS: Lily, white carnation and white lotus
ASSOCIATED CRYSTALS: Black pearl, obsidian and jet

MYTHOLOGY AND HISTORY

According to legend, opals were the tears of happiness shed by Zeus after he defeated the Titans. The earliest opals, about six thousand years old, have been found in a cave in Kenya.

DIVINATORY SIGNIFICANCE

Black opal is not used in divination.

HEALING AND THE ENVIRONMENT

Black opal absorbs pain or illness and replaces it with healing rainbow light. It eases chronic bone problems or weakness and any disease deep within the body tissue. Use it to counter side effects from X-ray or laser treatments and to reduce the toxicity of chemical treatments.

USES AT WORK AND HOME

It transforms the fears that hold us back from action into optimism and an eagerness to get on with life. It establishes order and helps us to formulate and put into practice logical steps towards completing any necessary task.

CHILDREN AND ANIMALS

Black opal helps children not to be afraid of being out in the dark or away from street-lights in the countryside. It eases animals with very poor eyesight and is good for guide dogs.

PSYCHIC ASSOCIATIONS

A power stone, black opal has been used throughout magical history by wizards and magicians and more recently in Wiccan rituals as a God stone (a white opal is the Goddess stone). It amplifies power magically and an amulet of black opal attracts good fortune.

RECHARGING ITS ENERGIES

It is very delicate: regularly recharge it only in water, to keep it hydrated.

BLACK PEARL

See also pearl (p40)

PROPERTIES

TYPE: Organic. Opaque
COLOUR: Lustrous black

SYMBOLIC ASSOCIATIONS

ZODIAC SIGN: Scorpio
PLANET: Moon
ELEMENT: Water
CANDLE COLOUR: Silver
GUARDIAN ANGEL: Raguel
CHAKRA: Sacral
HERBS, INCENSES AND OILS: Calamus, ambergris (synthetic), moonwort, lemon balm and violet
FLOWERS: Jasmine, night-scented stock and iris
ASSOCIATED CRYSTALS: Black opal, rainbow obsidian and apache tears

MYTHOLOGY AND HISTORY

Chinese myth says that the full moon produced so much heavenly dew from the discarded dreams and memories of men that it fell into the sea. Oysters came to the surface and opened their shells; the dewdrops fell inside and hardened into pearls. The black ones are all the sad thoughts transformed into beauty and hope by the moon mother. Black pearl is associated with the dark of the moon.

DIVINATORY SIGNIFICANCE

Black pearl in not used in divination.

HEALING AND THE ENVIRONMENT

Black pearl clears infections, especially lung or chest congestion, and protects against passive smoking. It is good for solid masses, whether organs, tissue or dense bone mass. It helps women in the perimenopausal phase and after the menopause: black pearl controls mood swings and adjusts their body to a deeper form of sexuality and harmony.

USES AT WORK AND HOME

A natural bringer of abundance, good luck and prosperity at home. It protects the owner against accidents, especially near water.

CHILDREN AND ANIMALS

It heals grief and helps children cope with their first experiences of evil in the world. It is not suitable for animals.

PSYCHIC ASSOCIATIONS

It is very magical for women, enabling them to contact their deeper wisdom. Use it for all women's mysteries and for channelling the wisdom of the Crone Goddess, for night astral travelling and for scrying by silver candlelight.

RECHARGING ITS ENERGIES

Keep away from heat or dryness. Polish with a silk cloth. Recharge with a dark pointed amethyst.

STAUROLITE

MYTHOLOGY AND HISTORY
Called fairy crosses, staurolites were thought to be a gift from the fey folk and were associated with fairy magic. Later they were carried by Crusaders. It is said they are the crystallized tears that fairies wept when they heard of the crucifixion. Staurolites have been carried for centuries as protective charms. The cross represents the meeting of the four elements.

DIVINATORY SIGNIFICANCE
Staurolite is not used in divination.

HEALING AND THE ENVIRONMENT
A very personal stone that will help you to balance your own energies, strengthen your skeletal formation and heal aspects of life that are holding back your spiritual development.

USES AT WORK AND HOME
Staurolite will give you a great deal of inner security that enables you to follow what you believe to be the right path. It is good for those who strive for the greater good of humankind, campaigners, aid workers and carers of seriously ill or disabled people. It protects all who travel, especially over long distances or for long periods.

CHILDREN AND ANIMALS
Use for children who have chronic illnesses. This stone is helpful for all beasts of burden.

PSYCHIC PROPERTIES
It was said that the possessor of a staurolite could command the four elements and so it is a powerful focus in any form of elemental magic. It is also helpful for personal power and good fortune. Use it wisely for personal gain.

RECHARGING ITS ENERGIES
Bury staurolite in a pot of earth or sand or in the garden for twenty-four hours.

PROPERTIES
TYPE: Twinned crystals of iron and aluminium silicate crosses

COLOUR: Black, dark reddish- or yellowy-brown, streaked with white, weathering to dull grey

SYMBOLIC ASSOCIATIONS
ZODIAC SIGN: Scorpio

PLANET: Pluto

ELEMENT: Four elements

CANDLE COLOUR: Burgundy

GUARDIAN ANGEL: Riehol

CHAKRA: Root

HERBS, INCENSES AND OILS: Basil, ambergris (artificial), all spice, pine and sagebrush

FLOWERS: Foxglove, lily of the valley and primrose

ASSOCIATED CRYSTALS: Banded agate, mahogany obsidian and petrified wood

SARDONYX

MYTHOLOGY AND HISTORY
From Classical times sardonyx has been much used for cameos, jewellery, mosaics and statues. It is associated with the god Mars, the hero Hercules and with saints. Traditionally, stones containing bands of black, white and red were said to signify humility, virtue and courage. A sardonyx talisman would bring marriage within the year.

DIVINATORY SIGNIFICANCE
To achieve what you want, you may need to negotiate through official channels and fill in what seems to be unnecessary paperwork.

HEALING AND THE ENVIRONMENT
It eases back and spinal pain, menstrual cramps, bowel or bladder problems and cleanses the body of blockages and impurities.

USES AT WORK AND HOME
Sardonyx will bring healing in the home either between a couple or parents and children. It is good for all legal matters and for obtaining justice, for all who work in lawmaking or enforcement and for civil-liberties campaigners. At work it offers the courage to be you, not intimidated by others.

CHILDREN AND ANIMALS
Children can benefit from the courage of sardonyx, especially if they do not fit in with the crowd. It helps find lost animals: hold it in your power hand and call the animal.

PSYCHIC ASSOCIATIONS
Sardonyx is used to amplify energies in fire or candle magic and in rituals to mend family or marital rifts. Make a stone pile or cairn of tiny pieces of onyx, naming a step you must take to overcome difficult odds for each piece. Add a stone and repeat the steps out loud every day.

RECHARGING ITS ENERGIES
Sprinkle a clockwise circle of rose petals or rose-based pot pourri round it and leave from dusk to dawn.

PROPERTIES
TYPE: Chalcedony with bands of sard

COLOUR: White and black, sometimes with reddish brown

SYMBOLIC ASSOCIATIONS
ZODIAC SIGN: Capricorn

PLANET: Mars

ELEMENT: Fire

CANDLE COLOUR: White

GUARDIAN ANGEL: Zagzagel

CHAKRA: Root

HERBS, INCENSES AND OILS: Anise, basil, cumin, cinnamon, musk (synthetic) and juniper

FLOWERS: Geranium, hibiscus and red tulip

ASSOCIATED CRYSTALS: Black onyx, brecciated jasper and jet

LABRADORITE

PROPERTIES
TYPE: Plagioclase feldspar
COLOUR: Grey, also blue, green and black (with grey). High-quality labradorite has iridescent flashes of red, blue, green, gold and silver
SYMBOLIC ASSOCIATIONS
ZODIAC SIGN: Scorpio
PLANET: Pluto
ELEMENT: Ice (the fifth element in the frozen north)
CANDLE COLOUR: Burgundy
GUARDIAN ANGEL: Raguel
CHAKRA: Solar plexus
HERBS, INCENSES AND OILS: Basil, hyssop, lemon, mugwort and tea tree
FLOWERS: Gardenia, blackthorn blossom and snowdrop
ASSOCIATED CRYSTALS: Rainbow moonstone, satin spar and snow quartz

MYTHOLOGY AND HISTORY
Named after Labrador, labradorite is associated with many of the ancient magical practices of the region, including knot rituals. Finnish labradorite was sometimes buried in fields as an offering to the powerful spirits of the land. In northern lands labradorite is said to have fallen from the Aurora Borealis. Spectrolite, a black iridescent labradorite, called shamans' stones, comes from Finland.

DIVINATORY SIGNIFICANCE
It may be a good time to strike out alone, whether in business or to follow a private dream – such as taking a short holiday to a place none of your family wishes to see.

HEALING AND THE ENVIRONMENT
Labradorite strengthens the immune system and repairs the aura. It is helpful for improving vision, especially at night, and so is a crystal to take with you for night driving. It also counters stress and psychological over-dependence, whether on other people, medicines, food, alcohol or tobacco.

USES AT WORK AND HOME
Labradorite will help if your home life has entered a rut or you feel that the fun has gone out of your life. At work, labradorite eases

changes whether of job, management or work practices. It is inspirational for fiction writers, playwrights and composers of songs or music.

CHILDREN AND ANIMALS
It helps children to express their imaginations creatively and to develop a sense of humour. It is a stone for guard and guide dogs.

PSYCHIC ASSOCIATIONS
It inspires novice and experienced psychics, especially if they feel out of touch with their gifts. Labradorite brings creative dreams.

RECHARGING ITS ENERGIES
Recharge when there is a rainbow in the sky or use a perspex rainbow on your window.

HEMATITE

HISTORY AND MYTHOLOGY
Like iron pyrites, polished hematite was traditionally used for magic mirrors, which supposedly had the power to reflect back negativity. Hematite was also considered powerful for divination purposes. In Ancient Egypt it was used magically in protective amulets (it was used as the ceremonial pillow to magically uplift the head of the deceased). The Ancient Egyptians also used hematite for healing diseases of the blood. Roman soldiers rubbed the red powder that came from the stone on their bodies to make them invulnerable. Some hematite has a reddish streak which, in rough-cut pieces, leaves a mark when rubbed against a harder stone: this led to the myth that the stone bled.

DIVINATORY SIGNIFICANCE
Start from where you are now, as you are now, and avoid falling into the old traps.

HEALING AND THE ENVIRONMENT

Hematite is one of the most powerful stones for self-healing and, if held over a painful place or the solar plexus chakra, will draw out pain, illness and muscle weakness, and calm racing blood pressure or pulse. As a stone of balance it is helpful to counter excessive menstrual bleeding.

USES AT WORK AND HOME

Known sometimes as the lawyer's stone, hematite will help with all legal wrangles or matters of injustice and is especially good for neighbourhood or boundary disputes. It also banishes irrational fears and helps you to avoid becoming too emotionally involved with the problems of others. Hematite overcomes fears of flying and reduces jet lag.

CHILDREN AND ANIMALS

It is too heavy for children and animals.

PSYCHIC ASSOCIATIONS

Hematite stimulates astral travel, while providing grounding and protective energies. It is good for all forms of psychic self-defence, land boundary and home protection.

RECHARGING ITS ENERGIES

Smudge hematite with sage or cedar.

PROPERTIES
TYPE: Iron oxide, a very heavy stone
COLOUR: Brilliant silvery black, steel-grey metallic, also dark red or reddish brown, with a red streak
SYMBOLIC ASSOCIATIONS
ZODIAC SIGN: Aries
PLANET: Mars
ELEMENT: Fire
CANDLE COLOUR: Silver
GUARDIAN ANGEL: Asrael
CHAKRA: Solar plexus / root
HERBS, INCENSES AND OILS: Dragon's blood, ginger, juniper, parsley and saffron
FLOWERS: Passion flower, red tulip and snapdragon
ASSOCIATED CRYSTALS: Bloodstone, red agate, iron pyrites

METEORITE

MYTHOLOGY AND HISTORY

The vast majority of meteorites originated in the asteroid belt between Mars and Jupiter, where there are many rock fragments. One of the most common types of stony meteorites is chondrite, which is unchanged since the solar system itself was formed 4,560 million years ago and is unlike any rock on earth. For thousands of years, meteorites that blazed across the skies and fell to earth were considered gifts from the deities. Some contained rich deposits of iron or crystals such as olivine (peridot) or even, occasionally, diamonds. However, they were sometimes regarded as a sign the gods were angry: meteorite showers opportunely appeared over Ireland when St Patrick was trying to persuade pagans that the Christian God was all-powerful. Meteorites symbolize akasha, the name given to the synthesis of all four elements to make something greater.

DIVINATORY SIGNIFICANCE

Meteorites are not used for divination.

HEALING AND THE ENVIRONMENT

Meteorites can be used to send healing to an absent person. They provide the impetus to give up a bad habit or overcome a phobia, especially if you have failed in the past.

USES AT WORK AND HOME

Used traditionally to protect against fire, meteorites have in the modern world been used as an amulet against bombs or hijacking.

CHILDREN AND ANIMALS

Their energies can be too unsettling to make them suitable for children and animals.

PSYCHIC ASSOCIATIONS

Primarily a magical stone, meteorite fragments contain unique energies that can aid you in any life transformation. Good for channelling information about possible life in other galaxies, for protection against unfriendly alien encounters and encouraging more positive experiences of otherworldly beings, especially in dreams or meditation. They help would-be and practising astrologers to improve their accuracy.

RECHARGING ITS ENERGIES

Meteorites hold energies well, so recharge only on the night of a lunar or solar eclipse, even if you cannot see it from where you live.

PROPERTIES
TYPE: Magnetic and alloyed with nickel and iron
COLOUR: Black, grey, brown
SYMBOLIC ASSOCIATIONS
ZODIAC SIGN: All
PLANET: The universe
ELEMENT: Spirit or Akasha
CANDLE COLOUR: Gold
GUARDIAN ANGEL: Michael
CHAKRA: All
HERBS, INCENSES AND OILS: Blessed thistle, frankincense, hyssop, myrrh and sandalwood
FLOWERS: Madonna lily, lotus and papyrus flower
ASSOCIATED CRYSTALS: Lodestone, iron pyrites and hematite

IRON PYRITES

PROPERTIES

TYPE: Iron sulphide

COLOUR: Silvery or dark grey/black with golden glints as chunky cubes, scattered through a cluster or polished as dull golden

SYMBOLIC ASSOCIATIONS

ZODIAC SIGN: Aries

PLANET: Mars/Pluto

ELEMENT: Earth

CANDLE COLOUR: Silver or grey

GUARDIAN ANGEL: Camael

CHAKRA: Solar plexus

HERBS, INCENSES AND OILS: Copal, cinnamon, dragon's blood, ginger and mint

FLOWERS: Bracken, flowering thorn and thistle

ASSOCIATED CRYSTALS: Gold, hematite and lodestone

MYTHOLOGY AND HISTORY

Also known as iron pyrites and fool's gold, from Palaeolithic times iron pyrites was regarded as a magical fire stone because it emitted sparks when struck. The Mayans and Aztecs used polished pyrites mirrors for divination. It has been a shamanic stone of power in a number of cultures.

DIVINATORY SIGNIFICANCE

Work with the polished golden nugget. This stone indicates that increased prosperity is coming your way through your own past efforts. Beware those who would spend your money for you.

HEALING AND THE ENVIRONMENT

Iron pyrites is good for relieving lung disorders, improving digestion, cell and bone health, and helping the body fight infections, viruses and fevers. It is protective for nurses, doctors and pharmacists and will help prevent carers of the chronically sick or elderly becoming ill and exhausted. Iron pyrites is good in rituals to restore the earth's rapidly depleting mineral sources.

USES AT WORK AND HOME

Use pyrites for brainstorming sessions, for all creative thinking and to give your ideas practical applications. Shiny gold pyrites in your workspace will repel negativity. At home

and work iron pyrites attracts good fortune and prosperity and brings harmony between people who live or work closely together.

CHILDREN AND ANIMALS

While not used for children, iron pyrites can help animals with skin problems and is good in the care of reptiles and insects.

PSYCHIC ASSOCIATIONS

Place iron pyrites in front of a mirror you are using for divination or scry directly into one by candlelight. Use for any channelling work connected with UFOs or aliens, for psychic protection and in all fire and candle rituals.

RECHARGING ITS ENERGIES

Pass it over the flame of a grey or silver candle.

PROPERTIES

TYPE: Opaque, naturally magnetized iron oxide. Occasionally gleaming

COLOUR: Black, dark grey

SYMBOLIC ASSOCIATIONS

ZODIAC SIGN: Capricorn

PLANET: Saturn/Mars

ELEMENT: Earth

CANDLE COLOUR: Purple

GUARDIAN ANGEL: Attarib

CHAKRA: Root/solar plexus

HERBS, INCENSES AND OILS: Cedar, cypress, patchouli, sandalwood and thyme

FLOWERS: Cactus, flowering wild garlic and wallflower

ASSOCIATED CRYSTALS: Copper, hematite and iron pyrites

LODESTONE

MYTHOLOGY AND HISTORY

For thousands of years and in different cultures, the lodestone has been valued in folk-magic and medicine. It was traditionally added to charm bags to attract luck (especially in gambling), money, love, passion and fidelity. During the Middle Ages one lodestone would be set in a woman's wedding ring and another given to the groom. It is also called magnetite. The male lodestones are pointed, the female square or rounded. Buy a pair that attract each other.

DIVINATORY SIGNIFICANCE

Lodestone is not used in divination.

HEALING AND THE ENVIRONMENT

Use male lodestones for men, female for women. They absorb pain or feverishness, infections and headaches. They clear blocks within the circulation, improve vision, regularize the heart, alleviate rheumatism and make wounds heal faster. They are good for overcoming male impotence. A lodestone on a woman's thigh pointing towards the womb is said to ease labour pains.

USES AT WORK AND HOME

You can draw money into your home and success into your work life by keeping a lodestone in your handbag or wallet with a few coins. For protection, set a male lodestone, point outwards, towards the door or the direction of hostility. It will effectively absorb negative vibes.

CHILDREN AND ANIMALS
It is too intense for children and animals.

PSYCHIC ASSOCIATIONS
The male-female attraction has made the lodestone a symbol of love and sex magic. Place a pair on your bedside table facing one another and bring them closer over a three-night period before sleep to attract love into your life. For increasing male potency, sprinkle an oil with associations with love (for example, sandalwood, rose or jasmine) over your lodestone. Hold the stone in your left hand, close your eyes and visualize successful lovemaking. Place the lodestone under the mattress before making love.

RECHARGING ITS ENERGIES
Lodestones traditionally are soaked in water on a Friday morning until noon, left in sunlight to dry, sprinkled with iron filings and kept in a red bag when not in use.

ZINC/SCHALENBLENDE

MYTHOLOGY AND HISTORY
Though it has been known since the Middle Ages, zinc has only recently been adopted in healing and in magic. It sometimes replaces lead, Saturn's traditional metal, whose dangers are now well understood.

DIVINATORY SIGNIFICANCE
Schalenblende is not used in divination.

HEALING AND THE ENVIRONMENT
A health bringer, schalenblende triggers the immune system to break down destructive material. It strengthens brain and red-blood-

cell function, improves the sense of smell and taste and aids vision. It reduces exhaustion, panic and insomnia, assists wound healing, and promotes the health of the prostate gland, genitalia and reproductive organs. It is a good amulet for preconception care. It acts as a radiation and pollutant shield.

USES AT WORK AND HOME
Zinc is a psychological insulator against the effects of sudden change. taking a detached view of a situation It is the stone of arbitrators, estate agents, trades union representatives, miners and geologists and anyone who works with computers or designs software. Place zinc near your computer as an anti-virus amulet.

CHILDREN AND ANIMALS
Zinc is not suitable for children and animals.

PSYCHIC ASSOCIATIONS
Magically it has replaced lead both as a fertility charm and in banishing magic to remove sorrow and destructive tendencies from one's life. Use it also for rituals concerning property.

RECHARGING ITS ENERGIES
Pass schalenblende over a silver-grey candle.

PROPERTIES
TYPE: Zinc sulphide. Opaque
COLOUR: Yellow brown/silver grey banded, blue, undulating look
SYMBOLIC ASSOCIATIONS
ZODIAC SIGN: Capricorn
PLANET: Saturn
ELEMENT: Earth
CANDLE COLOUR: Silvery grey
GUARDIAN ANGEL: Aftiel
CHAKRA: Root
HERBS, INCENSES AND OILS: Bistort, laurel, magnolia, oakmoss and tea tree
FLOWERS: Foxglove, night-scented stock and lupin
ASSOCIATED CRYSTALS: Copper, hematite and iron pyrites

APPENDIX

BIRTHSTONES

The concept of twelve different stones was found shown on a breastplate (excavated from a tomb dating from about 4000 bce) that was worn by the High Priest of Memphis in Ancient Egypt. Thereafter the Hebrews adopted the idea, assigning a stone to each of the twelve tribes of Israel, which their High Priest wore in four rows. The tradition evolved, with gems or crystals being assigned to the twelve angels, then the twelve Apostles and finally the twelve months. Birthstones came into fashion in the eighteenth century.

Birthstones are worn to attract good luck and happiness and over time become a repository of positive energies. Therefore you may wish to have a special ring, necklace or belt buckle containing your birthstone that you can wear for special occasions; the stone will become infused with love and joy and act as a talisman. Birthstones can accumulate health-giving energies and just holding your special stone can make you feel less stressed.

The table below is a combination of several traditions: I continue to adapt the list over the years as my own research dictates.

♈ ARIES *the Ram* 21 March–20 April Diamond Bloodstone	♎ LIBRA *the Scales* 23 September–23 October Opal Lapis lazuli
♉ TAURUS *the Bull* 21 April–21 May Emerald Rose quartz	♏ SCORPIO *the Scorpion* 24 October–22 November Coral Obsidian or Apache tear
♊ GEMINI *the Heavenly Twins* 22 May–21 June White sapphire Citrine	♐ SAGITTARIUS *the Archer* 23 November–21 December Ruby Turquoise
♋ CANCER *the Crab* 22 June–22 July Pearl Moonstone	♑ CAPRICORN *the Goat* 22 December–20 January Garnet Black onyx
♌ LEO *the Lion* 23 July–23 August Golden topaz Carnelian	♒ AQUARIUS *the Water Carrier* 21 January–18 February Amethyst Sugilite
♍ VIRGO *the Maiden* 24 August–22 September Blue sapphire Moss agate	♓ PISCES *the Fish* 19 February–20 March Aquamarine Jade

A DIVINATORY SET OF CRYSTALS

You can use any crystal in divination as long as it is a regular size (about that of a medium coin). Choose tumbled crystals that are not brittle and that do not have jagged edges that would scratch the other crystals. You can start with as few as eleven – one for each of the basic colours. In time you can add different shades of the basic colours and various stone types. However many or few crystals you use, the questioner will always intuitively choose the crystal/s that will answer his or her question.

WHITE: Clear crystal quartz or moonstone
PURPLE: Amethyst or purple fluorite
BLUE: Lapis lazuli or blue lace agate
GREEN: Malachite or jade
YELLOW: Citrine or yellow jasper
ORANGE: Carnelian or polished orange calcite
RED: Red agate or red tiger's eye
PINK: Rose quartz or rhodochrosite
GREY: Hematite or labradorite
BROWN: Tiger's eye or banded agate
BLACK: Obsidian or black onyx

CHAKRA CRYSTALS

Some crystals work with more than one chakra (see individual crystal entries). The more vibrant crystals will energize a chakra and softer ones gently unblock and calm the energy centres (see p9–10). Where I have listed a crystal type, choose the colour appropriate for the chakra colour.

THE ROOT OR BASE CHAKRA: RED

Bloodstone, garnet, iron pyrites, red and brown agate, red jasper, red and brown tiger's eye, obsidian and ruby.

THE SACRAL CHAKRA: ORANGE

Amber, orange aragonite, banded agate, carnelian, orange calcite, celestine, and all moonstones.

THE SOLAR PLEXUS CHAKRA: YELLOW

Aragonite, yellow calcite, citrine, chrysoberyl, jasper and golden topaz.

THE HEART CHAKRA: GREEN AND PINK

Green: Aventurine, amazonite, malachite, peridot and moss or tree agate.
Pink: Coral, rose quartz, pink chalcedony, rhodonite and rhodochrosite.

THE THROAT CHAKRA: BLUE

Blue aquamarine, blue lace agate, blue sapphire, lapis lazuli, sodalite, turquoise and violan.

THE BROW CHAKRA: PURPLE

Amethyst, charoite, lavender and purple fluorite, sugilite and lepidolite.

THE CROWN CHAKRA: WHITE

Apophyllite, clear quartz crystal, colourless fluorite, diamond, milky quartz, white sapphire and clear topaz.